Cambridge Approaches t
General editor: Jean Aitc.
Professor of Language and Communication,
University of Oxford

In the past twenty-five years, linguistics – the systematic study of language – has expanded dramatically. Its findings are now of interest to psychologists, sociologists, philosophers, anthropologists, teachers, speech therapists and numerous others who have realized that language is of crucial importance in their life and work. But when newcomers try to discover more about the subject, a major problem faces them – the technical and often narrow nature of much writing about linguistics.

Cambridge Approaches to Linguistics is an attempt to solve this problem by presenting current findings in a lucid and non-technical way. Its object is twofold. First, it hopes to outline the 'state of play' in key areas of the subject, concentrating on what is happening now, rather than on surveying the past. Second, it aims to provide links between branches of linguistics that are traditionally separate.

The series will give readers an understanding of the multi-faceted nature of language, and its central position in human affairs, as well as equipping those who wish to find out more about linguistics with a basis from which to read some of the more technical literature in books and journals.

Also in the series

The English Language
A Historical
Introduction

Second Edition

CHARLES BARBER
Formerly Reader in English Language and Literature, University of Leeds

JOAN C. BEAL
Professor of English Language, University of Sheffield

PHILIP A. SHAW
Lecturer in Old and Middle English, University of Sheffield

CAMBRIDGE
UNIVERSITY PRESS

University Printing House, Cambridge CB2 8BS, United Kingdom

Cambridge University Press is part of the University of Cambridge.

It furthers the University's mission by disseminating knowledge in the pursuit of education, learning and research at the highest international levels of excellence.

www.cambridge.org
Information on this title: www.cambridge.org/9781107693937

First published 1993
Fourth printing 1995
Canto edition 2000
Eighth printing 2007
Second edition 2009
4th printing 2011
Canto Classics edition 2012
7th printing 2017

Printed in the United Kingdom by Clays, St Ives plc

A catalogue record for this publication is available from the British Library

Library of Congress Cataloguing in Publication data
Barber, Charles Laurence.
  The English language : a historical introduction / Charles Barber,
Joan C. Beal, Philip A. Shaw. – 2nd ed.
     p.   cm. – (Cambridge approaches to linguistics)
  Includes bibliographical references and index.
  ISBN 978-0-521-85404-7 – ISBN 978-0-521-67001-2 (pbk.)
  1. English language – History. 2. Historical linguistics. I. Beal, Joan C.
II. Shaw, Philip A. III. Title. IV. Series.

PE1075.B265 2009
420.9–dc22   2008053625

ISBN 978-1-107-69393-7 Paperback

Contents

Figures

Preface to the second edition

In revising and updating Charles Barber's *The English Language: a Historical Introduction*, we have tried to interfere as little as possible with the overall tone and design of what has been a very popular and successful introductory textbook. Some revision was needed because of the advances of scholarship and opening up of new fields of research in the last decade of the twentieth century. This is particularly evident in chapters 9, 10 and 11: the study of Late Modern English gained momentum in the 1990s, the diversity of world Englishes has received much more attention in this period; and, of course, we are now in a position to review the twentieth century as a whole. In studying pre-modern languages, we are increasingly aware of the difficulties of simplistic equations of ethnicity with language, and there is a renewed emphasis on direct study of the epigraphic and manuscript records of early languages, along with increasing use of electronic corpora and computational approaches.

There has been some debate in recent years about whether it is appropriate to publish a 'history of English', given that there are many Englishes and many histories. In our experience of teaching an introductory module on this subject to first-year undergraduates, they need and appreciate a narrative which 'tells a story' simply and clearly without 'dumbing down' or glossing over difficulties. This is precisely what Barber's *The English Language: a Historical Introduction* has provided for the past fifteen years, and we hope that this new edition will continue to do so.

We are very grateful to a number of friends and colleagues who have provided information and advice. Alan M. Kent brought us up to date with the Cornish language situation, and Anthea Fraser Gupta provided a great deal of help with chapter 10. Mary Swan gave valuable advice on Old English. It goes without saying that any defects, errors or imperfections should be attributed to us.

Joan C. Beal and Philip A. Shaw
Sheffield, 2009

Preface to the first edition

Enormous numbers of ordinary people are fascinated by language, and have views about it, often strong. This book aims to provide material which will interest these general readers, and give them things to think about. Its central theme is the history of the English language, beginning with our remote Indo-European ancestors and working its way from Anglo-Saxon times down to the present day. Use is made of numerous short passages of English, to illustrate the varieties of the language in different times and places.

Many other languages are also given some attention. In the course of its history, English has been influenced by numerous languages, especially by Latin, by French and by the Scandinavian languages. In more recent times, colonization and worldwide trade have led to contributions to its vocabulary by the speech of many countries – from Greenland to South Africa, from India to Mexico. Something is therefore said about such languages, but nevertheless the main theme of the book is the English language.

But while there is widespread interest in language, there is also a good deal of prejudice and ignorance about it. Much of the ignorance is due to an absence of technical knowledge about such things as phonology and grammar: it is difficult, for example, to write coherently about pronunciation without some grasp of phonetics. I try to overcome this difficulty by giving a clear and simple introduction to the basic concepts of linguistics, which are not really difficult to grasp. Books written for specialists in the field are often obscure to the general reader. On the other hand, many popular books about language avoid technicalities, thus limiting their range and usefulness. This book tries to bridge the gap, by building on a basic theoretical structure while remaining easily accessible to the ordinary reader. As for prejudices about language, many of these arise from an absence of historical knowledge, and I hope that this history of English will help to clear some of them away.

But at the same time, you should try to enjoy language. English is extremely rich and varied, and it can be great fun just to listen to the speech of different groups and different individuals – to the speech of Australians, Scots, Irishmen, West Indians, to the speech of different social classes and different occupations, and to the latest modish inventions of the young. I hope that this book will help you to have fun!

In preparing this book, I have been fortunate to have the constant help and advice of Dr Jean Aitchison, the General Editor of the series. Without her penetrating and invariably constructive suggestions it would have been a much poorer work. Other friends and colleagues who have given valuable help include Karin Barber, David Denison, Stanley Ellis, Joyce Hill, Colin Johnson, Göran Kjellmer, Rory McTurk, Peter Meredith, Karl Inge Sandred and Loreto Todd. To all, my grateful thanks. For the errors and shortcomings which remain, I alone am to be held responsible.

I am also grateful to the publishers concerned for permission to quote the following copyright material: a passage of Nigerian pidgin from Loreto Todd's *Modern Englishes* (1990), by permission of Blackwell Publishers; two passages from G. N. Garmonsway's edition of Ælfric's *Colloquy* (1947), by permission of Methuen & Co.; a passage from the translation by B. Colgrave and R. A. B. Mynors of Bede's *Ecclesiastical History* (1969), two passages from Trevisa's translation of Higden's *Polychronicon* as reproduced in Kenneth Sisam's *Fourteenth Century Verse and Prose* (1921), and a passage from D. F. Bond's edition of *The Spectator* (1965), all by permission of Oxford University Press; and a passage from *The New English Bible* ©1970 by permission of Oxford and Cambridge University Presses. In some cases the version given in the text differs in small ways from that of the source, for example by the insertion of length-marks over vowels or the adoption of emendations.

Throughout the work, use is made of the traditional division of England into counties, before the local government changes of the 1970s (see the map at the beginning of the book). This can hardly be avoided, since the traditional county framework has been used by the majority of earlier works, including such major ones as the Survey of English Dialects and the publications of the English Place Name Society.

Charles Barber

The counties of England before 1974

Bedfordshire 25. Berkshire 34. Buckinghamshire 24. Cambridgeshire 20.
Cheshire 7. Cornwall 30. Cumberland 2. Derbyshire 8. Devon 31. Dorset 35.
Durham 3. Essex 28. Gloucestershire 22. Hampshire 36. Herefordshire 15.
Hertfordshire 27. Huntingdonshire 19. Kent 39. Lancashire 5.
Leicestershire 13. Lincolnshire 10. Middlesex 29. Norfolk 21.
Northamptonshire 18. Northumberland 1. Nottinghamshire 9. Oxfordshire
23. Rutland 14. Shropshire 11. Somerset 32. Staffordshire 12. Suffolk 26.
Surrey 37. Sussex 38. Warwickshire 17. Westmorland 4. Wiltshire 33.
Worcestershire 16. Yorkshire 6

1 What is language?

It is language, more obviously than anything else, that distinguishes humankind from the rest of the animal world. Humans have also been described as tool-making animals; but language itself is the most remarkable tool that they have invented, and is the one that makes most of the others possible. The most primitive tools, admittedly, may have come earlier than language: the higher apes sometimes use sticks as elementary tools, and even break them for this purpose. But tools of any greater sophistication demand the kind of human co-operation and division of labour which is hardly possible without language. Language, in fact, is the great machine-tool which makes human culture possible.

Other animals, it is true, communicate with one another, or at any rate stimulate one another to action, by means of cries. Many birds utter warning calls at the approach of danger; some animals have mating-calls; apes utter different cries to express anger, fear or pleasure. Some animals use other modes of communication: many have postures that signify submission, to prevent an attack by a rival; hive-bees indicate the direction and distance of honey from the hive by means of the famous bee-dance; dolphins seem to have a communication system which uses both sounds and bodily posture. But these various means of communication differ in important ways from human language. Animals' cries are not *articulate*. This means, basically, that they lack structure. They lack, for example, the kind of structure given by the contrast between vowels and consonants, and the kind of structure that enables us to divide a human utterance into words. We can change an utterance by replacing one word by another: a sentry can say 'Tanks

1

approaching from the north', or he can change one word and say 'Aircraft approaching from the north' or 'Tanks approaching from the west'; but a bird has a single indivisible alarm-cry, which means 'Danger!' This is why the number of signals that an animal can make is very limited: the Great Tit has about thirty different calls, whereas in human language the number of possible utterances is infinite. It also explains why animal cries are very *general* in meaning. These differences will become clearer if we consider some of the characteristics of human language.

What is language?

A human language is a signalling system. The written language is secondary and derivative. In the history of each individual, speech or signing is learned before writing, and there is good reason for believing that the same was true in the history of the species. There are communities that have speech without writing, but we know of no human community which has a written language without a spoken or signed one.

Vocal sounds

The vocal sounds which provide the materials for a language are produced by the various *speech organs* (see figure 1). The production of sounds requires energy, and this is usually supplied by the diaphragm and the chest muscles, which enable us to send a flow of breath up from the lungs. Some languages use additional sources of energy: it is possible to make clicking noises by muscular movements of the tongue, and popping noises by movements of the cheeks and lips, and such sounds are found in some of the African languages. It is also possible to use air flowing *into* the lungs, i.e. to utilize indrawn breath for the production of speech sounds in very short utterances. In English, however, we usually rely on the *outflow* of air from the lungs, which is modified in various ways by the position and shape of the organs that it passes through before finally emerging at the mouth or nose.

First the air from the lungs passes through the vocal cords, in the larynx. These are rather like a small pair of lips in the windpipe,

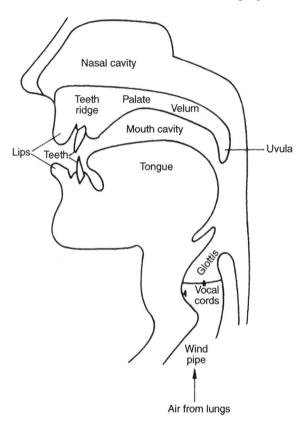

Figure 1 Main speech organs

and we are able to adjust these lips to various positions, from fully closed (when the flow of air is completely blocked) to wide open (when the flow of air is quite unobstructed). In one of the intermediate positions, the vocal cords vibrate as the air passes through, rather like the reed of a bassoon or an oboe, and produce a musical tone called **voice**. We can vary the pitch of our voice (how high or low the tone is on the musical scale), and it changes constantly as we speak, which produces the characteristic melodies of English sentences. The sounds in which voice is used are called **voiced** sounds, but some speech sounds are made with the vocal cords in the wide open position, and are therefore **voiceless** (or **breathed**). You can detect the presence or absence of voice by covering your ears with your hands: voiced sounds then produce a loud buzzing noise in the head. For example, if you cover your ears firmly and utter a long continuous *v* sound, you will hear voice; if you change it to an *f* sound, the voice disappears. In fact the English *v* and *f* are made in exactly the same way, except that one is voiced and the other voiceless. There are many other similar pairs in English, including *z* and *s*, the *th* of *this* and the *th* of *thing* (for which we can use the symbols [ð] and [θ]), and the consonant sounds in the middle of *pleasure* and of *washer* (for which we can use the symbols [ʒ] and [ʃ]). We can play other tricks with our vocal cords: we can sing, or whisper, or speak falsetto: but the two most important positions for speech are the voiced and the voiceless.

After passing through the vocal cords, the stream of air continues upwards, and passes out through the mouth, or the nose, or both. The most backward part of the roof of the mouth, called the *velum* or the soft palate, can be moved up and down to close or open the entrance to the nasal cavity, while the mouth passage can be blocked by means of the lips or the tongue.

In a **vowel** sound, voice is switched on, and the mouth cavity is left unobstructed, so that the air passes out freely. If the nasal passage is also opened, we get a nasal vowel, like those of French *bon* 'good' or *brun* 'brown', but for the English vowels the nasal passage is normally closed (though some American speakers habitually leave the door ajar and speak with a nasal 'twang'). The quality of a vowel is determined by the position of the tongue, lower jaw and lips, because these can change the shape of the cavity that the air passes through, and different shapes give different resonances. The tongue is the most important. If we raise part of our tongue, we divide the mouth passage into two cavities of different sizes, one at the back and one at the front; the quality of the vowel is, to a great extent, determined by the relative sizes of these two cavities. To describe any vowel sound, therefore, we specify the position of the highest part of the tongue: we can do this in terms of its height (open, half-open, half-close, close) and of its retraction (front, central, or back). A little experimentation with your finger in your mouth, or with a torch and a mirror, will show

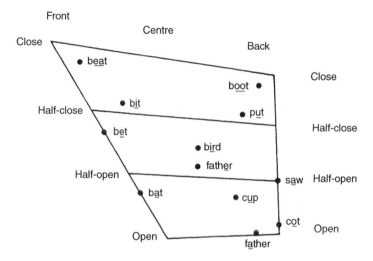

Figure 2 Vowel diagram: typical tongue positions for twelve vowels of present-day English (RP)

you the way your tongue changes position for different vowels. The different positions of the tongue to create different vowel sounds can be shown by means of a *vowel diagram*. This is a conventional-ized cross-section of the mouth cavity seen from the left-hand side, on which a vowel is marked as a dot, representing the position of the highest point of the tongue. Figure 2 shows a vowel diagram for twelve English vowels. The accent represented is usually called 'Received Pronunciation' (RP). It was historically the pronunci-ation of people from families in the south of England who had been educated at public schools such as Eton or Harrow. As we shall see in chapter 9, this became the most prestigious accent in England and is still used as a reference variety and in teaching English, but it has been calculated that a very small percentage of the population actually use this accent today. RP is similar to the general educated accent of south-eastern England, though not quite identical to it.

The quality of a vowel is also affected by the position of the lips, which can be spread wide, held neutral, or rounded more or less tightly. In most forms of English, lip-rounding plays no independent part, for it is an automatic accompaniment of the four backmost vowels, and the tightness of the rounding varies directly with the closeness of the vowel. You can easily check this with the help of a mirror and the vowel diagram (but it may not be true if you are Scottish or Irish). But this is not so in all languages: in French, the *u* of *lune* is made with a tongue-position similar to that of the *ea* of English *lean*, but is made with rounded lips, which gives it quite a different sound.

Vowels can also differ in length. In fact, the English vowels all have different lengths, but they fall into two broad groups, the long and the short. The short vowels are those heard in *pick, peck, pack, put, cut* and *cot*, together with [ə], the short central vowel which is heard in the *er of father* and the *a* of *about*.

The vowel diagram in figure 2 assumes that the vocal organs remain stationary while the vowel is uttered, but this is not always the case, for there are vowels in which the speech organs change their positions in the course of the sound. These are called **glides** or **diphthongs**. An example is the vowel heard in the word *boy*. Here the speech organs begin quite near the position they have for the vowel of *saw*, but almost immediately move towards the position they have for the vowel of *bit*, though they may not go all the way there. During most of the sound, the speech organs are moving, though they may remain in the initial position for a short time before the gliding movement begins. Other English diphthongs are heard in the words *hide, house, make, home, hare, here* and *poor* (though if you are from parts of the United States, Scotland or northern England you may use a pure vowel in some of these, especially in *home*). On the vowel diagram, diphthongs are represented by arrows, and examples are given in figure 3. Notice that our definition of a diphthong is concerned with *sound*, not with spelling. In popular usage, the *au* of *cause* and the *æ* of *mediæval* are often referred to as diphthongs, but these are not diphthongs in our sense of the word: they are pure vowels which happen to be represented in spelling by two letters (the digraph *au* and the ligature *æ*). Conversely, a diphthong may be represented in spelling by a single letter, like the *y* of *fly*.

We have spoken of diphthongs as single vowel sounds, not as combinations of two vowel sounds. One good reason for doing so is that a diphthong forms only one syllable, not two. A syllable is a

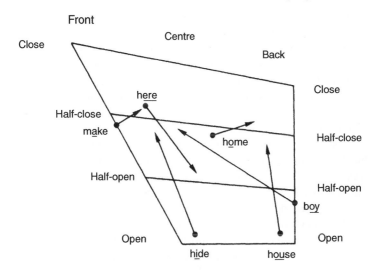

Figure 3 Vowel diagram: six diphthongs of present-day English (RP)

peak of prominence in the chain of utterance. If you could measure the acoustic power output of a speaker as it varies with time, you would find that it goes continually up and down, forming little peaks and valleys: the peaks are syllables. The words *lair* and *here* form only one peak each, and so only one syllable, whereas the words *player* and *newer* are usually pronounced with two peaks and so contain two syllables. It is thus desirable to distinguish between a diphthong (which is one syllable: for instance *face*) and a sequence of two vowels (which is two syllables: for instance *helium*). Alternatively, a diphthong can be analysed as the combination of a vowel with a semivowel (a non-syllabic glide, like the *y* in *yes*), and this analysis is adopted by many linguists, especially Americans.

In all vowels, the mouth passage is unobstructed. If it is obstructed at any time during the production of a speech sound, the resulting sound will be a **consonant**. In English, there are three main types of consonant: **fricatives, stops** and **sonorants**.

Fricatives are made by narrowing the air passage so much that the stream of air produces audible friction. In *f* and *v*, the constriction is made by pressing the lower lip against the top teeth, while in *th* ([θ] and [ð]) the tip of the tongue is pressed against the upper teeth. In *s* and *z*, the front of the tongue is pressed against the teeth-ridge (that is, the convex part of the roof of the mouth immediately behind the upper teeth), and the air allowed to flow down a narrow channel in the middle of the tongue, while for [ʃ] and [ʒ] the passage is made wider and flatter. The English *h* consonant can perhaps also be classed as a fricative, but in this case the friction occurs in the glottis, and the mouth passage is completely unobstructed.

In stop consonants, the flow of air from the lungs is completely blocked at some point, and pressure built up behind the blockage; then the blockage is suddenly removed, and there is an outrush of air. The exact sound produced will depend on where and how the blockage is made, and on the speed of the release. In *p* and *b*, the blockage is made by pressing the two lips together. In *t* and *d*, the tip of the tongue is pressed against the teeth-ridge (not against the teeth themselves, as in many other languages). In *k* and *g*, the back part of the tongue is lifted and pressed against the soft palate. In these six sounds, the release is very sudden. In *ch* (as in *church*) and *j* (as in *judge*), which are made in much the same position as *t* and *d*, the release of the blockage is slower, and this gives a different effect, so that *ch* sounds something like a *t* followed very rapidly by a *sh*. Stops with rapid release are called **plosives**, and those with slow release **affricates**. There is also a plosive called the **glottal stop**, in which the blockage is made by complete closure of the vocal cords. This was previously thought to be a feature of Cockney, but, as we shall see in chapter 11, its use is now widespread in many varieties of British English.

In the sonorant consonants, use is made of resonant cavities, as in the vowels, but there is some kind of obstruction in the mouth passage. The English sonorants are the nasals, *m*, *n* and *ng* (as in *sing*), the lateral consonant *l*, and the approximant *r*. In the nasals, the nasal passage is open but the mouth passage is blocked, the blockages being similar to those made for the plosives *b*, *d* and *g* respectively. In the lateral, the centre of the mouth is blocked by the tongue, while the air is allowed to escape down one side, or down both. In English these are all normally voiced, though they may become voiceless or partially voiceless under certain conditions, for example when they follow an *s*. In Welsh, you will hear an *l* sound (spelt *ll*, as in *Llanelli*) which is regularly voiceless, but this is a fricative consonant rather than a sonorant.

The *r* consonant has various realizations in different varieties of English, but in Received Pronunciation, and in much American English, it is an **approximant**. This is a consonant in which the articulators approach one another, but not closely enough to produce a fricative or a stop. In *r*, the tip of the tongue approaches the teeth-ridge, as if for *d*, but does not make contact, and the tongue is usually curled slightly backward, with the tip raised. In some varieties of English *r* is a trill, in which the tip of the tongue vibrates rapidly, or a flap, in which the tip of the tongue makes a single tap against the teeth-ridge. In some languages, the consonant written as *r* is a different sort of sound: in the best-known varieties of French and German, it is not made with the tip of the tongue, but with the uvula (the small fleshy appendage to the soft palate, which can be seen hanging at the back of the mouth), and in many Indian languages there is a retroflex *r* made by curling the tongue right back and articulating against the roof of the mouth.

In English, sonorant consonants can form syllables. It is sometimes asserted that every syllable must contain a vowel, but this is not so, as can be seen from words like *table* and *button*: in normal pronunciation, each of these has two syllables, the second of which contains no vowel. Syllabic *r* is very common in American speech, in positions where RP instead has the vowel [ə] (called 'schwa'), in words like *perceive*.

With the sonorant consonants we can also group the English semivowels, heard in the *y* of *yes* and the *w* of *wet*. A semivowel is a glide, like a diphthong; but, unlike a diphthong, it does not constitute a syllable. To make the *y* of *yes*, we put our tongue in the position for a short *i* (as in *pin*), and then glide to the position for the following *e*. Similarly, to make *w*, we put our tongue in the position for short *u* (as in *put*), and again glide to the following vowel.

Phonetic symbols

Even in this short account of the English speech sounds, it has already become apparent that it is difficult to discuss the subject without making use of special symbols. We have in English no single unambiguous spelling to represent the consonant sound in the middle of the word *pleasure* or the first vowel of the word *about*, or to distinguish between the voiced and voiceless *th* of *this* and *thing*, and for this reason we have already introduced the phonetic symbols [ʒ], [ə], [ð] and [θ] to represent these sounds. In the course of this book, we shall use phonetic symbols when they make things simpler and clearer, but shall often use ordinary letter symbols in cases where no ambiguity can arise. When we introduce a new phonetic symbol, we shall of course indicate what it stands for, but for convenience of reference we give below two tables in which all the symbols used are gathered together. In table 1.1, we give a list of symbols which can be used for the transcription of present-day English (Received Pronunciation), together with illustrative examples.

The examples assume Received Pronunciation. Speakers of General American (the most widespread accent in the United States) use the same vowel in *hot* as in *father*, pronounce the /r/ in *air* and *bird*, and lack the centring diphthongs /ɪə/, /ɛə/ and /ʊə/ (the word *here*, for example, being /hɪr/). The symbol [ː] is used to denote vowel-length, so that [ə] is short and [ɜː] long. In General American, however, vowel-length is less significant than in RP, and it is usual to transcribe it without using length-marks, so that for example *tree* is transcribed /tri/.

Similarly, the examples will not fit all speakers in Britain. If you are a northerner, you may well use the same vowel in *put* as in *cut*, where RP makes a distinction. If you are a Scot, you may use the same vowel in *put* as in *goose*. If you come from the West Midlands, or south Lancashire, or the Sheffield area, you may pronounce *sing* as /sɪŋg/, with a [g] after the [ŋ].

Diphthongs are represented by two symbols, the first showing the vowel position in which the diphthong starts, and the second showing the position towards which it glides. So the diphthong in the word *here* begins in about the same position as the [ɪ] of *pin*, and glides towards the central vowel [ə]. We therefore represent it by the notation [ɪə]. The symbol ['] is used to mark stress, and is placed before the syllable that is stressed, so that *admit* is transcribed [əd'mɪt].

Table 1.1 Phonetic symbols for the transcription of present-day English (Received Pronunciation)

I. VOWELS

Pure vowels

ɪ as in *sit* /sɪt/

e as in *pen* /pen/

æ as in *hat* /hæt/

ʌ as in *cup* /kʌp/

ɒ as in *hot* /hɒt/

ʊ as in *put* /pʊt/

ə as in *admit* /əd'mɪt/, *father* /'fɑːðə/

i: as in *tree* /triː/

ɑ: as in *far* /fɑː/, *father* /'fɑːðə/

ɔ: as in *saw* /sɔː/, *short* /ʃɔːt/

u: as in *goose* /guːs/, *few* /fjuː/

ɜ: as in *bird* /bɜːd/

Diphthongs

eɪ as in *make* /meɪk/

aɪ as in *time* /taɪm/

ɔɪ as in *boy* /bɔɪ/

əʊ as in *go* /gəʊ/

aʊ as in *loud* /laʊd/

ɪə as in *here* /hɪə/

ɛə as in *air* /ɛə/

ʊə as in *poor* /pʊə/ (but many speakers say /pɔː/)

II. CONSONANTS

Fricatives

f as in *far* /fɑː/

θ as in *thin* /θɪn/

s as in *sit* /sɪt/

ʃ as in *shoe* /ʃuː/

h as in *hit* /hɪt/

v as in *voice* /vɔɪs/

ð as in *this* /ðɪs/

z as in *zoo* /zuː/

ʒ as in *pleasure* /'pleʒə/

Stops

p as in *peel* /piːl/

t as in *took* /tʊk/

k as in *come* /kʌm/

ʧ as in *church* /ʧɜːtʃ/

b as in *bee* /biː/

d as in *deed* /diːd/

g as in *geese* /giːs/

dʒ as in *judge* /dʒʌdʒ/

Sonorants

m as in *make* /meɪk/

n as in *not* /nɒt/

ŋ as in *sing* /sɪŋ/, *finger* /'fɪŋgə/

l as in *leak* /liːk/

j as in *yes* /jes/

w as in *wait* /weɪt/

r as in *red* /red/

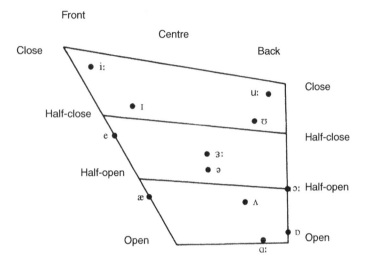

Figure 4 Vowel diagram for the pure vowels of present-day English (RP)

We can now redraw the vowel diagram of figure 2, using phonetic symbols. Figure 4 shows typical tongue positions for the pure vowels of Received Pronunciation in present-day English.

Table 1.2 gives a list of other phonetic symbols which will occur in the course of the book, again with illustrative examples. The table does not include diphthongs, since the pronunciation of these can be deduced from the two phonetic symbols used in their transcription.

This brief account has perhaps given some idea of the kind of vocal material used in the human signalling system. Let us now turn to the word *system*, which is crucial.

System in language

A language consists of a number of linked systems, and structure can be seen in it at all levels. For a start, any language selects a small number of vocal sounds out of all those which human beings are able to make, and uses them as its building blocks, and the selection is different for every language. The number of vocal sounds that a human being can learn to make (and to distinguish between) is quite large – certainly running into hundreds – and if

Table 1.2 Other phonetic symbols used

ɑ	like the *a* of *father*, but short; often heard in American pronunciation of words like *hot*.
a	as in French *la*, German *Mann*, Northern English *hat*.
aː	as in French *tard*, Australian English *park*.
æː	the long vowel often heard in the London pronunciation of words like *bad*, *man*.
ε	as in French *même*, German *Bett*; the starting position of the English diphthong heard in *air*.
εː	as in French *faire*, German *fährt*.
eː	as in German *zehn*; like the vowel of French *été* but lengthened.
ɔ	as in French *donne*, German *von*; like the vowel of English *law*, but short.
oː	as in French *chose*, German *wo*.
o	the corresponding short vowel, as in French *dos*.
øː	as in French *feu*, German *schön* (a long [eː] produced with rounded lips).
y	as in French *cru*, German *Hütte* (a short [i] produced with rounded lips).
yː	as in French *sûr*, German *führen* (a long [iː] produced with rounded lips).
x	as in *ch* of Scots *loch*, German *ach*.
ç	as in *gh* of Scots *night*, *ch* of German *ich*.
ɣ	a voiced velar fricative: like [g], but a fricative instead of a stop.
ʔ	the glottal stop: a plosive in which the blockage is made by complete closure of the vocal cords.

you know a foreign language you will also be familiar with speech sounds which do not occur in English, like the vowel of the French word *feu* or the consonant of the German *ich*. But out of all these possible sounds, most languages are content with a mere twenty or thirty as their basic material. In English, if you treat the diphthongs as independent sounds, the number is about forty-five; if you treat the diphthongs and the long vowels as combinations of a vowel and a semivowel, the number comes down to about thirty-five. Some languages are more modest in their demands: Italian uses only seven different vowels, and manages with twenty-seven basic sounds altogether; Hawaiian is said to manage with only thirteen. Some languages, on the other hand, use sixty or more.

You may have thought of an objection to our suggestion that English makes use of no more than forty-five basic sounds: pronunciation varies from speaker to speaker. Speakers from Texas, from Manchester, from Edinburgh, from New York use different sounds. Doesn't this mean, therefore, that there are hundreds of different sounds in English? This is obviously true. These variations, moreover, occur between different social groups as well as between different regions, for there are class accents as well as regional accents. Observe, however, that all these speakers use what is essentially the same *system* of sounds. When they pronounce the word *man*, they may all use rather different vowel sounds, but all these sounds occupy the same place in the system: they all contrast, for example, with a different vowel sound in *men*, but fail to contrast with the vowel sound heard in a whole number of other words, like *fan* and *mad*. Consequently, these different speakers can understand one another without too much difficulty. This assumes, of course, that many sounds will not vary greatly from one speaker to another, and this is in fact true: the *m* and the *n* of the word *man* are pronounced in pretty well the same way by native speakers of English all over the world, and it is only the vowel in the word that varies.

The phoneme

Not only do the forty-five basic sounds of English vary from region to region, from class to class, and even from speaker to speaker within a class or region: they also vary in a systematic way within the speech of each individual. These variations depend on the position of the sound – the other sounds that are adjacent to it, the part of the word that it occurs in. Take the English /p/ sound. This is a **voiceless stop**, made by blocking the flow of air through the mouth by pressing the two lips together, and then suddenly releasing the blockage by opening the lips. In the speech of most English people, the release of the /p/ is normally followed by a little rush of air, which makes a kind of *h* sound between the stop and the sound that comes next in the word; but when the /p/ follows an /s/ which belongs to the same syllable, this rush of air is missing, so that we use slightly different variants of the /p/sound in the words *park* and *spark*. You can test this by holding the palm of your hand about an inch in front of your mouth and speaking the two words aloud; in *park* you will feel a strong puff of breath on your hand, but in *spark* the puff is much reduced. If you listen carefully you can also *hear* the difference between these two different /p/ sounds, but you don't usually notice it in speech because it has no significance for the meaning of what is said: the difference between the two sounds is determined automatically by the neighbouring sounds, and is not used to distinguish between different words.

Another variant of the /p/ sound is heard before /m/, as in *topmost*: in this case the stop is released, not by opening the lips, but by letting the air flow out of the nose in an /m/ sound, and the lips are not opened until the end of the /m/. Yet another variant is often heard when /p/ comes at the end of a sentence, as when you say 'Can I take your cup?'; here it is common not to release the blockage at all, but just to leave the lips together at the end of the sentence. We see, then, that what we have called the English /p/ sound in fact consists of a whole group of sounds, slightly different variants being used according to the phonetic context.

This is true of the English speech sounds generally. If you listen carefully to your pronunciation of the initial /k/ in the words *keep* and *cool*, you will realize that they differ a good deal; and if you concentrate on the position of your tongue, you will find that the blockage is made much further forward in the former word than in the latter. Or listen to your pronunciation of the /iː/ sound in *bead* and in *beat*: in the first word the vowel is noticeably longer than in the second. Similarly you will probably find that you use different kinds of /m/ in the words *come*, *triumph* and *smooth*; different kinds of /l/ in the words *old*, *leak* and *sleek*; and different kinds of /uː/ in the words *do*, *cool* and *few*.

You may now feel inclined to ask what has happened to our forty-five basic sounds of English, the building blocks that the language is made up from. It has become clear, at any rate, that the word 'sounds' is hardly suitable: let us say instead that the sound system of English has forty-five basic terms or positions, each of which is represented by a whole group of related sounds. The sounds of any one group have a good deal in common, but there are small variations which depend on the context; these variations are normally unnoticed by the native speaker, because they are produced automatically, but they may be very obvious to a foreigner, whose language has a different sound system. Such groups of related and non-contrasting sounds are called **phonemes**, and we can now amend our earlier statement and say that the English language has about forty-five phonemes: the exact number depends on how you decide to treat diphthongs, and also varies slightly between different varieties of English. The variant forms of any phoneme are called the **allophones** of that phoneme.

In table 1.1, we have given only one phonetic symbol for each phoneme of present-day English, so that the same /p/ symbol would be used in transcribing *park* /pɑːk/ and *spark* /spɑːk/. A transcription of this kind is called a **phonemic** transcription, and is usually placed between oblique lines. But of course it is also possible to use a larger number of symbols, in order to show finer distinctions: so one could distinguish between the /p/ of *park* and that of *spark*, by transcribing [pʰɑːk] and [spɑːk]. If the transcription shows such finer distinctions, or if the transcriber does not wish to make a firm decision about the analysis of the language into phonemes, the transcription is usually placed within square brackets, and is called an **allophonic** or a **phonetic** transcription. Notice carefully the difference between *phonemic* (with an *m*) and *phonetic* (with a *t*): in a phonemic transcription there is one symbol, and only one, for each phoneme of the language; in a phonetic transcription there is no such limitation.

System can also be seen in the ways in which the phonemes can be combined into words. As far as we know, there is no English word *grust* or *blomby*, but there is no reason why there shouldn't be; whereas the groups *ngust* and *glbombr* (although perfectly pronounceable if you care to try) will immediately be rejected by a native speaker as not conforming to the pattern of English words. There are restrictions on the combinations in which English phonemes can occur. The /ŋ/ phoneme (as in *sing*) cannot occur at the beginning of a word, nor can the /ʒ/ phoneme (though in French a similar phoneme can, as in the word *je*, 'I'). Some of the short vowels, such as /æ/ (as in *man*) never occur as the last sound in a word, nor does /h/. (Don't be misled by the *spelling*, and say that there's an *h* sound in *oh*, or an *a* sound in *China*.) Again, at the beginning of a word we can have the cluster of consonants /spl-/, but not the cluster /stl-/; and you may care to amuse yourself by trying to work out which clusters of three consonants can in fact occur at the beginning of an English word. At the end of a word, we can have the cluster /-ðmz/ (as in *rhythms*) but not the cluster /-gbz/. And so on. These rules, of course, apply only to the English language; other languages have their own systems, and combinations that are impossible in English, and which may even seem quite jaw-breaking to us, may be perfectly normal in another language, and will not seem at all difficult or surprising to the speakers of that language, who are used to them.

Stress and rhythm

When we consider, not isolated words, but whole utterances, we notice such things as stress, pitch and rhythm, which are also systematic. We have already spoken of the small peaks of loudness which form syllables, but syllables themselves vary in loudness, and in any English utterance of any length there are syllables of many different degrees of loudness. They fall, however, into two main groups, those that are relatively prominent and those that are not; we can call these **stressed** and **unstressed syllables** respectively.

In English, stress is closely linked with rhythm. Large numbers of languages, including French and many of the languages of India, have a rhythm in which the syllables are evenly spaced: if a Frenchman speaks a sentence containing twenty syllables, and takes five seconds to speak it, then the syllables will follow one another pretty regularly at quarter-second intervals. But this is not true of English. Try speaking the following two sentences as naturally as you can, stressing in each the four syllables marked:

There's a néw mánager at the wórks todáy.
There's a néw bóss thére nów.

Although the first has eleven syllables, and the second only six, you will find that the two sentences take about the same time to speak. The reason for this is not hard to see: a speaker of English tries to space the *stressed* syllables evenly, so that both sentences contain four time-units. In the first sentence, the interval between *new* and *man-* is about the same as that between *man-* and *works*, so that the sequence *manager at the works* has to be taken very quickly. This characteristic of the English language plays a large part in the rhythm of English poetry, since a sequence of stressed syllables makes the verse move slowly, whereas a sequence of unstressed syllables makes it move fast.

Intonation

We have already mentioned the way in which the musical pitch of the voice changes during an utterance, giving the characteristic melodies of English. These melodies are called **intonation**. The use of intonation for conveying meaning can be shown very simply by speaking the two sentences:

(a) He's going to be there?
(b) He's going to be there.

In (a) we have a rising tone on the final stressed syllable, and in (b) a falling tone, and in many varieties of English this makes the difference between a question and a statement. These two are very common intonation patterns in English: (b) is used in statements and in 'wh- questions' (ones beginning with words like *which*, *where* and *who*), while (a) is used in questions which can be answered 'Yes' or 'No'. It is also possible to use a tone that falls and then rises: if you speak the word 'No' with falling–rising tone, you communicate doubt or encouragement (depending on the context); this is an example of the common use of intonation to communicate a mood or an attitude. Intonation can also be used to single out the part of the sentence that we want to emphasize. Take the sentence 'Is John going to wear those trousers?' We can select for special emphasis any word in this sentence except *to* ('*Is* John going to wear those trousers?', 'Is *John* going to wear those trousers?', etc.). If you examine what is going on when you speak the sentence with these various emphases, you will see that it is not just a matter of stressing the chosen word more strongly: you also begin it on a higher pitch than the other words, and use a falling tone on it.

In English, we only use musical pitch as a feature of a whole phrase: we use intonation to distinguish between different sentences, but not between different words. But in some languages, like Chinese, Thai and Yoruba, musical pitch is a distinguishing feature of the single word: if you change the intonation it becomes a different word. Such languages are called *tone languages*.

Morphology: words and morphemes

System is also found in the way words are constructed from smaller parts. Words are often defined as minimum free forms, i.e. the smallest pieces of language which can by themselves constitute a complete utterance. But they are not the smallest *meaningful* pieces of language: in the words *refill* and *slowly* we know perfectly well what *re-* and *-ly* mean, but these do not constitute words. The smallest meaningful element in a language is called a **morpheme**. So *re-* and *fill* are both morphemes. The former cannot exist except when joined to other morphemes, and so is a **bound morpheme**; but *fill* is also a word, and is therefore a **free morpheme**. A word may consist of one morpheme or of many: the word *unthoughtful* consists of three morphemes, whereas the word *molecule* is only one; and the word *I* is a single morpheme which is itself composed of a single phoneme.

Bound morphemes are used extensively in English for the formation of new words. Especially productive are prefixes (*un-, re-, de-*, etc.) and suffixes (*-ly, -ness, -ize*, etc.). We also make extensive use of bound morphemes when words change their form for grammatical purposes, as in *boy/boys* or *talk/talks/talking/talked*.

Lexical words and grammatical words

English words fall into a number of different grammatical categories – what were traditionally called 'the parts of speech', but which are now usually called word-classes. Obvious examples of word-classes are nouns (such as *brother, idea, library*), adjectives (such as *new, beautiful, young*), verbs (such as *come, annihilate, fraternize*) and pronouns (such as *you, I, who, anybody*).

Suppose now that we asked you to give us a complete list of the personal pronouns of present-day English (*I, he*, etc.). Would that be possible? Given a little time, you should be able to give us a list: *I, he, she, it, we, you* and *they*, together with their accusative forms *me, him, her, it, us, you* and *them*. You might too have noticed that there are also seven corresponding forms which are used before nouns (*my, his, her*, etc.), and seven corresponding possessive pronouns (*mine, his, hers*, etc.). But suppose we next asked you to give us a similar list of the nouns of present-day English. Would that be possible? We're afraid that, even given plenty of time and secretarial assistance, you would never finish the job. The moment you thought you had finished, you would discover that somebody had just invented a new word, for words are being coined all the time. You would have no idea whether a particular word would catch on, or whether it would disappear after a single use. Nor indeed could you be certain whether some old-fashioned words were dead or not: you might think a word was obsolete, but then hear somebody use it.

Nouns and personal pronouns, therefore, are quite different kinds of word-class. The personal pronouns form a closed system, whose members can be listed exhaustively. The nouns form an open-ended system, blurred at the edges, constantly changing. Of course, the system of pronouns changes with time: four hundred years ago there were the forms *thou, thee, thy* and *thine*, and there was no form *its*. But this is a long-term process: individuals cannot just invent a new pronoun, in the way they can invent a noun. These two different types are often called **lexical words** (open-ended class) and **grammatical words** (closed class). In the lexical class are nouns, verbs and adjectives. In the grammatical class are pronouns (*he, who, somebody*, etc.), conjunctions (*and, but, although*, etc.), auxiliaries (*must, might, would*, etc.), and determiners (words that go before nouns, like *the, a, this, every*). Prepositions (*on, by, in, in spite of*, etc.) are rather numerous, but still belong to the grammatical class. What were traditionally called adverbs fulfil different functions: some are verb-modifiers ('to run *quickly*'), some are sentence-modifiers ('*Undoubtedly*, ...'), and some modify adjectives or adverbs ('*extremely* happy', '*very* quickly'). And some are grammatical, others lexical: those formed from adjectives (*quickly, beautifully, contrariwise*) are lexical, but there is a group which is probably to be classed as grammatical (e.g. *then, there, very*, and ones identical in form with prepositions, like *by, in*, etc.). This is by no means an exhaustive account of the word-classes of present-day English, but will give you a starting-point.

Syntax

We also find that the rules for combining words into utterances form a system. We say 'the good old times', not 'the old good times', and 'a beautiful young American girl', not 'an American young beautiful girl'; and there is a complicated set of rules regulating the way a phrase of this kind is put together in English (rules which English speakers have obviously internalized).

Again, we say 'The dog bit John', and it seems almost like part of the order of nature that this shall mean that it was the dog that did the biting and John that suffered it. But it is not at all part of the order of nature: it is just one of the conventions of our language. In normal English sentences, the Subject ('The dog') comes before the Verb ('bit'), which itself comes before the Direct Object ('John'), and it is this word-order which tells us which is the biter and which the bitten. But this S–V–O word-order is not found in all languages: many languages, like Turkish and Classical Latin, have the equivalent of 'The dog John bit' (S–O–V); some, like Welsh, have the equivalent of 'Bit the dog John' (V–S–O). In some languages, for example Russian, the word-order is very free, and word-endings alone show which is the Subject ('biter') and which the Object ('bitten'). Nor is the word-order of 'The dog' universal: the order here is Determiner–Noun, which is obligatory in English, but some languages have the order Noun–Determiner. In Swedish, for example, 'dog' is *hund*, but 'the dog' is *hunden*, the definite article being attached to the end of the noun. In fact the permissible arrangements of words, and the meanings of particular arrangements, vary from language to language.

Lexical sets

System is also found in the realm of meaning. Words tend to form sets, and the meaning of a word depends on the other words in the set, with which it can be contrasted. This is very clear in sets of words denoting such things as military ranks (*captain*, *major, colonel*, etc.), where the meaning of each term depends on its position in the hierarchy. In Shakespeare's time, there were far fewer military ranks (usually about eight) than in the modern British army; an Elizabethan corporal or colonel, therefore, cannot be equated directly with a present-day one. In the sets of words for family relationships, the categories are different in different languages: Swedish has no word exactly corresponding to our *uncle*, but has *farbror* (paternal uncle) and *morbror* (maternal uncle). These categories also change with time, so that the Middle English word *nevew* (from which Modern English *nephew* develops) can refer to a nephew or a grandson. Earlier forms of our language also have categories which no longer exist: Old English has the term *sweostorsunu* (literally 'sister-son'), referring to a maternal nephew. Another obvious set is formed by words for colours, where different languages divide up the spectrum differently: for example, in Russian there is no single word corresponding to our *blue*, but two words, (a) *síniy* (roughly 'dark blue') and (b) *golubóy* (roughly 'light blue'). The sky can be either, but the sea can only be (a), while eyes are usually (b), though exceptionally dark-blue eyes can be (a). Again, the English system of colour terms has changed over time: Old English *brun* (Modern English *brown*), for instance, can refer to dark colours in general (such as that of the sea), as well as referring to the quality of being shiny (it is applied with this sense to helmets and swords, for instance). Other clear sets are series of words corresponding to degrees of intensity of some kind, like *hot, warm, lukewarm, cool, cold*: if any one of these terms were missing from the language, the meanings of the others would be different, since they would have to cover the same range of intensity in a smaller number of divisions. For instance, according to the *Oxford English Dictionary*, the word *pink* was a noun referring to a flower until 1674, when it was first used as a colour term. Before this date, speakers would have to use a phrase such as 'light red' to refer to the colour that we now know as pink.

Hierarchy

In these various intertwined systems that constitute a language, a large part is played by hierarchy. There is a hierarchy of units:

phoneme, morpheme, word, phrase, clause, sentence. Within the sentence itself, there is a hierarchical structure. Take a simple sentence:

(a) The women were wearing white clothes.

This can be divided into two parts, Subject and Predicate, in each of which there is a main part and a subordinate part. The Subject consists of a Noun Phrase ('The women'), in which a noun ('women') is the head, and a determiner ('The') is a modifier. The Predicate has as its head a Verb Phrase ('were wearing') which governs a Noun Phrase ('white clothes') as its Object. The Verb Phrase has a main verb ('wear') + *-ing* as its head, and an auxiliary ('were') as a subordinate part, while the Noun Phrase has as its head a noun ('clothes'), and an adjective ('white') as a modifier.

Now let us expand the sentence a little:

(b) The women in the house were wearing white clothes.

We have now added another modifier to the head 'women', namely the Preposition Phrase 'in the house'. This has a head, the preposition 'in', which governs the Noun Phrase 'the house', which itself has a head (the noun 'house') and a modifier (the determiner 'the'). The hierarchy of constituents thus extends downwards.

Let us try another expansion of our original sentence:

(c) The women who lived in the house were wearing white clothes.

We have now added a different modifier to the noun 'women', and this time it is a relative clause, 'who lived in the house'. This resembles a sentence, having a Noun Phrase as Subject (the relative pronoun 'who') and a Predicate consisting of a verb ('lived') as its head and a Preposition Phrase as modifier. This relative clause is an example of what is often called *embedding*: one sentence ('The women lived in the house') is embedded in another sentence ('The women were wearing white clothes'), of which it becomes a subordinate part. In traditional terminology, the embedded sentence is a *subordinate clause*. This explains why our hierarchy of constituents contained 'clause' as well as 'sentence'. Our original sentence (a) was also a clause, but an independent one, and we can say that Sentence (c) consists of a main clause and a subordinate clause.

This notion of hierarchy in sentence structure is of primary importance. For example, if we wish to change a sentence (for example, from a statement to a question, or from an affirmative to a negative form), we cannot do it by rules which just shuffle individual words around: the rules have to recognize the various units of the sentence and the ways in which they are subordinated to one another. For instance, if we want to turn the sentence 'The king is at home' into a question, we have to bring 'is' in front of the whole noun phrase 'the king' to produce 'Is the king at home?' 'The is king at home?' would be ungrammatical.

Language is symbolic

In all these ways a language shows system, and it is now perhaps clear, at any rate in a general way, what we mean when we say that a language is a system of vocal sounds. These sounds are *symbolic*. That is, they stand for something other than themselves, and their relationship to the thing that they stand for is not a necessary one, but arbitrary. There are a very few words which relate in a non-arbitrary way to the thing to which they refer. For instance, the word *cuckoo* refers to a bird whose call sounds somewhat like the word itself. Similarly, the word *quack*, referring to the call of a duck, is an approximation to the noise that ducks actually make. The vast majority of words, however, are purely symbolic, with no necessary relationship between the word or its sounds and the referent of the word. Thus English uses the word *cow* to refer to a large, domesticated bovine animal, while French refers to the same animal as a *vache*: neither word sounds like the animal in question, or relates to it in any other way, and the fact that these two language have very different words for the same animal demonstrates that the relationship between the word and its referent is essentially arbitrary.

The same kind of distinction applies to gestures: when a chimpanzee shows a companion that it is hungry by pretending to eat, it is using a representational gesture, but when a person nods their head to indicate assent (or, in some cultures, refusal) the gesture is arbitrary and therefore symbolic. Weeping is a sign of sorrow, blushing a sign of shame, and paleness a sign of fear, but these signs are *caused* by the emotional states in question, and so are not arbitrary or symbolic. When a person shakes their fist in anger, they are delivering a blow in pantomime, and the gesture is representational, but when the same person raises a clenched or flattened hand in a communist or fascist salute, they have moved into the realm of the purely symbolic.

Animal gestures and cries are largely non-symbolic. Usually they are either of the weeping and blushing kind, that is expressive cries or gestures, or they are representational, as when a chimpanzee pulls a companion in the direction it wants it to go. When a bird cries out on the approach of a predator, and so warns its companions, it is reacting automatically to the stimulus of seeing the enemy. Its cry triggers off reactions in its companions, which take to flight, but the bird utters the warning cry even if there are no companions present. The evolutionary process will obviously favour animals where such expressive cries trigger off suitable reactions, but the element of symbolism is small.

Its symbolical quality is one of the things that makes human language such a powerful tool. The expressive cry or trigger stimulus can refer only to the immediate situation, to what is present to the senses, but the symbolical utterance can refer to things out of sight, to the past and the future, to the hypothetical and the possible.

The functions of language

Language is used for more than one purpose. The person who hits their thumb with a hammer and utters a string of curses is using language for an expressive purpose: they are relieving their feelings, and need no audience but themselves. People can often be heard *playing* with language: children especially like using language as if it were a toy, repeating, distorting, inventing, punning and jingling. There is also a play element in the use of language in some literature. But when philosophers use language to clarify their ideas on a subject, they are using it as an instrument of thought. When two neighbours gossip over the fence, or exchange conventional greetings as they pass one another in the street, language is being used to strengthen the bonds of cohesion between the members of a society. Language, it seems, is a multipurpose instrument. One function, however, is basic: language enables us to influence one another's behaviour, and to influence it in great detail, and thereby makes human co-operation possible. Other animals co-operate, for example many primates, and social insects like bees and ants, and use communication systems in the process. But human co-operation is more detailed and more diversified than that found elsewhere in the animal kingdom. This human co-operation would be unthinkable without language, and it is obviously this function which has made language so successful and so important; other functions can be looked on as by-products. A language, of course, always belongs to a group of people, not to an individual. The group that uses any given language is called the *speech community*.

Language types

A human language, then, is a signalling system which operates with symbolic vocal sounds, and which is used by some group of people for the purposes of communication and social co-operation. There are over six thousand human languages spoken in the world today, which all fall under this definition of language, but nevertheless differ widely from one another. Various attempts have been made, therefore, to classify languages into different types.

One scheme distinguishes two main types of language, the analytic and the synthetic. An analytic language is one that uses very few bound morphemes, such as are seen in English prefixes and suffixes (*re*fill, slow*ly*) and in the inflections (grammatical endings) of English nouns and verbs (box*es*, talk*ing*, talk*ed*). Chinese, for example, is a highly analytic language: it has few bound forms, its words being mostly one-syllable morphemes or compounds of free morphemes. A synthetic language, by contrast, uses large numbers of bound morphemes, and often combines long strings of them to form a single word. Examples of highly synthetic languages are the Inuit languages and Turkish. Most languages lie between these extremes, for the synthetic–analytic division is not a sharp one: rather it is a continuous scale, a continuum, with languages occupying various points between the two extremes. Its weakness as a system of classification is that languages are mixed: some are more synthetic or more analytic in some respects, some in others.

It nevertheless has its uses: it makes sense, for example, to say that the English language in the course of its history has become less synthetic and more analytic.

Another well-known classification divides languages into four types: *isolating, agglutinative, flectional* (or *inflectional*) and *polysynthetic* (or *incorporating*). An isolating language uses no bound forms: words are invariable, and in the extreme case every word would consist of a single morpheme. Vietnamese and Chinese are examples of highly isolating languages. In agglutinative languages, such as Turkish and Finnish, there are many bound forms, and these are, as it were, stuck together to form words, without their shape being altered during the process: within a word, the boundaries between morphemes are clear-cut. In a flectional language, by contrast, the bound morphemes are not invariable, and a morpheme may signal several different features. For example, in Latin the noun *dominus* 'a master' has a genitive plural form *dominōrum*. The ending *-ōrum* signals three things: that the noun is plural, that it is genitive (so that the word means 'of masters') and that its gender is either masculine or neuter. But the ending *-ōrum* cannot be broken up into three pieces, each of which signals one of these things, whereas in an agglutinating language there would indeed be three different suffixes joined together to signal the three features. In a polysynthetic language, large numbers of morphemes, both grammatical and lexical, can be combined into a single word, as in the Inuit languages.

This fourfold system arose in the middle of the nineteenth century, and is still often used today. It is not wholly satisfactory, however. The various definitions given are not always completely clear, and the four classes are not quite mutually exclusive: the Inuit languages, for example, are both agglutinative and polysynthetic. For this reason, attempts have been made in recent years to establish different systems of language types. The two systems we have so far considered are both based on morphology, that is, the structure of words. Many recent linguists have instead concentrated on word-order, and tried to base a typology on it.

We have already noted that in English the normal order of the elements in a clause is Subject–Verb–Object, as in 'The dog bit John', whereas some languages prefer a different order: Classical

Latin, for example, normally has S–O–V order, as in 'Canis Marcum momordit', literally 'Dog Marcus bit', that is, 'The/A dog bit Marcus.' There are six possible combinations of Subject, Verb and Object, and five of them are certainly attested in living languages, while the sixth (O–S–V) probably also exists, in a few languages in South America. Again, in English an adjective normally precedes its noun, as in 'white clothes', but in some languages it usually follows it, as in French 'vêtements blancs', literally 'clothes white'. In French the possessive also follows the noun, as in 'la mort du roi', but in this case English has a choice: the possessive can come before the noun ('the king's death') or after it ('the death of the king'). In both English and French a relative clause comes after its governing noun, as in an example we have already seen: 'The women, who were wearing white clothes …'; but in some languages, such as Turkish, the order is the other way round. Again, both English and French use prepositions, which are placed before the noun phrase which they govern, as in the Preposition Phrase 'in white clothes', but some languages, again including Turkish, instead use postpositions, which are placed *after* the noun phrase which they govern. In Old English, however, both prepositions and postpositions were used.

One attempt to categorize languages by means of word-order divides them into those in which the head normally precedes the modifier ('operand–operator languages'), and those in which it normally follows it ('operator–operand languages'). So in operand–operator languages the Verb precedes the Object, the Noun precedes its adjectives and possessives and relative clauses, and the Preposition precedes the noun phrase which it governs; Welsh is an example of an operand–operator language. In operator–operand languages, the Object precedes the Verb, adjectives and possessives and relative clauses precede their Noun, and Postpositions are used instead of Prepositions; Turkish is an example of an operator–operand language. Unfortunately, a very large number of languages fail to conform exactly to either pattern: English, for example, is largely an operand–operator language, but places adjectives before the noun. Some advocates of the system therefore argue that the two types are ideals towards which languages strive: a mixed language is in process of transition from one type to the other. It is doubtful, however, whether this theory is supported by the actual data of language change.

There are some methodological difficulties with such word-order studies, especially in finding cross-language definitions for the categories used: it is not certain, for example, that all languages have parts of the sentence that can be categorized as Subject, Verb and Object. Some systems of language typology avoid this particular difficulty by using non-syntactic features for the classification: for example, it is possible to use semantic categories such as Agent, Instrument, Experiencer and Patient, instead of (or in addition to) syntactic categories like Subject and Object. None of the various approaches used, however, seems to have succeeded in establishing an all-embracing scheme of language types, and perhaps such an aim is in fact impracticable. They have, however, thrown much light on the structure of various languages and on the differences (and resemblances) between them.

Language universals

The study of language types has been closely linked to the search for language universals, that is, features which all languages possess, and must possess. Typology examines language variation, while the study of universals tries to establish the permissible limits of this variation, and both use the same kind of material. The search for linguistic universals was given considerable impetus by the work of Noam Chomsky. Because of the ease with which children learn language, Chomsky maintains that human language is innate: in the brain is a genetically transmitted 'language organ', which determines the syntactic and semantic properties of all languages. In Chomsky's view, therefore, all languages have the same underlying structure, and it should be possible to demonstrate the existence of universals. Not all specialists in the field, however, believe that *all* language universals are innate: some take the view that some universals may have psychological or functional explanations.

Some proposed universals are absolute, for example that all languages have vowels. It can be added that all languages have oral vowels (but not all languages have nasal vowels). There are also strong tendencies which are not quite universals: for example, nearly all languages have nasal consonants, but there are just a few that lack them. Some proposed universals are of the 'If A, then B' type: for example, 'If a language has V–S–O as its basic word-order, then it invariably has prepositions.' On the other hand, if a language has S–O–V as its basic word-order, then it will probably have postpositions; but this is not a universal, but a strong tendency, because there are counter-examples: Classical Latin, for example, has S–O–V as its basic word-order, but has prepositions. Universals of the 'If A, then B' type are called *implicational* universals; and tendencies of this type are similarly called implicational tendencies.

2 The flux of language

Languages sometimes die out, usually because of competition from another language. For example, Norn, a Germanic language related to Old Norse, was introduced to Orkney and Shetland by Viking settlers, and spoken there until the eighteenth century. Its use began to decline from the fifteenth century, when Norway ceded the islands to Scotland, and Scots was increasingly used instead. When a language officially becomes 'extinct' is sometimes difficult to determine: for instance, many histories of English state that Cornish 'died out' in 1777 when the last native speaker died. However, a small number of speakers continued to use and write in the language, and by the middle of the nineteenth century a revival was in process. The revival gathered pace in the twentieth century, and, according to *Ethnologue*, a number of people now use it as first language, some 1,000 use it as their everyday language, and 2,000 others speak it fluently. Cornish is now recognized as an official language of the United Kingdom, and as a Minority Language within the European Union. A language can also become dead in another way. Nobody today speaks Classical Latin as spoken by Julius Caesar, or Classical Greek as spoken by Pericles, or the Old Icelandic spoken by the heroes of the Norse sagas. So Classical Latin and Classical Greek and Old Icelandic are dead languages. But, although dead, they have not *died*: they have changed into something else. People still speak Greek as a living language, and this language is largely a changed form of the language spoken in the Athens of Pericles. The people who live in Rome today speak a language that has developed by a process of continuous change out of the language spoken there in the time of Julius Caesar, though Modern Italian developed out of the everyday language of the ancient Roman market-place and of the common soldiery, rather than out of the upper-class literary Latin that Caesar wrote. And the people who live in Iceland today speak a language that has developed directly out of the language of the great Icelandic sagas of the Middle Ages.

In fact all living languages change, though the rate of change varies from time to time and from language to language. The modern Icelander, for example, does not find it very difficult to read the medieval Icelandic sagas, because the rate of change in Icelandic has always been slow, ever since the country was colonized by Norwegians a thousand years ago and Icelandic history began. But the English, on the contrary, find an English document of the year 1300 very difficult to understand, unless they have special training; and an English document of the year 900 seems to them to be written in a foreign language, which they may conclude (mistakenly) to have no connection with Modern English.

Linguistic change in English

The extent to which the English language has changed in the past thousand years can be seen by looking at a few passages of English from different periods. Since it is convenient to see the same material handled by different writers, we have chosen a short passage from the Bible, which has been translated into English at many different times. The passage is from chapter XV of the Gospel according to Luke, and is the end of the story of the Prodigal Son. Here it is first in a twentieth-century translation, the New English Bible, published in 1961:

Now the elder son was out on the farm; and on his way back, as he approached the house, he heard music and dancing. He called one of the servants and asked what it meant. The servant told him, 'Your brother has come home, and your father has killed the fatted calf because he has him back safe and sound.' But he was angry and refused to go in. His father came out and pleaded with him; but he retorted, 'You know how I have slaved for you all these years; I never once disobeyed your orders; and you never gave me so much as a kid, for a feast with my friends. But now that this son of yours turns up, after running through your money with his women, you kill the fatted calf for him.' 'My boy,' said the father, 'you were always with me, and everything I have is yours. How could we help celebrating this happy day? Your brother here was dead and has come back to life, was lost and is found.'

You may feel that there is a certain unevenness of manner about that, but at any rate it is twentieth-century English, with little archaic or affected about it. Now let us look at the same passage as it appeared in the famous King James Bible of the year 1611:

> Now his elder sonne was in the field, and as he came and drew nigh to the house, he heard musicke & dauncing, and he called one of the seruants, and asked what these things meant. And he said vnto him, Thy brother is come, and thy father hath killed the fatted calfe, because he hath receiued him safe and sound. And he was angry, and would not goe in: therefore came his father out, and intreated him. And he answering said to his father, Loe, these many yeeres doe I serue thee neither transgressed I at any time thy commandement, and yet thou neuer gauest mee a kid, that I might make merry with my friends: but as soone as this thy sonne was come, which hath deuoured thy liuing with harlots, thou hast killed for him the fatted calfe. And he said vnto him, Sonne, thou art euer with me, and all that I haue is thine. It was meete that we should make merry, and be glad: for this thy brother was dead, and is aliue againe: and was lost, and is found.

We have no great difficulty in understanding that passage, but nevertheless there are numerous ways in which it differs from present-day English. In its vocabulary, there are words which seem to us archaic, or at least old-fashioned: *nigh* 'near', *meete* 'fitting', *transgressed* 'broke, violated', *commandement* 'commands, orders'. One word looks familiar, but has an unfamiliar meaning: *liuing* does not mean 'living' in our sense of the word, but rather 'income, property, possessions'. This sense still exists in the phrase 'to make a living'. In grammar, we notice the use of the personal pronoun *thou* and its accusative *thee*, together with the associated pronoun-determiner *thy*: and after *thou* the verbs have the inflection *-est* or *-st* (*gauest, hast*). The use of *thou* in the passage in fact shows the disadvantage of using translations for our illustrative material, for it does not reflect normal English usage in 1611. In Shakespeare's time, a father could address his son as *thou*, but the son could not, like the son in the passage, say *thou* in return without insulting his father: he would have to say *you* or *ye*. The usage in the passage is due to the influence of the original Greek. The passage uses the relative pronoun *which* ('thy sonne ... which hath deuoured') where we would use *who*. In word-order, notice the sequence Verb–Subject–Object in 'neither transgressed I ... thy commandement', and similarly Verb–Subject order in 'therefore came his father out'. The perfect tense of the verb *to come* is formed with the auxiliary *be*, not *have*: 'Thy brother *is* come', 'this thy sonne *was* come', where we would say 'has come', 'had come'. In the noun phrases *this thy sonne* and *this thy brother*, the determiner *this* and the pronoun-determiner *thy* occur together before the noun; today we would say 'this son of yours', 'this brother of yours'.

The spellings of the passage are quite close to modern ones, except for the use of *u* and *v*, which are not used to distinguish vowel from consonant: *v* is always used at the beginning of a word (*vnto*), and *u* is always used elsewhere (*serue, out, thou*). Notice, however, the spelling of *dauncing*, which does rather suggest a different pronunciation from *dancing*. There is in fact plenty of evidence to show that pronunciation in 1611 differed in many ways from pronunciation today, even when the spellings are the same. The vowels in particular were different, as we shall see later.

As our third example we can take the same passage as rendered by John Wycliffe, the first person to translate the entire Bible into English. Wycliffe died in 1384, and his translation probably dates from the last few years of his life. Like many Middle English texts, the passage uses two different kinds of letter *g*, namely *ʒ* and *g*. The *ʒ* (called 'yogh') is descended from Old English script, whereas *g* was used in writing Latin in the Anglo-Saxon period, and came to be commonly used in writing English after the Norman Conquest. In the passage, *ʒ* usually corresponds to a modern *y*, as in *ʒeeris* 'years'; but in *neiʒede* 'drew nigh, approached', it corresponds to a modern *gh*, and was probably pronounced [ç] (like the consonant of Modern German *ich*). The punctuation of the passage has been modernized.

Forsoth his eldere sone was in the feeld, and whanne he cam and neiʒede to the hous, he herde a symfonye and a crowde. And he clepide oon of the seruauntis, and axide what thingis thes weren. And he seide to him, Thi brodir is comen, and thi fadir hath slayn a fat calf, for he receyued him saf. Forsoth he was wroth, and wolde not entre. Therfore his fadir gon out, bigan to preie him. And he answeringe to his fadir seide, Lo, so manye ʒeeris I serue to thee, and I brak neuere thi commaundement, thou hast neuer ʒouun a kyde to me, that I schulde ete largely with my frendis. But aftir that this thi sone, which deuouride his substaunce with hooris, cam, thou hast slayn to him a fat calf. And he seide to him, Sone, thou ert euere with me, and alle myne thingis ben thyne. Forsothe it bihofte to ete plenteously, and for to ioye: for this thi brother was deed, and lyuede aʒeyn: he peryschide, and he is founden.

This is much more remote from Modern English, especially in vocabulary. There are many words and phrases which, while perfectly comprehensible, sound archaic or old-fashioned, like *forsoth* 'indeed' and *wroth* 'angry'. There are also words which are quite strange to the modern reader, like *neiʒede* 'approached' and *clepide* 'called'. There are familiar-looking words with unfamiliar meanings, like *symfonye* 'musical instrument', *crowde* 'fiddle', *largely* 'liberally, plenteously', *thyngis* 'goods' and *for* 'because' (in 'for he receyued him saf'). In grammar, there are noun-plural endings in *-is* (*thyngis, hooris*, etc.), verb-plural endings in *-en* or *-n* (*weren, ben*), verb past-tense endings in *-ide* (*clepide, axide*, etc.) and past participles ending in *-n* (*comen, founden*). In spelling, only *u* occurs in the passage, not *v*, but in Wycliffe's time they tended to be used interchangeably, and not distributed as they are in the 1611 passage: the use of *v* initially and *u* elsewhere was a printer's convention, which in England lasted until about 1630, but manuscripts often use the two letters indiscriminately. The passage also uses *i* instead of *j* (*ioye*); the letter *j* was in fact merely a variant of *i*, and the modern vowel–consonant distinction in their use was not established until about 1630. There are also numerous words where the spelling suggests a pronunciation different from our own – *whanne* 'when', *oon* 'one', etc. – though of course this piece of evidence alone is not sufficient for us to determine their pronunciation. The word-order of the passage, however, is very close to that of present-day English.

For our final example, we go back before the Norman Conquest, to a manuscript of the early eleventh century. Although Anglo-Saxon manuscripts do not distinguish short and long vowels, we mark long vowels by putting a macron (short horizontal line) over them, while short vowels are left unmarked. The symbol *þ* (called 'thorn') is equivalent to the modern *th*: the symbol *æ* (called 'ash') is pronounced like the vowel of the word *hat* in RP. The punctuation is modernized. As the English of this period is difficult for the modern reader, we give only the opening of the passage.

> Sōþlicē his yldra sunu wæs on æcere; and hē cōm, and þā hē þām hūse genēalæhte, hē gehȳrde þæne swēg and þæt wered. þā clypode hē ānne þēow, and ācsode hine hwæt þæt wǣre. þā cwæþ hē, þīn brōþor cōm, and þīn fæder ofslōh ān fætt cealf, forþām þe hē hine hālne onfēng.

Part of the difficulty of this lies in the number of unfamiliar words: *þā* 'when, then', *genēalæhte* 'approached', *swēg* 'noise', *wered* 'multitude, band', *þēow* 'servant', *ofslōh* 'killed', *forþām þe* 'because', *hine* 'him', *onfēng* 'received'; these are all words that have died out from the language. In the later passages, some of them are replaced by words borrowed from French after the Norman Conquest (*approached, servant, received*). Even words which have survived may be used in an unfamiliar sense: the word *æcere* has developed into our *acre*, but means 'field', and *hālne* has become our *whole*, but means 'well, safe'. Even words unchanged in meaning appear in unfamiliar spelling, like *yldra sunu* 'elder son', and were obviously pronounced differently from their modern counterparts.

The passage also differs from present-day English in the way words change their endings according to their grammatical function in the sentence. This could be demonstrated from many words in the passage but three brief examples will suffice. The word for 'field' is *æcer*, but after the preposition *on* it has to add the ending *-e* (pronounced as an extra syllable), and so in the text we have the expression *on æcere*. The expression for 'the house' is *þæt hūs*, but 'to the house' is *þām hūse*, and this is the form that appears in the text; *æcere* and *hūse* are the *dative case* of the nouns *æcer* and *hūs*. The normal word for 'was' is *wæs*, as in the first sentence of the passage, but there is also a form *wǣre* (the so-called subjunctive form) which has to be used in certain constructions, like 'ācsode hine hwæt þæt *wǣre*' ('asked him what it was'). This form is occasionally still used in Modern English, for instance in the phrase 'if I were rich'.

The passage also differs from present-day English in word-order. Translated literally word for word it runs as follows:

> Indeed, his elder son was in field; and he came, and when he the house approached, he heard the noise and the crowd. Then called he a servant, and asked him what it was. Then said he, Your brother came, and your father killed a fat calf, because he him safe received.

There we see three different types of word-order, different arrangements of Subject–Verb–Object. Some clauses have the normal present-day order of S–V–O: 'he heard the noise', 'your father killed a fat calf'. But some have the order V–S–O: 'then called he a servant', 'Then said he …' This construction often occurs when the clause begins with an adverbial expression, especially adverbs like *then* and *there*. Yet other clauses have the order S–O–V: 'when he the house approached', 'because he him safe received'. This word-order occurs in subordinate clauses, opened in this case by the conjunctions *because* and *when*. These three types of word-order are common in the earliest forms of English, and are still found in Modern German. One of the major syntactic changes in the English language since Anglo-Saxon times has been the disappearance of the S–O–V and V–S–O types of word-order, and the establishment of the S–V–O type as normal. The S–O–V type disappeared in the early Middle Ages, and the V–S–O type was rare after the middle of the seventeenth century. V–S word-order does indeed still exist in English as a less common variant, as in sentences like 'Down the road came a whole crowd of children', but the full V–S–O type hardly occurs today.

The English language, then, has changed enormously in the last thousand years. New words have appeared, and some old ones disappeared. Words have changed in meaning. The grammatical endings of words have changed, and many such endings have disappeared from the language. The membership of 'closed class' word-forms, the grammatical words, has changed: the system of personal pronouns, for example, has lost the forms *thou* and *thee*. There have been changes in word-order, the permissible ways in which words can be arranged to make meaningful utterances.

Pronunciation has changed. Taken all together, these changes add up to a major transformation of the language.

It can also be seen, even from the four passages that we have quoted, that the pace of change has varied. Between the New English Bible and the King James Bible there is a period of just three and a half centuries, but the differences between them are less than those between the King James Bible and Wycliffe's version, which are separated by only about two and a quarter centuries. The differences between the Wycliffe and the preconquest passage, too, are very great. It is conventional to divide the history of the English language into three broad periods, which are usually called Old English, Middle English and Modern English. No exact boundaries can be drawn, but Old English covers from the first Anglo-Saxon settlements in England (fifth century AD) to about 1100, Middle English from about 1100 to about 1500, and Modern English from about 1500 to the present day. These periods are often subdivided, giving such subperiods as Late Old English (c. 900–1100) and Early Modern English (c. 1500–1650).

Mechanisms of linguistic change

All living languages undergo changes analogous to those we have just seen exemplified in English. What causes such changes? There is no single answer to this question: changes in a language are of various kinds, and there seem to be various reasons for them.

The changes that have caused the most disagreement are those in pronunciation. We have various sources of evidence for the pronunciations of earlier times, such as the spellings, the treatment of words borrowed from other languages or borrowed by them, the descriptions of contemporary grammarians and spelling-reformers, and the modern pronunciations in all the languages and dialects concerned. From the middle of the sixteenth century, there are in England writers who attempt to describe the position of the speech organs for the production of English phonemes, and who invent what are in effect systems of phonetic symbols. These various kinds of evidence, combined with a knowledge of the mechanisms of speech production, can often give us a very good idea of the pronunciation of an earlier age, though absolute certainty is never possible.

When we study the pronunciation of a language over any period of a few generations or more, we find there are always large-scale regularities in the changes: for example, over a certain period of time, just about all the long [aː] vowels in a language may change into long [eː] vowels, or all the [b] consonants in a certain position (for example at the end of a word) may change into [p] consonants. Such regular changes are often called *sound laws*. There are no universal sound laws (even though sound laws often reflect universal tendencies), but simply particular sound laws for one given language (or dialect) at one given period. We must not think of a sound law, however, as a sudden change which immediately affects all the words concerned. If [b] changes to [p] in a given language, the change may first appear in words which are frequently used, and gradually spread through the rest of the vocabulary. Indeed, the sound law may cease to operate before all the relevant words have been affected, so that a few are left with the earlier pronunciation.

During childhood, we learn our mother tongue very thoroughly, and acquire a whole set of speech habits which become second nature to us. If later we learn a foreign language, we inevitably carry over some of these speech habits into it, and so do not speak it exactly like a native. For example, we have seen that in most phonetic contexts the English /p/ phoneme is pronounced with a following aspiration, producing a kind of [pʰ] sound, and the same is in fact true of the English /t/ and /k/ phonemes. But it is not true of the similar phonemes in French or Italian, where the voiceless plosives are pronounced without any following aspiration. Many English speakers of French and Italian, even competent ones, carry over their aspirated voiceless plosives into those languages, and this is one of many features that make them sound foreign to native speakers. In bilingual situations, therefore, the second language tends to be modified. Such modifications may not persist: an isolated immigrant to Britain will usually have grandchildren who speak English like their classmates whose grandparents were born in Britain, because the influence of the general speech environment (peer-group, school, work) is stronger than that of the home. But if a large and closely knit group of people adopt a new language, then the modifications that they make in it may persist among their descendants, even if the latter no longer speak the original language that caused the changes. This can be seen in Wales, where the influence of Welsh has affected the pronunciation of English, and the very characteristic intonation patterns of Welsh English have been carried over from Welsh, even among those who no longer speak it. Many historical changes may have been due to a linguistic substratum of this kind: a conquering minority that imposed its language on a conquered population must often have had its language modified by its victims.

Changes may also be due to contact between speakers of different dialects. In the long term, this can lead to the creation of a new variety of the language, as was the case in New Zealand, where English-speaking settlers from different parts of the British Isles came together in the nineteenth century, all bringing their own dialects. By the twentieth century, the variety that we now recognize as New Zealand English had emerged from this linguistic melting-pot. More recently, movement of people to New Towns, such as Milton Keynes in the south of England, commuting, greater ease of travel and new forms of communication have led to what has been termed 'dialect levelling', a process whereby the 'marked' or more regionally specific features of local dialects are replaced by more widespread ones, such as the glottal stop. This has been reported in the media as the spread of 'Estuary English', but, as we shall see in chapter 11, the reality is more complex.

Changes of this kind have often been attributed to 'fashion', or the prestige of the incoming feature. Some of the changes in accepted English pronunciation in the seventeenth and eighteenth centuries could be seen as consisting in the replacement of one style of pronunciation by another style already existing, and it is likely that such substitutions were a result of the great social changes of the period: the increased power and wealth of the middle classes, and their steady infiltration upwards into the ranks of the landed gentry, probably carried elements of middle-class pronunciation into upper-class speech. An example of this is the pronunciation of the final consonant in words such as *hunting*, *shooting* and *fishing*. Until the nineteenth century, it was perfectly acceptable to pronounce these as *huntin'*, *shootin'* and *fishin'*, with final /n/ rather than /ŋ/ (erroneously referred to as 'dropping the *g*', since, in phonetic terms, there is no /g/ to drop). However, the middle classes, no doubt influenced by the spelling, increasingly viewed the /n/ pronunciation as incorrect, so that this came to mark the speech of both the lower and the upper classes. Today the phrase *huntin'*, *shootin'* and fishin' is a stereotype of very old-fashioned aristocratic speech: otherwise the /m/ pronunciation is associated with lower-class and/or informal speech in most of the English-speaking world.

Another possible explanation for changes in pronunciation is that the imitation of children is imperfect: they copy their parents' speech, but never reproduce it exactly. This is true, but it is also true that such deviations from adult speech are usually corrected in later childhood. Perhaps it is more significant that even adults show a certain amount of random variation in their pronunciation of a given phoneme, even if the phonetic context is kept unchanged. This, however, cannot explain changes in pronunciation unless it can be shown that there is some systematic trend in the failures of imitation: if they are merely random deviations they will cancel one another out and there will be no nett change in the language. For some of these random variations to be selected at the expense of others, there must be further forces at work.

One such force which is often invoked is the principle of ease, or minimization of effort. We all try to economize energy in our actions, it is argued, so we tend to take short cuts in the movements of our speech organs, to replace movements calling for great accuracy or energy by less demanding ones, to omit sounds if they are not essential for understanding, and so on. Such changes increase the efficiency of the language as a communication system, and are undoubtedly a factor in linguistic change, though we have to add that what seems easy or difficult to a speaker will depend on the particular language that has been learnt. Suppose we have a sequence of three sounds in which the first and the third are voiced, while the middle one is voiceless: the speaker has to carry out the operation of switching off voice before the second sound and then switching it on again before the third. An economy of effort could be obtained by omitting these two operations and allowing the voice to continue through all three sounds. Such a change would be seen if the pronunciation of *fussy* were changed to *fuzzy*, the voiceless /s/ being replaced by the voiced /z/ between the two vowels. Changes of this kind are common in the history of language, but nevertheless we cannot lay it down as a universal rule that *fuzzy* is easier to pronounce than *fussy*. In Swedish, for example, there is no /z/ phoneme, and Swedes who learn English find it difficult to say *fuzzy*, which they often mispronounce as *fussy*. For them, plainly, *fussy* is the easier of the two pronunciations, because it accords better with the sound system of their own language.

The change from *fussy* to *fuzzy* would be an example of **assimilation**, which is a very common kind of change. Assimilation is the changing of a sound under the influence of a neighbouring one. For example, the word *scant* was once *skamt*, but the /m/ has been changed to /n/ under the influence of the following /t/. Greater efficiency has hereby been achieved, because /n/ and /t/ are articulated in the same place (with the tip of the tongue against the teeth-ridge), whereas /m/ is articulated elsewhere (with the two lips). So the place of articulation of the nasal consonant has been changed to conform with that of the following plosive. A more recent example of the same kind of thing is the common pronunciation of *football* as *foopball*. Sometimes it is the second of the two sounds that is changed by the assimilation. This can be seen in some changes that have taken place in English under the influence of /w/: until about 1700, words like *swan* and *wash* rhymed with words like *man* and *rash*; the change in the vowel of *swan* and *wash* has given it the lip-rounding and the retracted tongue-position of the /w/, and so economized in effort.

Assimilation is not the only way in which we change our pronunciation in order to increase efficiency. It is very common for consonants to be lost at the end of a word: in Middle English, word-final /-n/ was often lost in unstressed syllables, so that *baken* 'to bake' changed from /'baːkən/ to /'baːkə/, and later to /baːk/. Consonant clusters are often simplified. At one time there was a /t/ in words like *castle* and *Christmas*, and an initial /k/ in words like *knight* and *know*. Sometimes a whole syllable is dropped out when two successive syllables begin with the same consonant (*haplology*): a recent example is *temporary*, which in Britain is often pronounced as if it were *tempory*.

On the other hand, ease of pronunciation can lead to an extra phoneme being inserted in a word: in Old English, our word *thunder* was *þunor*, with no *d*. By normal development, *þunor* would have become **thunner*, not *thunder*, but at some stage a /d/ has been inserted in the pronunciation. Spellings with *d* are first found in the thirteenth century, and are completely normal by the sixteenth. Why was a /d/ inserted in the word? Probably because the pronunciation *thunder* actually calls for less precise movements of the speech organs. The /d/ arose from a slight mistiming in the transition from the nasal /n/ to the following phoneme (which was probably a syllabic /r/ rather than a vowel). This transition calls for two simultaneous movements of the speech organs: (1) the nasal passages are closed by the raising of the soft palate, and (2) the tongue is moved away from the teeth to unblock the mouth passage. If the two movements are not carried out simultaneously, but the nasal passages are closed before the tongue moves, a /d/ will be heard between the /n/ and the following phoneme, as the stop is released. Similar mistimings produced the /b/ in the middle of the words *thimble* and *bramble* (Old English *þymel*, *brēmel*). Sometimes, too, ease of pronunciation apparently leads us to reverse the order of two phonemes in a word (*metathesis*): this has happened in the words *wasp* and *burn*, which by regular development would have been *waps* and *brin* or *bren*.

The changes produced in pursuit of efficiency can often be tolerated, because a language always provides more signals than the absolute minimum necessary for the transmission of the message, to give a margin of safety: like all good communication systems, human language has built in to it a considerable amount of redundancy. But there is a limit to this toleration: the necessities of communication, the urgent needs of humans as users of language, provide a counterforce to the principle of minimum effort. If, through excessive economy of effort, an utterance is not understood, or is misunderstood, the speaker is obliged to repeat it or recast it, making more effort. The necessities of communication, moreover, may be responsible for the selection of some of the random variations of a phoneme rather than others, so that a change in pronunciation occurs in a certain direction. This direction may be chosen because it makes the sound inherently more audible: for example, open nasal vowels seem to be more distinctive in quality than close ones, and in languages which have such vowels it is not uncommon for a nasal [e] to develop into a nasal [a].

In considering such changes, however, we cannot look at the isolated phoneme: we have to consider the sound system of the language as a whole. The 'safeness' or otherwise of a phoneme for communicative purposes does not depend solely on its own inherent distinctiveness: it depends also on the other phonemes in the language with which it can be contrasted, and the likelihood that it may be confused with them. Let us imagine that in the vowel system of a language there is a short [e], as in *bet* (see for example the vowel diagram in figure 4, p. 12 above); in one direction from it there is a short [æ] (as in *bat*), and in another direction a short [ə] (as in the first syllable of *about*); but in the upward (closer) direction there is no short vowel, no kind of short [ɪ] for example. Suppose now that random variations occur in speakers' pronunciations of these three vowels. When the variations of [e] go too far in the direction of [æ] or [ə], the speaker will be forced to correct them, to avoid misunderstanding. But when the variations are in the direction of [ɪ], there is no such necessity for checking or correction. The result will be a shift in the centre of gravity of the [e], which will drift up towards [ɪ]. Moreover, the movement of [e] towards [ɪ] will leave more scope for variations in [æ], which may tend to drift up towards [e]. In this way, a whole chain of vowel changes may take place.

In this example we have assumed that the contrast between the three vowels is important enough in the functioning of the language for speakers to resist any changes which threaten this contrast. This will be the case if large numbers of words are distinguished from one another by these vowels, in other words if the contrast between them does a lot of work in the language. The functional load carried by a contrast is a major factor when speakers decide (unconsciously) whether to let a change take place or not. There may be forces in the system making for the amalgamation of two phonemes, and if there are very few words in the language which will be confused with one another as a result then there will not be much resistance to the change; but if serious confusion will be caused by the amalgamation it will be resisted more strongly, and perhaps be prevented.

This does not mean, on the other hand, that a phoneme with a small functional load will necessarily be thrown out of the system, either by being lost or by being amalgamated with another phoneme. It also depends on the degree of effort required to *retain* the phoneme, which may be quite small. For example, the contrast in English between the voiced /ð/ and the voiceless /θ/ phonemes carries a very small load; there are a few pairs of words that are distinguished from one another solely by this difference, like *wreathe* and *wreath*, and *mouth* (verb) and *mouth* (noun); but in practice the distinction between the two phonemes is of very small importance, and it would cause no great inconvenience if they were amalgamated, for example by both evolving into some third, different, phoneme. On the other hand, it takes very little effort to retain the distinction between them. They belong to a whole series of voiced and voiceless fricatives (/v/ and /f/, /z/ and /s/, /ʒ/ and /ʃ/), and so fall into a familiar pattern; and if we abolished the distinction between them we should not economize in the number of *types* of contrast that we made; we should still have to distinguish fricatives from other types of consonant, and between voiced and voiceless fricatives.

The stability of /ð/ and /θ/ thus results from the fact that they are, in André Martinet's terminology, 'well integrated' in the consonant system of English. An even better integrated group of consonants in present-day English is the following:

Voiceless plosives	/p/ /t/ /k/
Voiced plosives	/b/ /d/ /g/
Nasals	/m/ /n/ /ŋ/

Each of these three series uses the same places of articulation: the two lips pressed together for /p/, /b/, /m/; the tip of the tongue pressed against the teeth-ridge for /t/, /d/, /n/; the back of the tongue pressed up against the soft palate for /k/, /g/, /ŋ/. So, using only three articulatory positions, and three distinctive articulatory features (plosiveness, nasality, voice), we get no fewer than nine distinct phonemes. This group is very stable, because the loss of any one of the nine would produce negligible economy in the system: if, say, /ŋ/ were to disappear, we should still have to be able to produce nasality for /m/ and /n/, and we should still have to be able to articulate with the back of the tongue against the soft palate for /g/ and /k/. So even if /ŋ/ carried a very small load in the language we should still be unlikely to get rid of it. For the same reason, if there were a hole in the pattern, it would stand a good chance in time of getting filled. If there were no /ŋ/ in present-day English, but there was some other consonant which was not very well integrated in any subsystem, then any variations in this consonant that moved it in the direction of [ŋ] would tend to be accepted, because they would represent an 'easier' pronunciation – easier, that is, in terms of the economy (and therefore efficiency) of the system as a whole.

Changes in morphology, syntax, vocabulary and word-meaning, while they can be complicated enough, are less puzzling than changes in pronunciation. Many of the same causes can be seen at work. The influence of other languages, for example, is very obvious: nations with high commercial, political and cultural prestige tend to influence their neighbours: for centuries, French influenced all the languages of Europe, while today the influence of the English language is penetrating all over the world, largely because of the power and prestige of the United States. This influence is strongest in the field of vocabulary, but one language can also influence the morphology and syntax of another. Such influence may occur if languages in a given area are in intimate contact over an extended period, and also when a religion spreads and its sacred books are translated: in the Old English period there were many translations from the Latin, and there is some evidence that Latin syntax influenced the structure of Old English, at least in some of its written forms.

In the realm of vocabulary and meaning, the influence of general social and cultural change is obvious. As society changes, there are new things that need new names: physical objects, institutions, sets of attitudes, values, concepts; and new words are produced to handle them (or existing words are given new meanings). Sentimentality, classicism, wave mechanics, parliaments, post-Impressionism, privatization – these are human inventions just as much as steam engines or aircraft or nylon: and people inevitably invented names for them. Moreover, because the world is constantly changing, many words insensibly change their meanings. It is particularly easy to overlook shifts of meaning in words that refer to values or to complexes of attitudes: for example, in Shakespeare's day the adjective *gentle* meant a good deal more than 'kind, sweet-natured, mild, not violent', for it referred to high birth as well as to moral qualities, and had a whole social theory behind it.

As in pronunciation, so at the other levels of language we see the constant conflict between the principle of minimum effort and the demands of communication. Minimization of effort is seen in the way words are often shortened, as when *public house* becomes *pub*, or *television* becomes *telly*, and also in the laconic and elliptical expressions that we often use in colloquial and intimate discourse. But if economy of this kind goes too far, some kind of compensating action may be taken, as when in Early Middle English the word *ea* was replaced by the French loanword *river*, and in the seventeenth century the bird called the *pie* was expanded to the *magpie*. In such ways, the redundancy which has been removed from the language by shortenings may be reinserted by lengthenings.

There is also interplay between the needs of the users and the inherent tendencies of the language system itself. One way in which the language system promotes change, especially in grammar, is through the operation of **analogy**, which also tends to produce economy. Analogy is seen at work when children are learning their language. A child learns pairs like *dog/dogs*, *bed/beds*, *bag/bags*, and so on. Then it learns a new word, say *plug*, and quite correctly forms the plural *plugs* from it, by analogy with these other pairs. Analogy, then, is the process of inventing a new element in conformity with some part of the language system that you already know. The way in which analogy can lead to change is seen when the child learns words like *man* and *mouse*, and forms the analogical plurals *mans* and *mouses*. Ultimately such childish errors are usually corrected, but analogical formations also take place in adult speech, and quite often persist and become accepted. In Old English there were many different ways of putting a noun into the plural: for example, *stān* 'stone', *stānas* 'stones'; *word*

'word', *word* 'words'; *scip* 'ship', *scipu* 'ships'; *synn* 'sin', *synna* 'sins'; *tunge* 'tongue', *tungan* 'tongues'; *bēo* 'bee', *bēon* 'bees'; *bōc* 'book', *bēc* 'books'; *lamb* 'lamb', *lambru* 'lambs'. The form *stānas* has developed quite regularly into our plural *stones*, but, sometime during the past thousand years, all the others have changed their plural ending to the -(*e*)*s* type, by analogy with the many nouns like *stone*. The rarer a word is, the more likely it is to be affected by analogy. The unusual noun-plural forms in present-day English, which are the ones that have managed to resist the analogy of the plural in -(*e*)*s*, are mostly very common words, like *men*, *feet* and *children*, or at any rate are words which *were* very common a few centuries ago, like *geese* and *oxen*.

Language families

The process of change in a language often leads to divergent development. Imagine a language which is spoken only by the population of two small adjacent villages. In each village, the language will slowly change, but the changes will not be identical in the two villages, because conditions are slightly different. Hence the speech used in one of the villages may gradually diverge from that used in the other. If there is rivalry between the villages, they may even pride themselves on such divergences, as a mark of local patriotism. Within the single village, speech will remain fairly uniform, because the speakers are in constant contact, and so influence one another. The rate at which the speech of one village diverges from that of the other will depend partly on the degree of difference between their ways of life, and partly on the intensity of communication between them. If the villages are close together and have a good deal of inter-village contact, so that many members of one village are constantly talking with members of the other, then divergence will be kept small, because the speech of one community will be constantly influencing the speech of the other. But if communications are bad, and members of one village seldom meet anybody from the other, then the rate of divergence may well be high. When a language has diverged into two forms like this, we say that it has two **dialects**.

Suppose now that the inhabitants of one of the villages pack up their belongings and migrate *en masse*. They go off to a distant country and live under conditions quite different from their old home, and completely lose contact with the other village. The rate at which the two dialects diverge will now increase, partly because of the difference of environment and way of life, partly because they no longer influence one another. After a few hundred years, the two dialects may have got so different that they are no longer mutually intelligible. We should now say that they were two different **languages**. Both have grown by a process of continuous change out of the single original language, but because of divergent development there are now two languages instead of one. When two languages have evolved in this way from some earlier single language, we say that they are *related*. The development of related languages from an earlier parent language can be represented diagrammatically as a family tree, thus:

As we shall see later, this kind of diagram is in some ways inadequate, and we must certainly avoid thinking of languages as if they were people. But as long as we bear this in mind, we shall find that family trees are a convenient way of depicting the relationships between languages. Recently, scholars have begun to experiment with more nuanced methods for visualizing the relationships between languages, using the same software which geneticists use for analysing and diagramming relationships between genetically related populations. Such tools are better able to allow for, and represent visually, the effects of hybridization and the gradual divergence of related dialects. Various different sorts of diagram can be generated by these techniques, but a common form is a network indicating the distance between several languages, such as in figure 5.

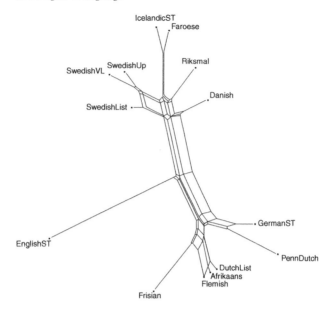

Figure 5 A language network

Languages descended from Latin

There are numerous examples in history of divergent development leading to the formation of related languages. For example, when the Romans conquered a large part of Europe, North Africa and the Near East, their language, Latin, became spoken over wide areas as the standard language of administration and government, especially in the western part of the empire. Then, in the fourth century of our era, the empire began to disintegrate, and, in the centuries which followed, was overrun by barbarian invasions – Huns, Slavs, Germans – and gradually broke up. In the new countries that eventually emerged from the ruins of the western empire, various languages were spoken. In some places, both Latin and the local languages had been swept away and replaced by the language of an invader – in England, by Anglo-Saxon, in North Africa, by Arabic. But in other places Latin was firmly enough rooted to survive as the language of the new nation, as in France, Italy and

Spain. But, because there was no longer a single unifying centre to hold the language together, divergent development took place, and Latin evolved into a number of different new languages. In general, the further a place was from Rome, the more the new language diverged from the original Latin.

In the early Middle Ages there was a whole welter of local dialects developed from Latin: each region would have its own local dialect. But, as the modern nation-states developed, these dialects became consolidated into a few great national languages. Today there are five national languages descended from Latin: Italian, Spanish, Portuguese, French and Romanian. There are also other languages derived from Latin which have not become national languages, but which are spoken by some large group with a common culture: such are Romansh (spoken in parts of Switzerland and of Italy), Provençal (spoken in southern France), Catalan (spoken in Catalonia and the Balearic Isles) and Sardinian (spoken in southern Sardinia). Languages descended from Latin are called *Romance* languages. We can draw a family tree of the Romance languages, thus:

Latin

Portuguese   Spanish   Italian   Provençal   French   Romansh, etc.

Each of the Romance languages has developed its own morphology and syntax, but they all bear signs of their common origin in Latin. The most obvious resemblances are in vocabulary: each language has undergone considerable changes in pronunciation, but the Latin origin of large numbers of words is quite evident. For example, the Latin word for 'good' is *bonus*: this has become Italian *buono*, Spanish *bueno*, French *bon*, Portuguese *bom* and Romanian *bun*. The Latin *homo* 'man' has become Italian *uomo*, Spanish *hombre*, French *homme*, Portuguese *homem* and Romanian *om*. The members of such a related group of words are said to be **cognate**.

The changes to Latin that ultimately saw it develop into different languages such as French, Spanish and Italian did not simply cause Latin to disappear. We have little documentary evidence dating from before the twelfth century AD for the languages that developed from Latin, but it is probable that many significant developments in Latin pre-date this period. However, Latin was probably used as a more or less standardized written form for these languages in the early Middle Ages. In non-Romance-speaking areas, however, such as Anglo-Saxon England, Latin was learnt as a second language, mainly for reading and writing. This use of Latin as a largely literary language may have contributed to its preservation as a fixed, literary language, which continued to be used for religious, educational and scientific purposes throughout the Middle Ages and well into the modern period. It is in this form that it influenced the lexis of many western European languages, especially English.

Some language families

This process of divergent development leading to the formation of new languages has occurred many times in human history, which is why there are now over six thousand different languages in the world. An examination of these languages shows that many of them belong to some group of related languages, and some of these groups are very large, constituting what we can call language families. A language which has arisen by the process of divergent development may itself give rise to further languages by a continuation of the same process, until there is a whole complex family of languages with various branches, some more nearly and some more distantly related to one another.

An example of such a family is the Semitic group of languages. At the time of the earliest written records this was already a family with many members: in Mesopotamia were the East Semitic languages, Babylonian and Assyrian, while round the eastern shores of the Mediterranean were the West Semitic languages, such as Moabite, Phoenician, Aramaic and Hebrew. The East Semitic languages have died out, and the most successful surviving Semitic language is undoubtedly Arabic, a South Semitic language which, with some dialectal variations, is spoken along the whole northern coast of Africa and in a large part of the Near

East. Also surviving are Syriac, Ethiopian and Hebrew, the last of which is a remarkable example of a language being revived for everyday use after a long period in which it had only been used for religious purposes.

But the Semitic languages are themselves related to another family, the Hamitic languages, and at some time in the remote past (certainly long before 3000 BC) there must have been a single Hamito-Semitic language which was the common ancestor of all Semitic and Hamitic languages. The language of ancient Egypt belonged to the Hamitic group; today, of course, the language of Egypt is a form of Arabic, but a descendant of the ancient Hamitic language of Egypt, Coptic, survived until about the fifteenth century, and is still used as the liturgical language of the Coptic Church. Surviving Hamitic languages are spoken across a large part of North Africa, and include Somali and the many dialects of Berber.

Another large language family is the Ural-Altaic. This has two main branches, the Finno-Ugrian and the Altaic (though some authorities deny that these branches are in fact related). The Finno-Ugrian group includes Hungarian, Finnish, Estonian and Sami, while the Altaic includes Turkish and Mongol. If you have ever visited Finland or Hungary, or seen newspapers from those countries, you may have been struck by the complete unfamiliarity of the language, whereas in most European countries there are many words that can be guessed, or which at any rate do not seem to be difficult to remember when once learnt. For example, the English numerals *one, two, three* are quite like German *eins, zwei, drei* and Swedish *en, två, tre*, and even French *un, deux, trois*; but the Finnish words are *yksi, kaksi, kolme*, and the Hungarian *egy, kettö, három*, which are quite strange to us. The reason is, of course, that English and most other European languages belong to a family quite unrelated to the Ural-Altaic.

A family with an enormous number of speakers is the Sino-Tibetan, which includes Thai, Burmese, Tibetan and the various dialects of Chinese (not all of which are mutually intelligible). Japanese is not related to this group (though it has been deeply influenced by Chinese), but may possibly be related to Korean. In southern India and Sri Lanka can be found Dravidian languages, which include Tamil and Telegu (or Telugu). In Malaya and the Pacific islands is the Malayo-Polynesian family, including Malayan, Melanesian and Polynesian. In Africa, there are numerous language families, including the Nilo-Saharan, the Niger-Congo and the Chadic. Of the better-known African languages, Yoruba and Igbo both belong to the Kwa branch of the Niger-Congo family, and Swahili and Zulu to its Bantu branch, while Hausa belongs to the Chadic family, which is perhaps related to Hamitic.

These are all families with large numbers of speakers, but there are many smaller ones, like the Inuit languages, various families of languages among the American Indians, the Papuan languages of Australia and New Guinea, and the Caucasian languages by the Caspian Sea, including Georgian. In addition, there are isolated languages which have no known family connections, such as Basque, spoken by nearly a million people in the French and Spanish Pyrenees.

Attempts have been made to demonstrate relatedness between various recognized language families, and thus to amalgamate them into superfamilies. To prove such relatedness, however, is quite another matter, after thousands of years of divergent development, and the proposed superfamilies must, at any rate for the present, be regarded as speculative.

Convergent development

The process of divergent development, then, has produced an enormous number of languages out of a smaller number of earlier ones (possibly out of one original one). There are, however, forces that work the other way, that may even reduce a language family or branch to a single language again. For example, Latin was only one of a number of related languages, dialects of Italic, which were spoken in the city-states of ancient Italy. At one time, some of these other Italic languages, such as Umbrian and Oscan, may have been at least as widespread and important as Latin. But as the Romans conquered Italy, their language conquered too, and eventually the other Italic languages died out. So we have the differentiation of a language into a number of variants, and then, for political reasons, one of these variants becomes dominant and the others disappear. Something similar has happened with the Semitic languages: many of these have died out, and one form, Arabic, has become the dominant one, because it was the language of the expansionist armies of Islam.

The same centralizing tendency can often be seen at work even when there is no question of conquest. Within a single political unit, like a modern national state, there is usually one form of the language which has higher prestige than the others, and which acts as a brake on the divergent tendencies in the language. This prestige-dialect may be the language of the ruling class, or it may simply be the educated speech of the capital, which is often the cultural as well as the administrative centre, and so exerts great influence on the rest of the country. Usually, such a prestige-dialect underlies the standard literary form of the language, which influences the whole country through books and education. The existence of a standard language discourages further divergence, because many people try to make their usage more like the standard, especially if they wish to make their way in administration and government, or if they are social climbers. It may also lead to the actual dying out of other dialects. In Middle English there were many dialects with distinct written representations, but the standard written form of Modern English is very largely descended from just one of them, a dialect of the East Midland region.

A standard literary language may continue to be influential even after the political decline of the group that made it important. An example of this is the Greek *koinē*, the standard literary language of the eastern Mediterranean from the time of Alexander the Great in the fourth century BC. This language was a modified form of the Attic dialect of Athens, which became the literary standard for the Greek-speaking world in the fifth century BC, when Athens was politically and culturally the dominant city of Greece. Athenian political dominance lasted less than a century, but the prestige of Athenian literature and of Athenian speech remained, and from it developed the *koinē*. This word means 'shared, common, popular', and it was indeed the common language of a large area for something like a thousand years. It is, for example, the language in which the New Testament was written. In the fourth century of our era, the sons of Constantine divided the Roman Empire, the younger son taking the eastern part and the elder son the western part, and this division became permanent. The administrative language of the western empire, ruled from Rome, was Latin; but the administrative language of the eastern empire, ruled from Constantinople, was the Greek *koinē*.

3 The Indo-European languages

We have talked about related languages and language families. What languages is English related to? If you know any European languages, you may well have been struck by resemblances between them and English. For example, German *Vater, singen, leben* and *Stein* resemble their English translations *father, sing, live* and *stone*. Resemblances alone do not prove relationship, however: the resemblances must be systematic. Consider then table 3.1, which shows a number of words of similar (but not necessarily identical) meaning in modern English, German and Swedish.

The thing to notice here is not just that the words look alike, but that there are regular correspondences: words with Southern British English /əʊ/ have German /aɪ/ (spelt <ei>) and Swedish /eː/ (spelt <e>). Such correspondences arise when related languages are produced by divergent development, because, as we have seen, the changes in pronunciation in any one language or dialect follow regular sound laws.

There are indeed certain anomalies in the table. German *Bein* does not mean 'bone' but 'leg'; the Swedish word *ben*, however, means both 'bone' and 'leg', and the same was once true of the German word. German *Reif* means 'ring, hoop', but formerly it also meant 'rope'. The English word *one* apparently does not fit the pattern, for it has the wrong pronunciation; if we go back a thousand years, however, we find that *one* is descended from an Old English word *ān* (pronounced with a long [ɑː], as in *father*), and the other words in the table also have this long *ā* in Old English: *stān, bān, āc, hām, rāp, gāt*. Obviously we should expect Modern English *one* to rhyme with *stone*, but something irregular has happened. In fact

Table 3.1 Similarities in English, German and Swedish

English	German	Swedish
stone	Stein	sten
bone	Bein	ben
oak	Eiche	ek
home	Heim	hem
rope	Reif	rep
goat	Geiss	get
one	ein	en

our present-day pronunciation of *one* derives from a different dialect from the other words listed above (perhaps to avoid confusion with *own*), but the expected pronunciation is found in *alone* and *atone*, which historically are derived from *all one* and *at one*.

The Germanic languages

This last example suggests that, when we look for family relationships between languages, it is desirable to go back to the earliest known forms of the languages. Table 3.2 shows the same seven words as they appear in Old English, Gothic, Old High German and Old Norse. Gothic was the language of the Goths, who were settled in the Black Sea area in the fourth century AD, but later formed relatively short-lived kingdoms in Italy and Spain; our knowledge of their language derives mainly from translations of parts of the Bible by Ulfilas, produced probably in the second half of the fourth century. Old High German was the ancestor of modern standard literary German, and survives in texts composed in the eighth to eleventh centuries AD. Old Norse was the early form of the Scandinavian languages, as found for example in the medieval Icelandic sagas, composed in the thirteenth and fourteenth centuries AD (though sometimes preserving skaldic verse which may have been composed in the ninth and tenth centuries AD). As we shall see in chapter 5, our written records of Old English consist mainly of texts composed in the eighth to eleventh centuries AD.

Table 3.2 Similar words in four ancient languages

Old English	Gothic	Old High German	Old Norse
stān	stains	stein	steinn
bān	–	bein	bein
āc	–	eih	eik
hām	haims	heim	heimr
rāp	raip	reif	reip
gāt	gaits	geiz	geit
ān	ains	ein	einn

Here again there are regular correspondences: words which have *ā* in Old English have *ai* in Gothic, *ei* in Old High German and *ei* in Old Norse. The spelling *ei* perhaps represented a pronunciation [ei] (somewhat like *ay* in English *may*), while Gothic *ai* perhaps represented [ai] (somewhat like the *i* of English *mine*). It seems likely that the original phoneme from which they all developed was similar to the Gothic one, though we cannot know exactly.

This is only one correspondence, but a fuller examination of these languages shows regular correspondences between their sound systems, and confirms that they are indeed related. The correspondences are not always obvious, and there are difficulties and complications. One source of confusion is seen if we examine the word *boat*, which comes from Old English *bāt*. In this case, however, the other languages fail to correspond. The German word is *Boot*, where we might have expected *Beiss (the asterisk shows that the form is a hypothetical one, and has not been recorded; the correspondence between final /t/ and /ss/ is normal). The Swedish form is not *bet, but *båt*, which would correspond to an Old Swedish *bāt*; and the usual Old Norse word is *bátr*. There is, however, a rarer Old Norse word *beitr*, found in poetry, and this does correspond to the English word, whereas the other forms seem to make no kind of sense. What is the explanation? What happened, almost certainly, is that the Scandinavians borrowed their *bátr* from Old English *bāt*: it is an example of a *loanword*, a word taken over bodily from one language to another. And the German word *Boot* was also borrowed from English, but at a later date, after Old English *ā* had developed into Middle English [ɔː] (a vowel similar to that of *law* in present-day Received Pronunciation).

Another source of complication can be illustrated by the word for a waste place. This is German *Heide*, Old High German *heida*, Swedish *hed*, Old Norse *heiðr* and Gothic *haiþi*. (The Old Norse letter <ð> was pronounced as [ð], and the Gothic letter which we transcribe as <þ> represented the sound [θ].) From this we might expect to find an English form **hoath*, but of course the word is in fact *heath* (though *hoath* does exist in English place-names). Our word *heath* is quite regularly descended from Old English *hǣþ*. In this case the clue to the difference from the other languages is given by the *-i* at the end of the Gothic word. It can be shown that, in prehistoric Old English, an [i] or [iː] or [j] caused a change in the vowel of the preceding syllable, provided it was in the same word. The prehistoric Old English form of *heath* was something like **hāþi* (note that this form corresponds regularly with Gothic *haiþi*); the final *-i* caused the *ā* to change to *ǣ*, and was later itself lost by a regular sound change. The regularity of these changes is confirmed by numerous Old English words that show the same development: consider, for instance, Old English *dǣlan* ('to divide'), *hǣlan* ('to heal') and *hǣlþ* ('health') versus Gothic *dailjan* and *hailjan* and Old High German *heilida*. In these cases the Gothic <ai> and Old High German <ei> would normally correspond to Old English <ā> (as in table 3.2), but the <j/i> that is still visible in the Gothic and Old High German words caused Old English <ā> to become <ǣ> before itself disappearing. Dependent sound changes of this kind (often called 'combinative changes') greatly complicate the task of establishing correspondences.

Although complicated, however, it can be done, and has been done for this group of languages. In addition to the languages already mentioned the group contains others, such as Dutch, Danish and Norwegian. The languages of this group are called *Germanic* languages. Besides the regular correspondences in their sound systems, they resemble one another closely in structure: they have the same or similar features of morphology and syntax. For example, in English there are two main ways of putting a verb into the past tense: in one group of verbs we change the vowel, as in *I sing, I sang*, while in the other we add an ending containing a

/d/ or a /t/, as in *I live, I lived*. Exactly the same is true in the other Germanic languages: German *ich singe, ich sang*, but *ich lebe, ich lebte*; Swedish *jag sjunger, jag sjöng*, but *jag lever, jag levde*.

English and French

English, then, belongs to the group of Germanic languages. But does this group form part of any larger family of languages? One possibility that may have occurred to you, if you know French, is a close relationship between French and English. Enormous numbers of English words closely resemble French words of similar meaning: to English *people* corresponds French *peuple*; *battle* is *bataille*; *to change* is *changer*, and one could easily give whole strings of French words of this kind – *musique, art, palais, collaboration, collision, danger, danse, machine*, and so on. This, however, is a false trail. You will remember that we need to look at the earliest recorded forms of a language when determining its family relationships. If we go back to the earliest recorded forms of English, all these words resembling French words simply do not exist. As we go back in time such words become fewer and fewer, and when we get back to the period before the Norman Conquest the vast majority have disappeared. They are in fact *loanwords*, taken from French, or in some cases direct from Latin. There are many such borrowed words in English, but they have not destroyed its essentially Germanic character and it retains typical Germanic structural features and a central core of Germanic words. Such are the common grammatical words (*the, and, is*), the numerals (*one, two, three*), and everyday lexical words for the closest members of the family (*father, mother, brother, son*) and for the parts of the body (*head, foot, arm, hand*). Such corewords are less often borrowed from other languages than more peripheral parts of the vocabulary, and so provide a better guide to family relationships.

The Indo-European languages

We see, then, that our attempt to compare Modern English with Modern French was misguided. We should instead have gone back to the ancestor of French, which is Latin, and compared it

Table 3.3 Numerals 1–10 in five ancient languages

	Latin	Greek	Sanskrit	Gothic	Old English
1	ūnus	heis	eka	ains	ān
2	duo	duo	dvau	twai	twēgen, twā
3	trēs	treis	trayas	–	þrīe
4	quattuor	tettares	catvāras	fidwor	fēower
5	quīnque	pente	panca	fimf	fīf
6	sex	hex	sat	saihs	siex
7	septem	hepta	sapta	sibun	seofon
8	octō	oktō	astau	ahtau	eahta
9	novem	ennea	nava	niun	nigon
10	decem	deka	dasa	taihun	tīen

with the earliest known forms of the Germanic languages, and we should have looked especially at grammatical features and at words from the central core of the vocabulary. Let us try a comparison of this kind, throwing in a couple of other ancient languages for good measure. We can begin with the numerals from one to ten: these are given in table 3.3 for Classical Latin, Classical Greek and Sanskrit, an ancient language of northern India; to represent the Germanic languages we give Old English and Gothic. Both here and later, the transcription of Greek and Sanskrit words has been simplified: such words have been put into the Latin alphabet, and accents omitted (macrons have, however, been used to mark long vowels throughout this table).

The resemblances between the Latin, Greek and Sanskrit are quite striking. Moreover, there are things that suggest regular correspondences: where Latin and Sanskrit begin a word with *s*, Greek begins it with *h*; where Latin and Greek have *o*, Sanskrit has *a*. The resemblances to the Germanic languages are less close, but nevertheless clear enough, and they would be even clearer if we took into account certain related words and variant forms: for example, in Greek there is a word *oinē*, which means 'the one-spot on a dice', and this corresponds more closely than *heis* to the Latin and Germanic words for 'one'. There are also signs of regular correspondences between the Germanic forms and the others. For

Table 3.4 Similarities in five ancient languages

Old English	Gothic	Latin	Greek	Sanskrit
fæder ('father')	fadar	pater	pater	pitar-
nefa ('nephew')	–	nepos	–	napāt
feor ('far')	fairra	–	perā	paras
faran ('go, fare')	faran	(ex)-perior	peraō	pr-
full ('full')	fulls	plēnus	plērēs	pūrna-
fearh ('pig')	–	porcus	–	–
feper ('feather')	–	penna	pteron	patra-
fell ('skin')	fill	pellis	pella	-

example, at the beginning of a word Germanic has *t* for their *d*, and it has *h* where they have *k* or *c*. Let us follow up just one possible correspondence. In the words for 'five', Greek and Sanskrit have *p* (*pente, panca*) where the Germanic languages have *f* (*fimf, fīf*). Can we find further evidence for this relationship? Consider table 3.4.

The words have the same or closely related meanings in the different languages. There are small variations: Sanskrit *napāt* means 'grandson', not 'nephew', but in fact Old English *nefa* could also mean 'grandson'. And in all these words we have Germanic *f* corresponding to *p* in the other three languages. Similar series of correspondences can be established for the other phonemes of these languages. And the correspondences are not confined to phonology (sound systems): the Germanic languages also show detailed resemblances to Latin, Greek and Sanskrit in morphology and syntax, for example in their inflectional systems (grammatical endings of words). It is certain that these languages are related.

But the family does not end here. Similar detailed resemblances, both in phonology and in grammar, can be demonstrated with a large number of other languages, including Russian, Lithuanian, Welsh, Albanian and Persian. In fact English belongs to a very extensive family of languages, with many branches. This family includes most of the languages of Europe and India, and is usually called Indo-European.

The branches of Indo-European

One branch of Indo-European is Indo-Iranian, or Aryan, so called because the ancient peoples who spoke it called themselves Aryas, from a root *ārya-* or *airya-*, meaning 'noble, honourable'; the very name of Iran is ultimately derived from the genitive plural of this word. The branch has two groups, the Indian and the Iranian. To the Indian group belongs the language of the ancient Vedic hymns from north-west India, which go back by oral tradition to a very remote past, perhaps to about 1200 BC, though the first written texts are much later. A later form of this language is Classical Sanskrit, which was standardized in the fourth century BC, and has since been the learned language of India (rather like Latin in western Europe). Modern representatives of the group are Bengali, Hindi, and other languages of northern India, together with some from further south, like Sinhalese. The other Aryan group, Iranian, includes Modern Persian, and neighbouring languages such as Ossetic, Kurdish and Pashto (or Pushtu), the official language of Afghanistan. An ancient form of Iranian is found in the Avesta, the sacred writings of the Zoroastrians, perhaps dating back to 600 BC.

Another branch with ancient texts is Greek, which has a literature from the seventh century BC. The Homeric epics, which were long handed down by oral tradition, go back even earlier, to the ninth or tenth century BC (though not to the time of the Trojan War itself, which was about 1200 BC). Some years ago, tablets from Crete written in a script called Minoan Linear B were deciphered by Michael Ventris, and revealed a form of Greek which was in use there in about 1400 BC. The Greek branch includes all the various ancient Hellenic dialects, and it is from one of these, Attic, that Modern Greek is descended.

Two branches which have some things in common are the Italic and the Celtic. For example, both branches have a verb-inflection in *-r*, used to form the passive voice, as in Latin *amātur* '(he/she/it) is loved', and Welsh *cerir fi* 'I am loved'. The *-r* ending is similarly found in deponent verbs, that is ones which are passive in form but active in meaning: corresponding to the Latin deponent verb *sequitur* '(he/she/it) follows' is Old Irish *sechithir*.

Italic consisted of a number of dialects of ancient Italy, including Oscan, Umbrian and Latin. The earliest Latin texts date from the third century BC. Of the other Italic languages we have only fragments.

Celtic, once widely diffused over Europe, can be divided into three groups: Gaulish, Britannic and Gaelic. Gaulish was spoken in France and northern Italy in the time of the Roman Republic, and was spread abroad by military expeditions to central Europe and as far as Asia Minor. It died out during the early centuries of the Christian era, and is known only from a few inscriptions and from names of people and places preserved in Latin texts. Britannic was the branch of Celtic spoken in most of Britain before the Anglo-Saxon invasions. It survived into modern times in three languages: Cornish, which is known in texts from the fifteenth century; Welsh, which has literary texts going back to the eleventh century; and Breton, which has literary texts from the fourteenth century. Breton is not a descendant of Gaulish: it was taken across to Brittany by refugees from Britain during the period of the Anglo-Saxon conquests. Gaelic was the Celtic language of Ireland. It spread to the Isle of Man in the fourth century, and to Scotland in the fifth, thus giving rise to the three main branches of Gaelic – Irish Gaelic, Scottish Gaelic and Manx. Its earliest records are inscriptions from the fourth or fifth century AD. A characteristic difference between Britannic Celtic and Gaelic Celtic is the treatment of Indo-European *kw*, which appears as *p* in Britannic but as *c* in Gaelic: Welsh *pen* 'head', *pair* 'cauldron', but Old Irish *cenn*, *coire*. For this reason the two groups of languages are sometimes called 'P-Celtic' and 'Q-Celtic'.

Among the distinctive phonological characteristics of Celtic are the treatment of Indo-European *p*, and the treatment of Indo-European long *ē*. In most positions, Indo-European *p* was lost in Celtic: with Latin *plēnus* and Greek *plērēs* compare Old Irish *lan* and Welsh *llawn* 'full', and with Latin *pater* compare Old Irish *athir* 'father'. (The *p* in Welsh *pump* 'five' is not from Indo-European *p* but from Indo-European *kw*: compare Latin *quīnque*.) In Celtic, Indo-European long *ē* became long *ī*: with Latin *rēx* 'king' compare Old Irish *rī* (genitive *rīg*), Gaulish *-rīx* and Welsh *rhi*.

Another two branches of Indo-European that have things in common are Baltic and Slavonic. The Baltic languages include

Lithuanian, Lettish (or Latvian) and Old Prussian (which died out around the end of the seventeenth century). The Slavonic branch has many members, which fall into three main groups: Eastern Slavonic includes Russian, Ukrainian and Byelorussian; West Slavonic includes Polish, Czech and Wendish; while South Slavonic includes Serbo-Croat, Slovenian and Bulgarian. The earliest recorded Slavonic, called Old Church Slavonic, is the language of certain religious writings of the tenth and eleventh centuries AD, emanating from Bulgaria.

There are still three minor branches unmentioned: Albanian, Armenian and Tocharian (an extinct language of Chinese Turkestan, which has some affinities with Italic and Celtic). Then there is the large Germanic branch. And finally we have to add Anatolian, of which the main representative is Hittite, one of the languages of the Hittite empire in Asia Minor round about 1500 BC, which is recorded in numerous texts in a cuneiform writing. Hittite is certainly related to Indo-European, though much of its vocabulary is non-Indo-European. Some scholars have argued that it represents a very early branching-off from the parent language.

Even from this brief survey, you will see what an enormous and complicated family the Indo-European languages are – and a glance at the numbers of speakers given by *Ethnologue* reveals how large a part they play in the modern world. Altogether, over 2,500 million people speak an Indo-European language as their first language today: of these, over 400 million speak a Germanic language, over 600 million a Romance language, over 500 million an Indian language, and around 280 million a Slavonic language; the other branches are all small. The next largest family is the Sino-Tibetan family, with over 1,000 million native speakers. The Afro-Asiatic, Austronesian and Niger-Congo families have over 300 million speakers each: put together, they account for around the same number of speakers as the Sino-Tibetan family, and only a fraction of the number of speakers of Indo-European languages.

Grouping the Indo-European languages

We have noted above some of the distinctive features of the different branches of the Indo-European family tree, and we have considered how regular correspondences between different Indo-European languages allow us to demonstrate their interrelatedness. But how do we actually produce a family tree from this sort of evidence? The evidence of regular phonological correspondences discussed above has been of great importance in the traditional method of establishing language family trees since the nineteenth century. Scholars have used the 'comparative method', which relies on painstaking scrutiny of correspondences in (mainly) phonology and morphology in order to determine groups of languages with shared innovations. An example noted above was that of P-Celtic and Q-Celtic. An important example which takes us back to some of the earliest distinctions between varieties of Indo-European is the split between the Eastern and Western branches of the Indo-European family:

The major subdivisions of the Western branch are as follows:

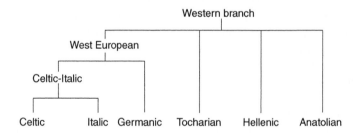

And these are the major subdivisions of the Eastern branch:

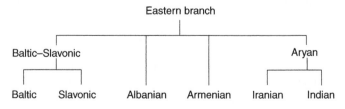

The first division into an Eastern Group and a Western Group is important. The groups are marked by a number of differences in phonology, grammar and vocabulary. One of the distinctive differences in phonology between the two groups is the treatment of palatal *k* in the common ancestor of all the Indo-European languages, a hypothetical language that we usually term 'Proto-Indo-European'. This palatal *k* appears as a velar [k] in the Western languages, but as some kind of palatal fricative, [s] or [ʃ], in the Eastern languages. Thus the word for 'hundred' is Greek *he-katon*, Latin *centum*, Tocharian *känt*, Old Irish *cet*, and Welsh *cant* (the *c* in each case representing [k]), but in Sanskrit it is *satam*, in Avestan *satəm*, in Lithuanian *szimtas* and in Old Slavonic *seto* (modern Russian *sto*). For this reason, the two groups are often referred to as the *Kentum* languages and the *Satem* languages. On the whole, the Kentum languages are in the west and the Satem languages in the east, but an apparent anomaly is Tocharian, right across in western China, which is a Kentum language. The division into Kentum and Satem languages had already taken place when we get our first glimpse of Indo-European round about 1500 BC.

Although our family tree has some value, however, it is not entirely satisfactory, because there are always some points on which a language shows the closest resemblance to a language which is *remote* from it on the tree. Greek and Sanskrit are in different major branches, but nevertheless resemble one another a good deal in syntax, and to some extent in vocabulary. Greek and Iranian are in different major branches, but they agree in changing Indo-European *s-* at the beginning of a word into *h-*: the word for 'seven' is Latin *septem*, Sanskrit *saptan* and Old English *seofon*, but in Greek it is *hepta* and in Old Iranian *haptan*. Moreover, no amount of juggling with the family tree can completely remove discrepancies of this kind. In fact, it is impossible to depict the relationships of the Indo-European languages in an entirely satisfactory way by means of a model in which branches divide and subdivide.

These facts make sense if we envisage Proto-Indo-European as consisting of a number of dialects *before* the divergence into distinct languages began (which is what could be expected anyway). For, under such conditions, changes will spread from various centres within the region, and the boundaries of one change will not necessarily coincide with those of another. The speakers in a given area may pick up one new pronunciation from their neighbours to the east, and another from their neighbours to the west, so that their speech combines features of different dialect regions. At the same time, another change may spread down from the north, and stop halfway across their area, so that some of them have it and some not. In this way, dialect features will appear in various permutations and combinations throughout the whole region.

This, in fact, is the kind of situation which is often found in studies of modern dialects. One small example of this is given in figure 6, which shows the dividing lines, or **isoglosses**, for two pairs of features in the traditional rural dialects of northern England. One line shows the boundary between two pronunciations of the vowel of the word *house*: north of the line, it is a pure vowel, [u:], while south of the line it is some kind of diphthong, [au] or [əu]. The second line shows the limit of occurrence of one particular word, namely, *lop*, meaning 'flea': this word is found only east of the line, not west of it; it is in fact a loan from Scandinavian, and it looks as though it has spread across the region from the east. The crucial point is that these two lines run in quite different directions, and cut one another, so that all possible combinations of the four features occur.

To return to Proto-Indo-European, this model enables us to see how a Kentum language, Tocharian, can occur in the Far East. We can imagine the fricative pronunciation of palatal *k* as an innovation in Proto-Indo-European that spread over the eastern part of the original Indo-European speech area from some focus. But it need not have spread over the whole of the eastern part of the speech area, and there could well have been a region on the eastern edge, occupied by Proto-Tocharian, which the innovation never reached. At the same time, we should also note that languages can converge as well as diverge. For instance, French *cent* ('hundred') is now pronounced with an initial [s], due to a sound change which occurred in the last two millennia: this does not mean that French belongs to the Satem languages, rather it has independently developed a pronunciation which resembles that which is common among such languages.

The problems involved in establishing large-scale language families, and the complexities of the comparative method, have

Figure 6 Two intersecting isoglosses

led some scholars to experiment with computational methods for grouping language families using statistical data. Morris Swadesh is strongly associated with pioneering such approaches, although his was not the first effort in this direction. In the 1950s, Swadesh proposed a method of dating the processes of development of language families, which is usually called 'glottochronology'. This method relies on the idea (discussed above) that certain very common words – a language's core vocabulary – are highly resistant to change. Swadesh therefore compiled lists of 100 and 200 meanings that he believed to be fundamental to all cultures (or at least to Indo-European cultures; recently it has been realized that Swadesh's meanings are not always appropriate outside the

Table 3.5 Words used in four languages with corresponding meanings

Meaning	French	English	Danish	German	Cognation
all	tout	all	al	alle	ABBB
and	et	and	og	und	ABCB
animal	animal	animal	dyr	Tier	ABCC
ashes	cendre	ashes	aske	Asche	ABBB
at	à	at	ved	an	AABC
back	dos	back	bag	Rucken	ABBC
bad	mauvais	bad	ond	schlecht	ABCD
bark (of a tree)	écorce	bark	bark	Rinde	ABʔBʔC
because	parce que	because	fordi	weil	ABCD
belly	ventre	belly	bug	Bauch	ABCC

Indo-European languages, and lists have been devised for working with other language families). The words that possess these meanings in a language were likely, in Swadesh's view, to form the core vocabulary of the language, and to be very resistant to change. Based on Swadesh's meaning lists, one can create tables of the words used in different languages with corresponding meanings. Table 3.5 presents just ten such meanings (the first ten of a 200-word list compiled by Isidore Dyen), in four languages, in order to show how the method works.

For each of the meanings listed, Dyen made a judgement as to which of the various words representing those meanings were cognates, that is, words that existed in the common ancestor of the languages in which they are found. In table 3.5, for instance, English *all* and German *alle* are cognates, but English and French *animal* are not, as the French word was borrowed into English during the later Middle Ages (Old English had the word *dēor*, cognate with German *Tier*). Making such judgements requires expertise in the languages concerned, and in the traditional comparative method, discussed above. This table demonstrates the difficulties involved, as Dyen was unable to decide for certain whether or not the English and Danish words *bark* are cognate, and listed them as 'doubtfully cognate'. They are clearly related to one another, but it is probable that

English borrowed the word *bark* from Old Norse as a result of Viking settlement in northern and eastern parts of England (on which, see chapter 6). We have highlighted groups of cognates in our table, based on Dyen's decisions as to which words are cognate.

Having established the cognates in the list, the next step is to calculate the percentages of shared cognates in each pair of languages. Since we are only dealing with four languages, this is relatively straightforward: German and English share cognates for 'all', 'and' and 'ashes', three out of the ten slots we are using, which can be expressed as 30%. German and Danish share cognates for 'all', 'animal', 'ashes' and 'belly': 40%. English and Danish are harder to calculate, due to the doubt over the cognacy of 'bark'. Linguists working in this area have used various calculations to deal with such cases, but for our purposes we will adopt the simple-minded approach of counting 'bark' as a half cognate, giving us a figure of 35% (full cognates existing in the slots 'all', 'ashes' and 'back'), French only has a cognate with the English for 'at', giving 10% as the figure for English–French, but 0% for German–French and Danish–French. For ease of dealing with comparisons of large numbers of languages, such percentages are usually tabulated in a 'similarity matrix' like this:

	French	English	Danish	German
French	100	10	0	0
English	10	100	35	30
Danish	0	35	100	40
German	0	30	40	100

This matrix can then be used to group languages into families according to their similarity to one another. There are various methods for doing this, and the question of the best method or methods is complex: we will therefore outline a simple method, described by Isidore Dyen and his colleagues, which can be carried out manually (given time, patience and a lot of paper!). This method is known as 'the pair-group clustering method'. The first step is to find the pair of languages with the highest percentage of cognates, and we join these two languages together, to show that they have a common ancestor. This allows us to draw the first part of a family tree of the languages:

German–Danish

German   Danish

We can then repeat this process with the next most similar pairing, and so on until we have grouped all the languages. However, in order to do this, we need to be able to compare the remaining languages not with German and Danish individually, but with German and Danish as a group. We therefore amalgamate German and Danish into a single column. There are various methods for calculating the values for this combined column: one is to take the minimum of the two values that compare German and Danish to each of the other languages, which would give a new value of 30% for German–Danish against English. An alternative is to take the maximum of these two values, which would give 35%, and we could also average the two values (note that German–Danish against French will always produce 0%, since there are no cognates between German or Danish and French in our sample). These methods are fairly basic, and more complex approaches are available, but for the sake of simplicity, we will simply take the maximum, producing a new similarity matrix as follows:

	French	English	German–Danish
French	100	10	0
English	10	100	35
German–Danish	0	35	100

Based on this matrix, we can repeat our first step, noting that the next highest pairing is English with German–Danish, and thus we add English to our tree with a common ancestor (which we can call Primitive Germanic) with German–Danish higher up the branch:

We can now combine the English column of our similarity matrix with the German–Danish column, using the same method as before:

	French	PGmc
French	100	10
PGmc	10	100

As there are now only two columns in the matrix, it is fairly obvious that the next step is to add French to the tree, but with a common ancestor higher up the branch than the common ancestor of English, German and Danish:

This method is not without its problems – most obviously its tendency to construct trees consisting entirely of binary splits – but with the application of more sophisticated methods of calculating and representing the interrelationships indicated by the data, it has potential. This stage of the process of glottochronology concerns itself solely with grouping languages, and does not attempt to use these data for dating language development. Most scholars doubt the validity of glottochronology, but work on this sort of data as evidence for grouping (but not dating) languages has recently attracted renewed attention and favour. We can refer to this area of study as 'lexicostatistics', to distinguish it from glottochronology.

The extra step that glottochronology applies on top of lexicosta-tistics is to use the similarity figures to calculate approximate dates for the periods when languages began to diverge from one another. By taking languages whose dates of divergence are already known, and looking at the lexicostatistical data generated for these lan-guages, we can calculate an average rate of retention of core vocab-ulary per millennium. For example, we can date the divergence of French and Italian from around the period when the Roman Empire began to disintegrate into medieval successor states in the fifth cen-tury AD, leading to Latin developing into distinct regional varieties that eventually formed the separate French and Italian languages (actually this is a considerable simplification, but we should bear in mind that this method is itself a way of abstracting a simple, over-arching pattern from data that may have many complexities). If we then look at Dyen's data, and find that 'bad' is the only meaning slot in our subsample of ten meanings for which French and Italian do not share cognates (the Italian word listed is *cattivo*), we could say that over the period from around AD 500 to around AD 2000, Italian and French retained 90% of their shared core vocabulary. This would give us a retention rate of around 93.33% per millen-nium, and we could then apply this rate to our data for French, English, German and Danish. German and Danish have 40% shared vocabulary, therefore we must divide 93.33 by 40 to give the number of millennia since the common ancestor of German and Danish began to split apart to form these two languages: this gives a dating of around two and a third millennia ago (i.e. around the fourth century BC). Similar calculations for the common ancestor of English and German–Danish, and for the common ancestor of French and the Germanic languages, give dates around the seventh century BC and the eighth millennium BC, respectively.

Our results are clearly nonsense, but rather more plausible results can be achieved by using Swadesh-lists of 100 or 200 words, and by basing the calculation of retention rate per millennium on a wider sampling of languages whose divergence dates can be determined on extra-linguistic grounds. Nevertheless, the glottochronological method has many extremely serious weaknesses. The model has been developed using the Indo-European languages, and it is not clear that retention rates calculated on the basis of these languages are applicable to other language families. More than this, it is quite clear that the assumption of a uniform rate of retention of core vocabulary across different languages is simply not valid: in drawing our tree, the data led us to see English as more distantly related to Danish and German than they are to one another, but in fact this is not consonant with the results of application of the comparative method to the Germanic language family (see chapter 4 for a discussion of this family). English appears to have had a much lower retention rate than other Germanic languages over the last millennium or so, and, as will become clear in later chapters, there is plenty of evidence to show why this has been the case. Some languages, on the other hand, seem to have had much higher retention rates than others: Icelandic is a case in point, and we should not be surprised at this, as the speech of small, emigrant populations (Iceland was settled, starting around the later ninth century AD, mainly by relatively small numbers of settlers from mainland Scandinavia and Viking populations in parts of the British Isles) can often be conservative in comparison to the language of their homeland. These are just some of the main objections to glottochronology, and, although techniques have been developed which attempt to address some of these objections, glottochronology is not now widely accepted by historical linguists.

Who were the Indo-Europeans?

The Indo-European family of languages, with its numerous branches and its millions of speakers, has developed, if we are right, out of some single language, which must have been spoken thousands of years ago by some comparatively small body of people in a relatively restricted geographical area. This original language we can call Proto-Indo-European (PIE). The people who spoke it we can for convenience call Indo-Europeans, but we must remember that this does not imply anything about race or culture, only about language. People of very different races and cultures can come to be native speakers of Indo-European languages: such speakers today include Indians, Afghans, Iranians, Greeks, Irishmen, Russians, Mexicans, Brazilians and Norwegians. It is probable, of course, that the speakers of Proto-Indo-European, living together in a limited area, had a common culture, whatever race or races they consisted of. But who were they? Where did they live? And how did their language come to spread over the world?

The traditional view has been that the Indo-Europeans were a nomadic or semi-nomadic people who invaded neighbouring agricultural or urban areas and imposed their language on them. The archaeologist Colin Renfrew has however argued that we do not necessarily have to envisage conquering armies or the mass movement of populations. He believes that the initial expansion of the Indo-Europeans was simply the pushing out of the frontiers of an agricultural people, who over centuries introduced agriculture into the more thinly populated country round their periphery, inhabited by hunters or food-gatherers. This process would require a longer time-scale than the traditional view of mass migration: Renfrew thinks that the expansion began in about 7000 BC, whereas the traditional view had dated it to 4000 BC or later. The geneticist Stephen Oppenheimer has shown that a large proportion of the genetic make-up of the population of the British Isles derives from Neolithic movement of peoples, a fact that could be seen as supporting Renfrew's dating. At the same time, caution is necessary, as languages do not necessarily require large-scale migrations to spread to new areas

But, whatever the method by which the dispersal of the Indo-European languages began, where did it begin from? It is plain, for a start, that the Indo-Europeans did not live in any of the advanced cultural centres of the ancient world, such as the Nile valley, Mesopotamia, or the Indus valley. The language recorded in ancient Egyptian hieroglyphic inscriptions, for instance, is non-Indo-European. When speakers of Indo-European languages appeared in such places it was as intruders from outside. They appeared on the fringes of the Mesopotamian area around 1500 BC, when a dynasty with Indo-European names is found ruling a non-Indo-European-speaking people, the Mitanni, who lived on the upper Euphrates. At about the same time, Hittite was being used in Anatolia, and some of the Aryas (whose language belonged to the Indo-Iranian branch of Indo-European) were in north-west India: their earliest records, the Vedas, suggest that at this time they were in the Punjab, and were in conflict with the earlier inhabitants of India.

In Europe we have no very early records of Indo-European-speaking groups, except for the Greeks. From Ventris's decipherment of Minoan Linear B we know that a form of Greek, Mycenean, was in use in Crete and on the Greek mainland by 1400 BC. The records of Italic are later, dating from around the sixth century BC onwards, but we can perhaps equate the Italic-speaking peoples with an archaeological culture that appeared in northern Italy in about 1500 BC, and spread southwards. However, we should be wary of equating archaeological cultures with ethnic groups or speakers of a particular language. The Celtic-speaking peoples also first become visible in the region of the Alps, with inscriptions from around the fifth century BC onwards. The Germanic-speaking peoples are first heard about from Greek and Roman authors during the first century BC; they were then living mainly east of the Rhine in parts of what are now Germany and the Netherlands, and also in Scandinavia. Our earliest records of Germanic languages come in the form of inscriptions in the runic alphabet, mainly from the fourth century AD onwards, but with a handful of earlier examples, dating back perhaps as far as the first century AD. We also have Germanic personal names and place-names recorded in Latin texts and inscriptions of the Roman imperial period. At the same time, Slavic-speaking groups were living north of the Carpathians, mainly between the Vistula and the Dnieper; they appear to have been living there for many years before they began to expand in the early years of the Christian era, but we do not have significant written records of the Slavic languages before the central Middle Ages.

The Indo-European languages of which we have early records had already diverged markedly from one another. It seems likely, therefore, that the divergence of these languages must have begun by 3000 BC at the latest, and it may well have begun very much earlier. But where did it begin from? Here one of the sources of evidence is the lexis of the languages themselves.

The Proto-Indo-European vocabulary

Words which occur in a large number of Indo-European languages, and which cannot be shown to be loanwords, were presumably a part of the vocabulary of Proto-Indo-European. But if the words existed, then the things denoted by the words existed too, and must have been familiar to the people who spoke the language. In this way, we can deduce what kinds of animals and plants the Indo-Europeans were familiar with (and hence what part of the world they lived in), what stage of culture they had reached and so on.

The method, indeed, has dangers. For example, the absence of a word from most of the languages does not prove that the Indo-Europeans were unacquainted with the object in question: loss of words is a common happening in all languages, and when peoples have been widely dispersed and met widely different conditions, we must expect that many of them will lose large numbers of words. On the other hand, the absence of a whole group of words, covering an entire field of activity, may well be given some weight.

Another danger is that we may be deceived by loanwords. When a group of people learn a new technique or become familiar with new objects, they often take over the appropriate names from the people from whom they learn the technique or acquire the objects. So several branches of the Indo-Europeans may well have borrowed the vocabulary of, for example, agriculture from the same people, or from peoples speaking similar languages. While, however, it is likely that the Celts and the Germans might borrow the same words from their neighbours, it is not very likely that they would also borrow the same words as the Indians and Iranians. We can guard against the danger of loanwords by giving the most weight to words that are found both in European and in Asiatic languages, and only such words are counted as original Indo-European in what follows.

The common vocabulary thus obtained gives some support to the traditional view that the Indo-Europeans, before their dispersal, were a nomadic or semi-nomadic pastoral people. They had cattle and sheep, for there are common words for both of these: for example, our *ox* is Welsh *ych*, Sanskrit *uksan-* and Tocharian *okso*, and our *ewe* is related to Latin *ovis* and Sanskrit *avi-*. Cattle were obviously highly prized: the Old English word *feoh*, corresponding to Sanskrit *pacu-* and Latin *pecu*, meant both 'cattle' and 'wealth'; the Latin word for 'money, wealth' was *pecunia*, and cattle figure prominently in the early writings of Indo-European peoples. They also had other domestic animals, including the dog, and possibly the pig and the goose (but whether these were all domesticated by Indo-European speakers is uncertain: they may, for instance, have known geese only as wildfowl), but there is no common word for the ass, nor for the camel – our name for this animal goes back, via Latin and Greek, to a loan from a Semitic language. The Indo-Europeans certainly had horses, for which a rich vocabulary has survived, and they also had vehicles of some kind, for there are words for wheel, axle, nave and yoke. They had cheese and butter, but no common word for milk has survived, which shows how chancy the evidence is. No large common vocabulary has survived for agriculture: such a vocabulary is found in the European languages, but this may obviously date from after the dispersal. There are, however, common words for grain, and Greek and Sanskrit have cognate words for plough and for furrow, so there is some support for Renfrew's view that the Proto-Indo-Europeans were agriculturalists. There is however no common word for beer (which is an agriculturalist's product). On the other hand, there is no common vocabulary for hunting or fishing.

There are a number of common words for tools and weapons, including arrows, and there is evidence to suggest that at one time the tools and weapons were made of stone: the Latin verb *secāre* 'to cut' is related to *saxum* 'a stone, rock', and the latter is identical with Old English *seax*, which meant 'knife'. At one time, it seems, a stone could be a cutting implement. The speakers of Proto-Indo-European knew metal, however, for there are two common words for copper and bronze, one of which survives as our *ore* (Latin *aes*, Sanskrit *ayas*), and we can plausibly reconstruct a Proto-Indo-European word for silver. There is, however, no common terminology for the techniques of metallurgy. The vocabulary shows a familiarity with pottery and also with weaving. There are also words for house, door and roof/thatch, which might suggest a dwelling more substantial than a tent, but there is no common word for window.

They knew both rain and snow, but their summer seems to have been hot, which suggests a continental climate. The wild animals they knew included wolves, bears, otters, mice, hares and beavers, but apparently not lions, tigers, elephants or camels, so presumably they lived in a cool temperate zone. There has been some argument about the common Indo-European words for the beech tree, the eel and the salmon. The beech does not grow in north-eastern Europe, or anywhere east of the Caspian, so it has been argued that the home of the Indo-Europeans must have been further west. The eel and the salmon are not found in the rivers that flow into the Black Sea, so it has been argued that this region too must be ruled out. There are, however, two weaknesses in this argument. The first is that the climate has changed: around 4000 BC, the climate of southern Russia was wetter and warmer than it is today, and there were many more trees, especially along the banks of streams and rivers; these trees almost certainly included beech. The second weakness is that we cannot be absolutely certain that these words originally referred to the species in question. For example, it is possible that the word for 'salmon' (German *Lachs*, Swedish *lax*, Russian *losósi* 'salmon', Tocharian *laks* 'fish') did not originally refer to the true salmon, but to a species of *Salmo* found north of the Black Sea.

It seems that rivers and streams were common, but there is no word for the sea or the ocean, so they were apparently an inland people. There is a word for a ship, seen in Latin *navis* and Sanskrit *naus*, but originally this may well have been the name of a vessel used for crossing rivers, or for fishing in them.

There is a large common Indo-European vocabulary for family relationships, and it seems that the family played an important role in their social organization. The linguistic evidence suggests that this family went by male descent, and that when a woman married she went to live with her husband's family. For example, there is a widespread Indo-European word for daughter-in-law (seen in Latin *nurus*, Greek *nuos*, Sanskrit *snusā*), but no such widespread word for son-in-law; and there are common words for husband's brother, husband's sister, and husband's brothers' wives, but no such common words for the wife's relatives.

This view of the Indo-European family is supported by the Indo-European names of gods. There are a few common to the European and Asiatic languages, and they seem originally to have been personifications of natural forces; they do not, however, include a great mother goddess or an earth goddess. Prominent among them, however, is a sky god: the names of the Greek Zeus, the Sanskrit Dyaus and the Old English Tīw (whose name survives in our word *Tuesday*) all appear to be reflexes of a single Proto-Indo-European word. Zeus and Dyaus, at least, can plausibly be interpreted as sky gods. In historical times, we sometimes find societies with Indo-European languages which have a great mother goddess, for example Minoan Crete. The names of such deities, however, appear not to be of Indo-European origin, and it is to be presumed that the cult has been taken over from a non-Indo-European-speaking people. Nevertheless, mother goddesses with Indo-European names do appear to have existed in some Indo-European speech communities (for instance, among Celtic and Germanic-speaking groups), although these goddesses do not appear to have been great mother goddesses.

The home of the Indo-Europeans

A certain amount has emerged from all this about the culture of Proto-Indo-European speakers, but not enough to pin it down to a particular locality. Claims have been advanced for several different areas as the Indo-European homeland: Scandinavia and the adjacent parts of northern Germany, the Danube valley, especially the Hungarian plain, Anatolia (now in Turkey) and the steppes of southern Ukraine, north of the Black Sea.

At one time the Scandinavian theory found a good deal of support, especially in Germany, and was often linked with a belief that the Germanic peoples were the 'original' Indo-Europeans. But the theory has serious weaknesses. Scandinavia does not tally very well with the evidence from comparative philology: it is a maritime region (whereas there is no common Indo-European word for sea or ocean), and it is not very suitable terrain for horse-drawn vehicles, which belong rather to the steppes. Nor is there an Indo-European word for amber, which was one of the most sought-after products of the Baltic region. This theory cannot be considered remotely plausible, but it sheds an interesting light on the preoccupation of late nineteenth- and early twentieth-century philologists with the politics of pan-Germanism, whose worst excesses found expression in National Socialist ideologies.

In the 1920s, a case was put forward by the archaeologist V. Gordon Childe for locating the Indo-European homeland in the steppes of Ukraine, north of the Black Sea. He argued that speakers of Proto-Indo-European should be identified with a certain 'corded-ware' or 'battle-axe' culture in that region. More recently, this line of argument has been developed by another archaeologist, Marija Gimbutas. She groups together a number of cultures (including Childe's 'corded-ware') under the title 'Kurgan', and argues that the bearers of these cultures were the Proto-Indo-Europeans. The material evidence from these cultures certainly corresponds well with the comparative linguistic evidence discussed above, and also with what we know historically about the early Indo-European-speaking peoples. Gimbutas places the original Indo-Europeans rather further to the east than Childe had done, north of the Caucasus range and around the lower Volga (north of the Caspian Sea). She dates the early Kurgan settlements in this region to the fifth millennium BC, claiming that, between 4000 BC and 3500 BC, the Kurgan culture spread westward as far as the Danube plain, and in the following five hundred years was to be found in the Balkans, Anatolia, much of eastern Europe, and northern Iran. Between 3000 BC and 2300 BC, continuous waves of Kurgan expansion or raids affected most of northern Europe, the Aegean area, the eastern Mediterranean area, and possibly Palestine and Egypt. The 'Peoples of the Sea' who raided and settled the coasts and islands of the eastern Mediterranean were possibly Kurgan.

As we have seen, however, Renfrew has challenged Gimbutas's position, arguing that the Indo-European expansion began in Anatolia in about 7000 BC, and consisted in the slow spread of agriculture into the more sparsely populated land occupied by hunter–gatherers. He points out, moreover, that the spread of a material culture does not necessarily mean the actual movement of a people. In 2003 the psychologists Russell Gray and Quentin Atkinson published, in a letter to *Nature*, a glottochronological analysis of the Indo-European languages, which, they claim, supports the Anatolian theory: despite their attempts to answer some of the objections to glottochronology noted above, however, few linguists would accept their findings. The Russian linguists Gamkrelidze and Ivanov put great emphasis on the evidence of Semitic loanwords in early Indo-European, and place the Indo-European homeland around eastern Anatolia, to the south of the

Caucasus range and west of the Caspian Sea. They date it to the fifth to fourth millennium BC, and identify the Indo-European speech community with archaeological cultures from this area. Their model supposes initial migrations from this area into the eastern Mediterranean and the area to the north of the Black Sea. The latter area was, in their view, a secondary Indo-European homeland, in which the common ancestor of most of the Indo-European languages of Europe developed. This represents a compromise between the Anatolian and the Kurgan hypotheses, with a primary homeland in the Anatolian region and a secondary homeland corresponding to the Kurgan area.

If Gimbutas is right, the peoples speaking the Proto-Indo-European language were a semi-nomadic pastoral people in the Chalcolithic stage of culture (that is, using stone tools and some copper-based metal tools), living on the south Russian steppes in the fifth millennium BC, where they formed a loosely linked group of communities with common gods and similar social organization. After 4000 BC, when the language had developed into a number of dialects, they began to expand in various directions, different groups ending up in Iran, India, the Mediterranean area and most parts of Europe. We should not, however, discount the idea that the Indo-European languages may have spread through transmission of culture rather than migration, and it may be that both the Anatolian and the Kurgan hypotheses capture some aspects of what must have been a lengthy and complex process of linguistic development.

4 The Germanic languages

The branch of Indo-European that English belongs to is called Germanic, and includes German, Dutch, Frisian, Danish, Swedish and Norwegian. All these languages are descended from one parent language, a dialect of Indo-European, which we can call Proto-Germanic (PG). Round about the beginning of the Christian era, the speakers of Proto-Germanic still formed a relatively homogeneous cultural and linguistic set of groups, living in the north of Europe. We have no records of the language in this period, but we know something about the people who spoke it, because they are described by Roman authors, who called them the *Germani*. One of the best-known of these descriptions is that written by Tacitus in AD 98, called *Germania*.

Early Germanic society

Tacitus describes the Germani as living in scattered settlements in the woody and marshy country of north-western Europe. He says that they do not build cities and keep their houses far apart, living in wooden buildings. They keep flocks, and grow grain crops, but their agriculture is not very advanced, and they do not practise horticulture. Because of the large amount of open ground, they change their ploughlands yearly, allotting areas to whole villages, and distributing land to cultivators in order of rank. The family plays a large part in their social organization, and the more relatives a man has the greater is his influence in his old age. They have kings, chosen for their birth, and chiefs, chosen for their valour, but in major affairs the whole community consults together; and the freedom of the Germani is a greater danger to Rome than the despotism of the Parthian kings. Chiefs are attended by companions, who fight for them in battle, and who in return are rewarded by the chiefs with gifts of weapons, horses, treasure and land. In battle, it is disgraceful for a chief to be outshone by his companions, and disgraceful for the companions to be less brave than their chief; the greatest disgrace is to come back from a battle alive after your chief has been killed; this means lifelong infamy. The Germani dislike peace, for it is only in war that renown and booty can be won. In peacetime, the warriors idle about at home, eating, drinking and gambling, and leaving the work of the house and of the fields to women, weaklings and slaves. They are extremely hospitable, to strangers as well as to acquaintances, but their love of drinking often leads to quarrels. They are monogamous, and their women are held in high esteem. The physical type is everywhere the same: blue eyes, reddish hair and huge bodies. The normal dress is the short cloak, though the skins of animals are also worn; the women often wear linen undergarments. Very few of the men have breastplates or helmets, and they have very little iron. They worship Mercury, sometimes with human sacrifices, and sacrifice animals to Hercules and Mars. It is likely that Tacitus intended Mercury, Hercules and Mars as translations or equivalents for Germanic deities, and these are sometimes glossed by modern authors as Woden, Thunor and Tiw. There is, however, no clear evidence to support the view that Tacitus knew or intended these particular Germanic gods. They set great store by auspices and the casting of lots. Their only form of recorded history is their ancient songs, in which they tell of the earth-born god Tuisto and his son Mannus, ancestor of the whole Germanic race; the various sons of Mannus are the ancestors of the different Germanic tribes. And Tacitus goes on to give an account of each of these tribes, its location and peculiarities.

To some extent, Tacitus is undoubtedly using the Germani as a means of attacking the corruptions of Rome in his own day: they are the noble savages whose customs are, in many ways, a criticism of Roman life. But at the same time he obviously has access to a great deal of genuine information about the Germani, and many of the details of his account are confirmed by what we know about the Germanic-speaking peoples in later times. When he wrote, they were already pressing on the borders of the Roman Empire, and Tacitus recognized them as a danger to Rome. Earlier they had probably been confined to a small area of southern Scandinavia and northern Germany between the Elbe and the Oder, but round about 300 BC they had begun to expand in all directions, perhaps because of overpopulation and the poverty of their natural resources. In the course of a few centuries they pushed northwards up the Scandinavian peninsula into territory occupied by Finns. They expanded westwards beyond the Elbe, into northwest Germany and the Netherlands, overrunning areas occupied by Celtic-speaking peoples. They expanded eastwards round the shores of the Baltic Sea, into Finnish or Baltic-speaking regions. And they pressed southwards into Bohemia, and later into southwest Germany. At the same time, the territory to their south ruled by Rome was also expanding, and by the time of Tacitus there was a considerable area of contact between Romans and Germani along the northern frontiers of the empire. There was a good deal of trade, with a number of recognized routes up through Germanic territory to the Baltic; there was considerable cultural influence by the Romans on the Germani (many of whom served their time as mercenaries in the Roman legions); and of course there were frequent clashes.

The branches of Germanic

Perhaps as a result of this expansion of the Germanic-speaking peoples, differences of dialect within Proto-Germanic became more marked, and we usually distinguish three main branches or groups of dialects, namely North Germanic, East Germanic and West Germanic.

To North Germanic belong the modern Scandinavian languages – Norwegian, Swedish, Danish, Icelandic, Faroese and Gutnish (the language of the island of Gotland). The earliest recorded form of North Germanic (Old Norse) is found in runic inscriptions from about AD 300; at this period it shows very little trace of dialectal variations, and it is not until the Viking Age, from about AD 800 onwards, that we begin to see evidence of it breaking up into the dialects which have developed into the modern Scandinavian languages. Here is a family tree for the North Germanic languages:

North Germanic differs from the other Germanic languages in a number of points of phonology and grammar. For example, Proto-Germanic /j/ is lost at the beginning of a word, so that corresponding to English *year*, German *Jahr* and Gothic *jēr* we find Old Icelandic *ár* and Modern Swedish *år*. Proto-Germanic initial /w/ was lost before certain rounded vowels, so that corresponding to English *worm* and *wolf* we find Old Icelandic *ormr* 'snake' and *ulfr* 'wolf', both of which were also used as Scandinavian forenames. We have already noticed an example of one North Germanic grammatical peculiarity, the development of a postposed definite article: corresponding to the English forms *a dog* and *the dog* we find Swedish *en hund* and *hunden*. But if there is also an adjective before the noun, there has to be an element of the definite article both before and after: *the big dog* is Swedish *den stora hunden*.

The East Germanic dialects were spoken by the tribes that expanded east of the Oder around the shores of the Baltic. They included the Goths, and Gothic is the only East Germanic language of which we have any record. Round about AD 200 the Goths migrated south-eastwards, and settled in the plains north of the Black Sea, where they divided into two branches, the Ostrogoths east of the Dnieper and the Visigoths west of it. The main record of Gothic is the fragmentary remains of a translation of the Bible, made by the Bishop Wulfila or Ulfilas in the fourth century AD. The Gothic kingdoms were shortlived, but a form of Gothic was being spoken in the Crimea as late as the seventeenth century, and a few words of it were recorded by the Flemish ambassador to the Ottoman court, Ogier Ghiselin de Busbecq. It has since died out, however, and no East Germanic language has survived into our own times. Here is a family tree for the East Germanic languages:

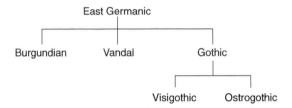

One of the phonological characteristics of Wulfila's text is that the Proto-Germanic short vowels /e/ and /o/ appear as *i* and *u*: the verb 'to steal' is Old English and Old High German *stelan*, and Old Icelandic *stela*, but Gothic *stilan*; and corresponding to English *God* and German *Gott* we find Gothic *guþ*.

To West Germanic belong the High German dialects of southern Germany, the Low German dialects of northern Germany (which in their earliest recorded form are called Old Saxon), Dutch, Frisian and English. The language most closely related to English is Frisian, which was once spoken along the coast of the North Sea from northern Holland to central Denmark, but which is now heard only in a few coastal regions and on some of the Dutch islands. The groups who migrated to Britain and formed the Anglo-Saxon kingdoms probably included Frisians, as well as groups who were near neighbours of the Frisians on the continent. It has often been supposed that there was a prehistoric Anglo-Frisian dialect, out of which evolved Old English and Old Frisian. Here is a family tree for the West Germanic languages:

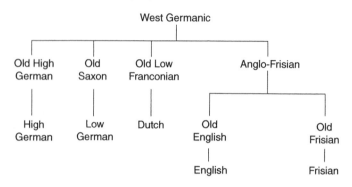

One of the phonological characteristics of the West Germanic languages is the development of numerous diphthongs, often found in positions where North and East Germanic have a pure vowel plus a consonant. So the Old Norse *hǫggva* and Modern Swedish *hugga* correspond to the Old English verb *hēawan* 'to cut, hew', and to Old English *brēowan* 'to brew' corresponds Old Swedish *bryggja*, Modern Swedish *brygga*. One lexical form found only in West Germanic is the word *sheep* (Dutch *schaap*, German *Schaf*, Old Frisian *skēp*), which has no known cognate elsewhere. Gothic used the forms *awi-* and *lamb*, while the Old Norse word was *fār* (Old Swedish) or *fær* (Old Icelandic): the Faroes are the 'Sheep Islands' (Old Icelandic *Færeyjar*).

The expansion of the Germanic-speaking peoples did not, of course, end in the time of Tacitus. During the break-up of the Roman Empire, Germanic groups travelled all over Europe and the Mediterranean: Goths swept through Spain and Italy, Vandals invaded North Africa, Franks and Burgundians settled in France, Anglo-Saxons occupied southern Britain. Later still, Scandinavian Vikings harried many coastal areas of Europe, and established kingdoms in England, Ireland, Normandy and Russia. Often, however, such conquests were made by relatively small groups, whose language ultimately disappeared: Gothic and Vandal did not survive anywhere; Frankish disappeared in France, and French is a Romance language; the Vikings did not establish their language permanently anywhere except in Iceland and the Faroes. Of course, the Germanic languages often left traces on the languages that supplanted them: French has a few hundred loanwords from Germanic, including the word *guerre*, 'war'; the Langobards, or 'long beards', left their name in *Lombardy* when they invaded Italy in the sixth century AD; and the very name of *Russia* is a Scandinavian loanword. And, even though so many dialects died out, there were in earlier times a great number of Germanic dialects spoken in Europe. Their consolidation into a small number of national languages was due to the rise of the modern nation-states: as we have seen, the existence of a coherent and centralized political unit favours the triumph of a single dialect (a prestige-dialect or standard literary language) within its area.

We have no records of the Proto-Germanic language from which all these languages are descended. We can, however, reconstruct it to quite a considerable extent by comparing the various daughter languages. Especially valuable are languages with early literary records. We can also learn a good deal by comparing our reconstructions with the forms found in the other branches of Indo-European. Further minor sources of information are the Germanic names recorded by Latin and Greek authors, and the words borrowed from Proto-Germanic by other languages. For example, the Finnish word *kuningas*, meaning 'king', is plainly borrowed from Germanic, and it preserves a more archaic form of the word than any of the Germanic languages themselves (for example, Old Norse *konungr*, Old High German *kuning*, Old English *cyning*); the Proto-Germanic form was probably **kuningaz*.

The inflectional system of Proto-Germanic

The Proto-Germanic language, reconstructed in this way, has close affinities with the other Indo-European languages, together with certain peculiar developments of its own. Like the postulated Proto-Indo-European language, Proto-Germanic is a highly *inflected* language: that is, in its grammar it makes great use of variations in the *endings* of words. Not much of the Indo-European system of inflections is left in Modern English, which prefers other grammatical devices, and to get a better idea of what an inflected language is like, you need to look at something like Classical Latin, or Modern German.

The English sentence *The master beat the servant* could be rendered in Latin, word for word, as *Dominus verberāvit servum*, though Classical Latin would normally prefer the order *Dominus servum verberāvit*. The important point is, however, that altering the order of the Latin words cannot alter the basic meaning of the sentence: if we write *Servum verberāvit dominus*, we are adopting a rather unusual word-order, and giving special emphasis to the word 'servant', but it still means 'The master beat the servant.' English uses word-order to indicate who is the beater and who the beaten, but in Latin this information is carried by the inflections *-us* and *-um*. If we wish to say that the servant beat the master, we must change these endings, and write *Servus dominum verberāvit*. In grammatical terminology, we are inflecting the nouns *servus* and *dominus* for **case**: the ending *-us* shows the nominative case, used for the subject of the sentence, and the ending *-um* the accusative case, used for the object of the sentence.

Latin nouns, moreover, have other inflections, which to some extent do the work that in Modern English is performed by prepositions (words like *of* and *with*). Thus the noun *dominus* has the following set of inflections:

	Singular	Plural
Nominative	dominus 'a master'	dominī 'masters'
Vocative	domine 'master!'	dominī 'masters!'
Accusative	dominum 'a master'	dominōs 'masters'
Genitive	dominī 'of a master'	dominōrum 'of masters'
Dative	dominō 'to, for a master'	dominīs 'to, for masters'
Ablative	dominō 'by, with, from a master'	dominīs 'by, with, from masters'

The Latin noun, it will be seen, has six different cases, and there are separate inflections for the singular and the plural.

Latin inherited its system of case inflections from Proto-Indo-European, and a somewhat similar system was inherited by Proto-Germanic, though both Latin and Proto-Germanic reduced the number of case distinctions: for all practical purposes, they had only five or six cases, whereas Proto-Indo-European had at least eight. The cases preserved in Proto-Germanic were the nominative (showing the 'beater' relationship), the accusative (the 'beaten' relationship), the genitive ('of'), the dative ('to' or 'for') and the instrumental ('by'). There are also traces of a vocative case (used in addressing somebody) and of a locative (corresponding to 'at'). As in Latin, there were separate inflections for the singular and the plural. In Proto-Indo-European, there had also been inflections for the *dual* number, that is, to indicate that there were *two* of a thing, but the dual survives only vestigially in the Germanic languages.

In Proto-Germanic, as in other Indo-European languages, there was no single set of case inflections used for all nouns alike, but several different sets, some nouns following one pattern, and others another. That is, there were various **declensions** of nouns. All nouns, moreover, had grammatical gender: every noun had to be either masculine, feminine or neuter. This grammatical gender had no necessary connection with sex or with animacy: the names of inanimate objects could be masculine or feminine, and the names of sexed creatures could be neuter. The words for *he, she* and *it* had to be used in accordance with grammatical gender, not in accordance with sex or animacy. This is still, to some extent, the case in Modern German, where for example *das Mädchen* 'the girl', being neuter, has to be referred to as 'it', while *die Polizei* 'the police', being feminine, has to be referred to as 'she'.

So far we have been dealing with nouns, but similar considerations apply to adjectives (words like *good, happy, green, beautiful*). These were also inflected in Proto-Indo-European, and had to be put in the same case and number as the noun they were attached to. Moreover, adjectives had different inflections for different genders, and had to agree with the noun in gender. So in Latin the noun *dominus* 'master' is masculine, and 'a great master' is *magnus dominus*; but *domus* 'house' is feminine, and 'a great house' is *magna domus*; while *opus* 'work' is neuter, and 'a great work' is *magnum opus*. In Proto-Indo-European, the adjective inflections had been essentially the same as the noun inflections, but in many of the daughter languages they became distinguished from them in various ways. This happened in Proto-Germanic, which developed two distinct sets of inflections for the adjectives, called the strong and the weak declensions of the adjective. The distinction between the strong and the weak forms of the adjective has not survived in Modern English, but it can still be found in many of the other Germanic languages. In Modern Swedish, for example, 'a good friend' is *en god vän*, but 'my good friend' is *min goda vän*. In the first phrase, the strong form of the adjective is used (*god*); in the second, the weak form (*goda*). In Swedish, the weak form is used after the definite article, after words like *this* and *that*, and after possessive words like *my* and *your*; otherwise the strong form is used. In Old English, similarly, the strong form of the adjective was used in *gōd mann* ('a good person'), and the weak form in *se gōda mann* ('the good person').

Proto-Germanic, like Proto-Indo-European, also had a system of cases for the pronouns, articles and similar words. Where Modern English has the one form *the*, Proto-Germanic had a whole series of forms according to the case, number and gender of the noun that followed. This was still so in Old English, where 'the woman' is *se wīfmann* (masculine), 'learning' is *sēo lār* (feminine) and 'the woman' is *þæt wīf* (neuter). The declension of the definite article is still found in Modern German, where the non-native learner early on learns the pattern *der, die, das*. Similarly with the personal pronouns (*I, you, he*, etc.), which had different forms for different cases. Here, Proto-Germanic preserved dual forms as well as plurals, and these are found in some of the daughter languages. In Old English, there is a form *ic* meaning 'I', and a form *wē* meaning 'we', but also a form *wit*, meaning 'we two'. Similarly, *þū* is singular 'thou', *gē* is plural 'you', and *git* is dual 'you two'.

Proto-Indo-European also had a great array of inflections for its verbs. Proto-Germanic retained many of these, but it simplified the system. For example, it had only two tenses of the verb, a present tense and a past tense: there were forms corresponding to *I sing* and *I sang*, but no distinct forms with such meanings as 'I shall sing', 'I have sung' and so on. Within these two tenses, however, Proto-Germanic had different endings for different persons and numbers, like Latin, in which 'I sing' is *cantō*, 'he/she sings' is *cantat*, 'they sing' is *cantant* and so on. Like Latin, Proto-Germanic had two sets of inflections for the verbs, one indicative and one subjunctive. The indicative was the normal form, while the subjunctive was used in various constructions implying doubt, uncertainty, or unreality. The subjunctive forms have been largely lost in Modern English, which instead uses modal auxiliaries (*might, should,* etc.), but relics of them remain, for example in the use of *be* instead of *is* (as in the expression *if need be*), and in the difference between *he was* (indicative) and *he were* (subjunctive), as in the sentences 'If *he was* there he will tell us about it' and 'If *he were* here he would tell us about it.' Like Latin, Proto-Germanic had inflections to mark the passive; these did not survive in Old English, but are found in Gothic, where *haita* means 'I call', while *haitada* means 'I am called.'

It was in the verbs that Proto-Germanic made one of its own distinctive developments. From Proto-Indo-European it had inherited a whole series of verbs that showed change of tense by changing the vowel of their stem, like Modern English *I sing, I sang,* or *I bind, I bound*; these are called **strong** verbs. This alternation of vowels for grammatical purposes is highly characteristic of the Indo-European languages, and there were large numbers of strong verbs in Proto-Germanic. Alongside these strong verbs, however, Proto-Germanic invented a new type, called **weak verbs**. In these, the past tense is formed by adding an inflection to the verb-stem, as in *I walk, I walked*. This inflection had various forms: in Gothic, 'I seek' is *sōkja,* 'I sought' *sōkida*; 'I anoint' is *salbō,* 'I anointed' *salbōda*; 'I have' is *haba,* 'I had' *habaida*. There we have the endings *-ida, -ōda* and *-aida*. All, however, have the consonant *d,* and either this or some other dental/alveolar consonant appears in the weak past-tense inflection in all the Germanic languages. In Proto-Germanic the inflections must have contained either a [d] or a [ð]. The origin of the weak conjugation of verbs is uncertain; one theory is that the ending was originally a part of the verb 'to do', rather as though 'he walked' had developed out of 'he walk did'; but no single theory seems able to explain all the facts. What is certain is that the weak verbs have become the dominant verb-forms in the Germanic languages. In Old English, for example, the weak verbs are already the majority. Since then, many strong verbs have changed over to weak, like the verb 'to help', which formerly had the past tense *healp,* but now has *helped*. And nearly all new verbs formed or borrowed by the language are made weak: for example, sixteenth-century loans such as *imitate* (from Latin) and *invite* (from French) have past tenses like *imitated, invited*; and when, in recent times, we invent a new verb such as *blog* (formed from the noun), it seems inevitable that the past tense shall be *blogged*. So today the strong verbs, which were the original type, are a small minority, and weak verbs are the norm.

The phonology of Proto-Germanic

In pronunciation, Proto-Indo-European underwent considerable changes in developing into Proto-Germanic (PG). The history of pronunciation in any language is full of detail and complication, and here we can consider only a few of the more prominent developments. One big change is in the matter of accent. The accent on a syllable depends partly on stress (acoustic loudness), partly on intonation (musical pitch), but some languages rely more on one than on the other. Proto-Indo-European probably made great use of musical accent, but in Proto-Germanic the stress accent became predominant. At the same time, there was a strong tendency in Proto-Germanic to adopt a uniform position for the stress on a word, by putting it on the first syllable. This was not the case in Proto-Indo-European, where the accent could fall on any syllable of a word, whether prefix, stem, suffix or inflection. This so-called 'free accent' can still be seen in Classical Greek: for example, the Greek word for 'mother' is *métēr*, with the accent on the first syllable, but the genitive case ('of a mother') is *mētéros*, with the accent on the second syllable, or *mētrós* (a contracted form) with the accent on the final syllable. The tendency in Proto-Germanic to stabilize the accent on the first syllable of a word, together with the adoption of a predominantly stress type of accent (and also perhaps a tendency towards the even spacing of stressed syllables), had profound consequences. Above all, it led to a weakening and often to a loss of unstressed syllables, especially at the end of a word, and this is a trend which has continued in the Germanic languages throughout their history. For example, the Proto-Indo-European form of the infinitive of the verb 'to bear' was something like **bheronom*, which in Proto-Germanic became something like **beranan*. The final *-an* had been weakened and then lost before any of the Germanic languages were recorded, and the Old English

Table 4.1 The First Sound-Shifting

Aspirated voiced stops		Voiced stops		Voiceless stops		Voiceless fricatives
bh	⟶	b	⟶	p	⟶	f
dg	⟶	d	⟶	t	⟶	θ
gh	⟶	g	⟶	k	⟶	h

form is *beran*. Then the final *-an* became *-en,* giving early Middle English *beren*. In the course of the Middle English period the final *-n* was lost, and the word became *bere,* which was still a two-syllable word (with the final *-e* probably pronounced [ə]). At the end of the Middle English period, this final *-e* was lost in its turn, and the modern form has simply the single syllable *bear*. Similar processes of attrition, though not always as drastic as this, have taken place in the other Germanic languages.

The phoneme system of Proto-Indo-European was reconstructed by a series of nineteenth-century scholars, culminating in the work of Karl Brugmann near the end of the century. Since then, additional evidence has come to light, notably the discovery of Hittite, and there have been great developments in linguistic theory. Some of Brugmann's views have therefore been challenged. For example, it has been suggested that Brugmann's PIE phoneme *b* did not in fact exist. On the evidence of Hittite, it has been argued that there was an additional series of consonants unknown to Brugmann, called laryngeals. Gamkrelidze and Ivanov have produced an alternative analysis of the PIE consonant system: what Brugmann called voiced stops were in fact, they argue, glottalized voiceless stops. The debate continues, and in what follows we keep close to the traditional analysis.

In Proto-Indo-European as thus reconstructed, there was a rich array of stop consonants. This system underwent great changes in Proto-Germanic. The most important series of changes is called 'the First Sound-Shifting', or sometimes 'Grimm's Law', after the early nineteenth-century philologist Jacob Grimm, who analysed it. The main features of the First Sound-Shifting are shown in table 4.1.

A few examples will show what is meant. PIE /p/ became Germanic /f/:

Latin	Greek	Sanskrit	Gothic	Old English
pedem	poda	padam	fōtus	fōt 'foot'
pecus	–	pacu	faihu	feoh 'cattle, money'
piscis	–	–	fisks	fisc 'fish'

PIE /t/ became Proto-Germanic voiceless /θ/; in some cases this has become voiced /ð/ in Modern English, as in the word *thou*:

Latin	Greek	Sanskrit	Old Norse	English
trēs	treis	trayas	þrír	three
tenuis	tanaos	tanu	þunnr	thin
tū	tu	tvam	þú	thou

Greek *tu* is the Doric form: the Attic dialect has *su*.

PIE /k/ became in Germanic the [x] sound heard in Modern German *ach* or Scots *loch*. In Old English and other early Germanic languages it often appears with the spelling *h*. It was lost between vowels in prehistoric Old English, but can be seen in this phonological context in other Germanic languages. For example:

Latin	Greek	Welsh	Gothic	O.H. German	English
cordem	kardia	craidd	hairto	herza	heart
centum	-katon	cant	hund	hunt	hund(red)
decem	deka	deg	taihun	zehan	ten

The Indo-European voiced stops /b/, /d/ and /g/ became, in Germanic, the corresponding voiceless stops /p/, /t/ and /k/. The /b/ occurred only rarely in Proto-Indo-European, but examples of its development to Germanic /p/ can perhaps be seen in the English words *deep* (Lithuanian *dubs*), *thorp* (Lithuanian *troba* 'house', Latin *trabs* 'beam') and *sleep* (related to Old Slavonic *slabu* 'weak'). The following are examples of the change from /d/ to /t/:

Latin	Greek	Sanskrit	Gothic	English
edō	edō	admi	itan	eat
decem	deka	daca	taihun	ten
vidēre	oida	veda	witan	to wit

In this last example, the Latin word *vidēre* means 'to see', and the remainder mean 'to know' or 'I know'. In Old English there was a verb *witan* 'to know', and from this we get the expression *to wit*, meaning 'namely'. The same root is seen in *witness* and *unwitting*.

The change of Indo-European /g/ to Germanic /k/ is seen in the following examples:

Latin	Greek	Gothic	English
ager	agros	akrs	acre
genus	genos	kuni	kin
gelidus	–	kalds	cold

Proto-Indo-European had a series of phonemes which appeared in Sanskrit as *bh*, *dh* and *gh*, and in Greek as the letters φ (phi), θ (theta) and χ (chi; transliterated in the Latin alphabet as *ph*, *th* and *ch* respectively). The exact nature of the original sounds is disputed, but traditionally they have been called aspirated voiced stops, and represented by the symbols *bh*, *dh* and *gh*. In table 4.1 they are shown as changing into Proto-Germanic /b/, /d/ and /g/. However, this is not quite accurate, for in Proto-Germanic they almost certainly became the corresponding voiced fricatives. In many positions, however, they did develop into voiced stops in the various Germanic languages. The English verb *to bear* corresponds to Sanskrit *bharami* and Greek *phēro*; *brother* corresponds to Sanskrit *bhrātar* and Greek *phrātēr* 'clansman'; *door* is cognate with Greek *thura*; *red* is related to Sanskrit *rudhiras*; and Greek *chēn* is related to German *Gans* and English *goose*.

In addition to the three rows of phonemes shown in table 4.1, it is believed that in Proto-Indo-European there was also a series of stops with labialization (lip-rounding), namely gʷh, gʷ and k^w. PIE k^w became PG /hw/: corresponding to Latin *quod*, we find Old Saxon *hwat* and Old English *hwæt* (Modern English *what*). PIE g^w became PG /kw/: Old English *cwene* 'woman', which became Modern English *quean*, corresponds to Greek *gunē* 'woman'. PIE g^{w}h appears in the Germanic languages either as *w* or as *w*, according to position, as in Old Norse *gunnr*, Old English *gūþ* 'battle, war' and Old English *snīwan* 'to snow'.

We do not know the exact dates of the First Sound-Shifting, but it may have begun around the fifth century BC, and possibly took several centuries to complete. It was followed by a smaller series of changes, usually called 'Verner's Law', in which voiceless fricatives became voiced if the preceding syllable was unstressed, but otherwise remained unchanged. Thus the Old English verb *snīþan* 'to cut' has a past participle *sniden*, in which the stop /d/ is the normal Old English development of a Primitive Germanic voiced fricative /ð/, indicating that the stress pattern of the pre-Old English ancestor of this verb differed between the infinitive and past-participle forms. This may have taken place in the first century of our era. Finally came the fixing of the accent on the first syllable of the word, which cannot have taken place until after the operation of Verner's Law.

The Proto-Germanic vowel system

Proto-Germanic also made changes in the PIE vowel system, though these were less extensive than the consonant changes. The three most important vowels in Proto-Indo-European were *a*, *e* and *o*, each of which could be either short or long. There were also short *i* and *u*, which could operate either as unstressed vowels or as approximants (i.e. [j] and [w]) according to their position, and could also be combined with any of the three main vowels, long or short, to form diphthongs. There were also a disputed number of vowels used only in unstressed syllables, and a number of syllabic consonants.

In tracing vowel changes in Proto-Germanic, or any of the later Germanic languages, we always have to distinguish between stressed and unstressed syllables, since these give different results. Henceforward, when we talk about vowel changes we shall be referring to stressed syllables unless we specify otherwise. For Proto-Germanic, let us look at just two vowel changes in stressed syllables: PIE short *o* became PG *a*, and PIE long *ā* became PG *ō*. Examples of the change from *o* to *a*:

Latin	Greek	Old Irish	Gothic	Old High German	
octō	oktō	ocht	ahtau	ahto	'eight'
hortus	chortos	gort	gards	gart	'yard, garden, enclosure'
hostis	–	–	gasts	gast	'stranger, guest, enemy'

The stressed syllable in Germanic is the first in the word, and it is there that the change is seen. Examples of the change of *ā* to *ō*:

Latin	Greek	Old Irish	Gothic	Old Norse	Old English	
frāter	phrātēr	brāthir	brōþar	brōþer	brōþor	'brother'
māter	mātēr	māthir	–	mōþer	mōdor	'mother'

As noted above, the Greek *phrātēr* meant 'clansman', not 'brother'. The Greek *mātēr* is from the Doric dialect, other dialects having *mētēr*.

The vowels played an important part in the grammar of Proto-Indo-European, because of the way they alternated in related forms (as in our *sing, sang, sung*), and this system descended to Proto-Germanic. There were several series of vowels which alternated in this way. Each member of such a series is called a **grade**, and the whole phenomenon is known as **gradation** (or **ablaut**). One such series in PIE, for example, was short *e*, short *o* and zero: originally, the zero grade probably appeared in unaccented syllables. This series was used in some of the strong verbs: the *e* grade appeared in the present tense, the *o* grade in the past singular, and the zero grade in the past plural and the past participle (in which the accent was originally on the ending, not the stem). This is the series that was used in *sing, sang, sung*, though this fact has been obscured by the vowel changes which took place in Proto-Germanic. The original PIE stems of these words were something like *$seng^wh$-* (*e* grade), *$song^wh$-* (*o* grade), and *sng^wh-* (zero grade).

In Proto-Germanic these became **sing-*, **sang-*, **sung-*, as seen for example in Old English *singan* ('to sing'), *sang* ('he/she sang'), *sungon* ('they sang'), *gesungen* ('sung'). The *e* changed to *i* because of the following *ng*, a normal combinative change in Proto-Germanic. PIE short *o* regularly changed to PG *a*, as we have already seen. The *u* appeared in the zero-grade form through the influence of the following syllabic *n*: in Proto-Germanic, the PIE syllabic consonants *m*, *n*, *l* and *r* became *um*, *un*, *ul* and *ur* so that a syllable that originally had no vowel often appears in the Germanic languages with *u*.

Gradation is not confined to verbs, however. We see the alternation of *e* and *o* grades in the Greek verb *lego* 'I speak' and the related noun *logos* 'speech', and this same alternation, ultimately, lies behind the Modern English pairs *bind* and *band*, *ride* and *rode*, *learn* and *lore*. In some cases, related words appear with different grades in different languages; these must go back to variant forms in PIE. For example, the PIE word for 'knee' had the variant forms **gen-*, **gon-*, **gn-*. The *e* grade appears in Latin *genu* and the *o* grade in Greek *gonu*. In the Germanic languages it is the zero grade **gn-* that appears: by Grimm's Law this becomes *kn-*, as in Gothic *kniu* and Old English *cnēo* 'knee'.

These, then, are some of the main developments in Proto-Germanic: simplification of the inflectional system of PIE; the introduction of the weak declension of the adjective; the introduction of the weak verbs; the great consonant change known as the First Sound-Shifting (or Grimm's Law), and the smaller change known as Verner's Law; the change from predominantly pitch accent to predominantly stress accent; the fixing of the accent on the first syllable of the word; and of course a host of lesser changes, both in grammar and in pronunciation.

The vocabulary of Proto-Germanic

Some of the vocabulary of Proto-Germanic also seems to be peculiar to it, since it is not paralleled in other Indo-European languages. In some cases this may be pure chance, a word having been preserved by Germanic and lost by the other branches, but no doubt some of the words were invented or acquired by the Germanic peoples after the dispersal of the Indo-Europeans. Among the words peculiar to Germanic are a number that have to do with ships and seafaring: words to which there are no certain correspondences in other Indo-European languages include *ship, sail, keel, sheet, stay* ('rope supporting a mast'), possibly *float,* and *sea* itself. This tallies with the view that the Indo-Europeans originally lived inland: nautical vocabularies would then be developed independently by those peoples that reached the coast and took to the sea.

Proto-Germanic speakers borrowed a number of words from neighbouring speech communities, especially Celtic and Latin speakers, who were on a higher cultural level and so had things to teach them. Groups speaking Celtic languages were skilled in metallurgy, and the Germanic words for iron and lead (seen for example in Old English *īren, lēad*) were probably borrowed from them. From the Romans were borrowed many words to do with war, trade, building, horticulture and food – all fields where the Germani learnt a good deal from their southern neighbours. The word *pile* (OE *pīl*) 'pointed stake' is from Latin *pīlum* 'javelin', and goes back to these early days, as does the word *street* (OE *strǣt*), taken from the Latin (*via*) *strāta* 'paved (road)', a tribute to the impression made on the Germans by Roman military roads. Tacitus described the Germans as living in wooden houses, but they learnt a good deal about building from the Romans, and borrowed the words which in Modern English have become *wall, tile, chalk, mill* and *pit* (from Latin *puteus* 'a well'). They also learnt Latin trading terms, for there was a good deal of traffic between the two areas: the loans include the words which have become *pound, mile, cheap, monger* and *mint* (originally meaning 'coin, money', from Latin *monēta*). Tacitus said that the Germans did not grow fruit trees or cultivate gardens, but again they seem to have been willing to learn, for they borrowed the words *apple, plum* and *pear*, not to mention *wine*. As has happened so often since, culinary refinements also came to the north of Europe from the Mediterranean: the very word *kitchen* was borrowed from Latin, and so were *pepper, peas, mint* (the herb), *cheese, butter, kettle* and *dish*. To judge from the linguistic evidence, the early Germanic languages were not so much impacted by Roman law, ideals of order, and so on, as by more concrete manifestations of Roman civilization – roads, buildings and food. Nevertheless, some Latin loanwords in the Germanic languages, such as Old English *cāsere* 'emperor' (from Latin *caesar*) do suggest that Roman ideas of governance had an impact on Germanic-speaking groups.

The influence of Latin also extended to bound morphemes. The Germanic languages share the suffix which usually appears in Modern English as *-er* (Old English *-ere*), as in Old English *bōcere* 'scribe' and *sangere* 'singer' (compare Gothic *bōkareis* and Old Norse *sǫngare*). This suffix appears to have been an early borrowing from the Latin suffix *-ārius*, as in *cūpārius* 'a cooper, a barrel-maker' (from Latin *cūpa* 'a vat, a cask') and *molīnārius* 'a miller' (from Latin *molīna* 'a mill'). The borrowing of a suffix from Latin reinforces the impression that at least some Germanic-speaking groups had extensive contacts with the Latin language. Moreover, we have quite a bit of documentary evidence for this from the later Roman period, when Germani frequently served in the Roman army (sometimes rising to the highest ranks) and a number of Germanic tribal groups were settled within the borders of the Roman Empire, particularly around the lower Rhine.

5 Old English

During the three or four centuries after Tacitus wrote his *Germania*, the Germanic peoples were in a state of flux and movement. We know little of their history in this turbulent period of migration and expansion, but we do know that, towards the end of these centuries of flux, Germanic-speaking groups settled in England. There is some archaeological evidence that Saxons settled in East Anglia and the Vale of York while Britain was still a Roman province, but the main settlements were made after the Roman legions had withdrawn from Britain in AD 410, and the traditional accounts of the landing of Hengest and Horsa in Kent place it in the year 449.

The Anglo-Saxon settlement of Britain must not be thought of as the arrival of a unified invading army, but rather as the arrival and penetration of various uncoordinated bands in different parts of the country, beginning in the middle of the fifth century and going on all through the sixth. The processes of struggle and assimilation with Celtic-speaking Britons were lengthy, and Anglo-Saxon domination in England was not assured until late in the sixth century. We know little about these developments: it was the age of King Arthur, and there are more legends than hard facts. But by about 700, the Anglo-Saxons had occupied most of England (the exceptions being Cornwall and an area in the north-west) and also a considerable part of southern Scotland. Wales remained a British stronghold.

Anglo-Saxons and Britons

Debate continues as to the exact nature of the Anglo-Saxon settlements. Some scholars have seen them as the arrival of a ruling minority who assumed control over British populations, whereas others envisage larger groups of settlers. Such groups may in some cases have lived alongside and integrated with British populations, while in some cases they may have replaced existing British populations. The Germanic language of the incomers became the dominant one, and there are few traces of Celtic influence on Old English (OE); indeed, the number of Celtic words taken into English in the whole of its history has been very small. The names of some English towns were taken over from the Britons, for example London and Leeds. Rivers often have Celtic names: Avon and Ouse are Celtic words for 'water' or 'stream'; Derwent, Darent and Dart are all forms of the British name for 'oak river'; the Thames is the 'dark river'; while Trent has been interpreted as meaning 'trespasser', that is, a river with a tendency to flood. Among county names, Kent and Devon are Celtic, and so are the first elements in Cornwall and Cumberland; the latter means 'the land of the Cymry (that is, the Welsh)', and testifies to the long continuance of British power in the north-west. A few words for topographical features also suggest Celtic influences, such as OE *cumb*, a word for a type of valley that may have been influenced by the Old British term from which modern Welsh *cwm* developed.

These few Celtic words in Old English were merely a drop in the ocean, however. Even in English place-names, where Old British left its biggest mark, Celtic forms are far outnumbered by English ones, and only in areas where the Anglo-Saxons penetrated late are Celtic names at all common for villages. There are an enormous number of place-name elements of English derivation. Among the common ones are *ton* (often from OE *tūn* 'enclosure, farmstead', but also a fairly common development of OE *dūn* 'large hill with a level top'), *ham* (OE *hām* 'homestead' and *hamm* 'area enclosed (generally) by water, such as a water meadow'), *ley* (OE *lēah* 'glade, wood'), *worth* (OE *worþ* 'enclosure'), *field* (OE *feld* 'open country') and *ing* (OE *-ingas* 'the people of'). Thus Nottingham (OE Snotingaham) was 'the homestead of Snot's people', Buckingham was 'the meadow of Bucca's people', Langley was 'a long wood' and Aston and Easton were 'eastern farmstead (or village)'.

The failure of Old British to influence Old English to any great extent does not mean that the Britons were all killed or driven out.

There is in fact evidence that a considerable number of Britons lived among the Anglo-Saxons, but their language quite possibly had no prestige compared with that of the Anglo-Saxons. Whether or not the prestige associated with the language of a political elite would have been sufficient in itself to achieve the replacement of Old British with Old English remains an open question. The example of the Norman Conquest, as we shall see in chapter 6, suggests that this is unlikely, but we cannot rule it out. Alternatively, one might suppose that the Anglo-Saxons had settled in such large numbers that there could be no question of their absorption by the Britons, but recent work on the genetic make-up of the population of the British Isles has called this model into question. The Old English word *wealh*, which originally meant 'foreigner', seems usually to have been used to mean 'Briton, Welshman', but is also used to mean 'servant, slave' in some texts, which illustrates both the survival of Britons among the Anglo-Saxons, and their low status in some contexts. The OE *wealh* has survived as the second syllable of *Cornwall*, and also in the word *walnut* (OE *wealh-hnutu* 'foreign nut, walnut'). Our word *Welsh* is from the related adjective, OE *wylisc*.

Angles, Saxons, Jutes – and others

The piecemeal way in which the Anglo-Saxons settled in England led to a profusion of small kingdoms, and no doubt to dialect differentiation. In any case there were probably dialect differences from the start, for the incomers came from more than one Germanic tribe. Bede, writing in about 730, tells us about this:

> They came from three very powerful Germanic tribes, the Saxons, Angles, and Jutes. The people of Kent and the inhabitants of the Isle of Wight are of Jutish origin and also those opposite the Isle of Wight, that part of the kingdom of Wessex which is still today called the nation of the Jutes. From the Saxon country, that is, the district now known as Old Saxony, came the East Saxons, the South Saxons, and the West Saxons. Besides this, from the country of the Angles, that is, the land between the kingdoms of the Jutes and the Saxons, which is called *Angulus*, came the East Angles, the Middle Angles, the Mercians, and all the Northumbrian race (that is those people who dwell north of the river Humber) as well as the other Anglian tribes.

The land of the Old Saxons was in north-west Germany (in Schleswig-Holstein, and perhaps further west too along the North Sea coast), and we can assume that the Saxons who settled in England came from this region. The Angles probably came from slightly further north, from the Danish mainland and islands. The Jutes are more obscure: they may have come from Jutland, which is what Bede's account might suggest, but there is little clear evidence for the homeland of the Jutes. There is also evidence that, in addition to Angles, Saxons and Jutes, the Germanic settlers in Britain included Frisians, and probably groups from other Germanic-speaking tribes, such as the Suebi (who give their name to Swabia in modern Germany).

Whatever their exact origins, these groups were in any case closely related in language and culture, and eventually came to regard themselves as one people. For example, the word *Engle* 'the Angles' came to be applied to all the Germanic settlers in Britain, and the related adjective *Englisc* was similarly applied to all these peoples and their language, not just to the Angles. Political union came slowly, however. In the early days there was a medley of petty kingdoms, and some of their names are preserved in our modern counties: Essex, Middlesex and Sussex were the realms of the East, Middle and South Saxons, while Norfolk and Suffolk were the north and south folk of the East Angles; the names of others survive only in the history books, like the kingdoms of the Deirans in Yorkshire and the Bernicians in Northumberland. By a process of conquest and amalgamation, this medley of kingdoms was eventually reduced to seven, sometimes called the Heptarchy: Northumbria (southern Scotland and England north of the Humber), Mercia (in the West Midlands), East Anglia, Essex, Sussex, Kent and Wessex (based on central southern England). The approximate positions of these seven kingdoms are shown in figure 7. Different kings managed to establish their suzerainty over other kingdoms at various times, but these dominations were often personal and temporary. In very broad terms, we can see a gradual shift southwards of the centres of power and civilization. In the seventh century, Northumbria was very powerful, and was a great centre of learning. In the eighth century this leadership passed to Mercia, and in the ninth century to Wessex; and it was the kings

Figure 7 Britain before the Vikings

of Wessex who finally unified the country. In the late ninth century, the kings of Wessex, notably King Alfred, saved the south and west of England from the Danes, and in the tenth century Alfred's successors reconquered the north and the east. In the second half of the tenth century, Edgar not only ruled all England, but was recognized as overlord of Wales and Scotland as well. From this time, the unity of England was durable: the king might be Danish, like Cnut, or half-English, like Edward the Confessor, or Norman French, like William the Conqueror, but in any case he ruled a single country.

The West Saxon literary language

For various reasons connected with Viking settlement in the north and east of England, and its unification under the West Saxon kings, a written form of the West Saxon dialect developed, towards the end of the Anglo-Saxon period, as a literary language that influenced written forms of the language outside the areas in which it was spoken. The surviving texts from the Old English period have traditionally been grouped into four main dialects: West Saxon, Kentish, Mercian and Northumbrian (the last two often being grouped together as Anglian); but the surviving representatives of these dialects are in fact the products of a small number of centres of textual production, and there were certainly other varieties of which we have no records. Figure 8 is a traditional dialect map of Anglo-Saxon England, showing the areas to which the four main dialects can be assigned: but in fact this map is misleading, presenting boundaries that are essentially the political boundaries of four major kingdoms of early Anglo-Saxon England: Northumbria, Mercia, Wessex and Kent. Our evidence really relates to a few small areas within these kingdoms, and of the spoken dialects of most parts of Anglo-Saxon England we have little or no idea. The bulk of our records, moreover, are in the West Saxon dialect. Many of the earlier manuscripts were destroyed in the Viking conquests of the north and midlands, and in the later part of the period there was a tendency for the manuscripts to be copied by West Saxon scribes and so put into West Saxon form. For example, the Old English epic poem *Beowulf* was possibly composed in an Anglian dialect, but the only surviving manuscript copy contains a fair number of West Saxon features.

One interesting thing is that, although a West Saxon variety became an influential literary language in the late Anglo-Saxon period, it is not the direct ancestor of modern standard English, which is mainly derived from an Anglian dialect (but not, it should be pointed out, any of the Mercian or Northumbrian varieties represented in extant Old English texts). One difference between West Saxon and Anglian is preserved in the modern words *weald* (from West Saxon) and *wold* (from Anglian): before certain consonant groups a vowel became diphthongized in West Saxon but not in Anglian, the

Figure 8 The main dialect areas of Old English

Old English forms being Anglian *wald* and West Saxon *weald*, both meaning 'forest'. The same difference is seen in the word for 'cold': Anglian *cald*, West Saxon *ceald*. The modern word is quite regularly descended from the Anglian form; the West Saxon form would have produced a modern word **cheald*. Another West Saxon characteristic was the use of the diphthongs *ie* and *īe*, which did not exist in the other dialects. The West Saxon verb 'to hear' was *hȳran*, which could be expected to develop into a modern form **hire* or **hure*; our word *hear* is in fact quite regularly descended from an Anglian form, *hēran*. In addition to such phonological differences, the Old English dialects differed in small ways in grammar and vocabulary.

Christianity and writing

We know little about the Anglo-Saxons until after their conversion to Christianity, which introduced them to the use of the Roman alphabet for writing extensive texts. As elsewhere in medieval Europe, writing was in the hands of clerics, whose priorities generally lay with the production of materials of Christian spiritual instruction, so that we learn little about the ways of the heathen English from their writings. Some evidence of pre-Christian traditions has, however, remained fossilized in the language. The heathen gods Tīw, Wōden, Thunor ('thunder', corresponding to the Scandinavian Thor) and Frīg have given their names to Tuesday, Wednesday, Thursday and Friday; but these names are translations of the Latin *martis dies* ('day of Mars'), *mercurii dies* ('day of Mercury'), *iovis dies* ('day of Jove') and *veneris dies* ('day of Venus'), and it is not clear whether these translations were the work of pagans or Christians. More remarkably, the goddess Ēastre has probably given her name to the Christian festival of Easter, apparently because the pre-Christian English had a month named after her which usually fell around the time of year when the Christian festival of Easter took place. The pagan deities named in the days of the week are also commemorated in place-names such as Tuesley, Wednesbury and Thunderfield, and pagan cult sites are attested by place-names like Harrow (OE *hearh* 'temple') and Wye in Kent (OE *wīg* 'idol, shrine').

The conversion of the English to Christianity began in about the year 600, and took a century to complete. It was carried out from two directions, the Celtic church penetrating from the northwest and the Roman church from the south-east. With Christianity came the Latin model of writing. The English already had one form of writing, runes, but these were used only for short inscriptions, not for texts of any length. Runes had been used by the Germanic peoples from at least the third century AD, for carving or scratching inscriptions on stone, metalwork or wood: the word *book* (OE *bōc*) originally meant 'beech', while it is clear that the OE verb *wrītan* could mean both 'write' and 'scratch'. The word *rune* (OE *rūn*) also meant 'mystery, secret', and some inscriptions were perhaps thought to have magical power. It is unclear how and where the runic alphabet originated, but it has clear similarities with Greek and Italic alphabets (among which the Roman alphabet is the best known, and the one we use today). Because of their use in inscriptions, runes have acquired a decidedly angular form, as straight lines are easier to scratch (especially into wood) than curved lines. The best-known inscriptions are the Scandinavian ones, and the earliest English inscriptions use forms of the runic alphabet that closely resemble those in contemporaneous use elsewhere in Germanic-speaking areas. However, the English developed in the seventh century a distinctive form of the runic alphabet which, from its first six letters, is known as the 'futhorc' (ᚠᚢᚦᚩᚱᚳ = **fuþorc**). When the clerics introduced writing to England, they used a version of the Latin alphabet, but eked it out with runic symbols from the futhorc: for example, they used the symbol ᚹ ('wynn') to represent the OE /w/ phoneme.

In modern editions of OE texts (at any rate ones designed for students), it is customary to give the Latin letters their modern form, to use *w* instead of 'wynn', and to use special symbols only for some of the letters that represent a departure from the Latin alphabet. It is also common in modern editions to mark long vowels by putting a macron (short horizontal line) over them, while leaving the short vowels unmarked; the original OE manuscripts do not mark vowel-length. We shall follow modern conventions in these matters.

The preservation of Old English

The quantity of surviving texts in Old English is small in comparison to Middle English, and extremely small in comparison to Modern English. There is an ongoing project to produce a definitive dictionary of Old English (the *Dictionary of Old English*), based at the University of Toronto. This project has assembled an electronic corpus containing a copy of every single text in Old English currently known, and they estimate that this corpus is only about six times the size of all the surviving plays and poems by Shakespeare. Although previously unknown texts do very occasionally come to light, we should not expect this corpus to grow very much. It is true, also, that the corpus does not contain a copy of the text of every manuscript copy of Old English texts: where a text is known from more than one manuscript copy, it is nevertheless usually only represented by a single copy in the corpus. It is clear that we possess only a fraction of the Old English textual material originally produced, but the size of this fraction is very hard to determine: we might conceivably have half the Old English texts ever written, or only a tenth or a hundredth of them.

There are, however, some ways in which we can estimate the scale of Old English textual production: we know that the population of England was much smaller in the early Middle Ages than it now is, and that writing was restricted to elites, especially ecclesiastics. The surviving manuscripts containing Old English can often be traced to a relatively small number of important monastic centres, and the number of surviving manuscripts of a text can sometimes give an indication of its popularity and dissemination during the period. It is noteworthy, therefore, that Old English poems rarely exist in more than one copy, and that most of them are preserved in four main manuscripts, while some sorts of prose text (for instance, homilies, and the *Anglo-Saxon Chronicle*) often exist in several copies. It is likely that our corpus of Old English texts provides a rather more substantial sample of some sorts of writing than of others. We should bear in mind the unevenness of our data in studying Old English language. Much of what follows is based on numerous scholars' painstaking surveys of the data, undertaken before the *Dictionary of Old English Corpus* existed; but we have also checked some details against the *Corpus*. Nevertheless, we should bear in mind the incompleteness of our data: the following is a description not of Old English as a whole, but of what we know and can reconstruct of Old English, and especially of the literary Late West Saxon variety.

The pronunciation of Old English

Old English script used the six vowel symbols *a*, *e*, *i*, *o*, *u* and *y*, and a seventh one, *æ*, called 'ash'. All of these could represent both long and short vowels. The probable pronunciations represented by the symbols are shown in table 5.1. The pronunciations are those of early West Saxon, as far as they can be reconstructed.

Table 5.1 The vowel sounds of Old English, Early West Saxon

Symbol	Pronunciation	Resembling the vowel of
a	[ɑ]	Southern English *bath*, but shorter
æ	[æ]	Southern English *hat*
e	[e]	French *elle*, German *Bett*
i	[i]	German *sie*, English *tree*, but shorter
o	[o]	German *wo*, French *chose*, but shorter
u	[u]	English *room*, but shorter
y	[y]	French *cru*, German *Hütte*
ā	[ɑ:]	Southern English *bath*
ǣ	[æ:]	Southern English *bad*
ē	[e:]	French *été* (lengthened), German *zehn*
ī	[i:]	German *sie*, English *tree*
ō	[o:]	German *wo*, French *chose*
ū	[u:]	English *room*
ȳ	[y:]	French *sûr*, German *führen*

All the symbols represent pure vowels, not diphthongs. To represent diphthongs, the Anglo-Saxons used digraphs (sequences of two symbols): *ea*, *eo*, *io* and *ie*. The spellings *ea* and *eo* probably represented the pronunciations [æɑ] and [eo] (or perhaps [eu]); they too could be either short or long. The spelling *io* appears mainly in early texts, where it appears to represent a distinct diphthong, which later fell together with the sound represented by *eo*. The digraph *ie* probably also once represented a diphthong, but even in early West Saxon texts it seems already to have fallen together with the sounds represented by *i/y*. Non-West-Saxon texts also use the digraph *oe*; this however does not represent a diphthong, but the close-mid front rounded vowel [ø(:)], that is, some kind of [e(:)] with lip-rounding.

Turning now to consonants, the use of double consonants was different from the one we are used to. In Modern English spelling, we use double-consonant symbols in two-syllable words to show that the preceding vowel is short: the spellings *written* and *copper* are used for words pronounced /'rɪtn/ and /'kɒpə/ in present-day Received Pronunciation, which have short vowels; a single consonant symbol is used if the preceding vowel is long or is a diphthong, as in *writer* and *coping*. But in Old English this is not so: the fact that a single consonant symbol is used tells us nothing about the length of the preceding vowel. The Old English words for 'written' and 'copper' are *writen* and *copor*; these had short vowels, and were probably pronounced ['writen] and ['kopor]. However, we do find OE spellings with doubled consonants, like *assa* 'ass', *bucca* 'he-goat' and *cuppe* 'cup'. In such words the double-consonant symbol indicates that the consonant was in fact pronounced double or long, rather as in Modern Italian or Modern Swedish. The kind of pronunciation to aim at is heard in Modern English words like 'mis-spell', 'book-case' and 'lamp-post' (as contrasted with 'dispel', 'bookish' and 'lampoon', which have single [s], [k] and [p]).

Old English script normally uses sixteen consonant symbols, which in modern editions are usually reproduced as *b, c, d, f, g, h, l, m, n, p, r, s, t, þ, ð* and *w*. For *w* the scribes in fact used the runic symbol ƿ ('wynn'), and for *g* they used ȝ ('yogh'), and some modern editions retain these. A few other symbols are sometimes found, for example *x*, which stands for *cs/ks* or *hs*. Many of the symbols present no difficulty: the letters *b, d, l, m, p, t* and *w* each represent a single phoneme which can be pronounced as in Modern English. The other symbols call for comment.

Old English had no symbol *v*: the symbol *f* was used to represent both [f] and [v]. The reason is that, in Old English, [f] and [v] were members of the same phoneme: they were allophones. When this phoneme occurred within a word (that is, not initially or finally) before a voiced sound, and was not doubled, it was pronounced [v]; in all other positions it was pronounced [f]. So [f] was used in *fæder* 'father', *fīf* 'five', *'hæft* 'handle' and *pyffan* 'to puff', while [v] was used in *giefan* 'to give', *seofon* 'seven', *hræfn* 'raven' and *lifde* 'he lived'. The pronunciation often corresponds to modern usage, but not always, since OE *fīf* was [fi:f], whereas our *five* is [faɪv]; and, unlike our word *puff*, OE *pyffan* was pronounced with a double [-ff-].

There were two other such pairs in Old English. There was a symbol *s*, but not normally a symbol *z*, and for a similar reason: [s] and [z] were allophones, and the rules for their distribution were exactly the same as for [f] and [v]. So [s] occurred in *sǣ* 'sea', *hūs* 'house', *stānas* 'stones', *west* 'west' and *cyssan* 'to kiss', while [z] occurred in *nosu* 'nose' and *bōsm* 'bosom'.

The third pair that behaved in this way were the voiceless [θ] (as in *thin*) and the voiced [ð] (as in *this*). To represent this phoneme, the scribes used two symbols: the runic symbol þ, called 'thorn', and the symbol ð, called 'eth', which was based on the Latin character *d*. They did not, however, use one of these symbols for the voiceless sound and the other for the voiced, but used them both indiscriminately; this is only to be expected, since native speakers of a language do not usually notice differences between allophones of a single phoneme. For simplicity, we will use only thorn in transcriptions from Old English. The distribution of the allophones was exactly the same as in the other two pairs: thus the voiceless [θ] was used in *þegn* 'thane, attendant', *trēowþ* 'good faith', *þes* 'this' and *moþþe* 'moth', while the voiced [ð] was used in *baþian* 'to bathe' and *fæþm* 'embrace'.

In all three cases, Old English has a single phoneme consisting of a pair of voiced and voiceless allophones, where Modern English has two separate phonemes. The Old English arrangement was not inherited from Proto-Germanic, but arose in prehistoric Old English by processes of assimilation.

The letter *k* was not normally used, [k] being represented by *c* in most cases. However, when in prehistoric Old English this [k] preceded a front vowel, it developed into a palatal stop instead of a velar one, that is, it was articulated further forward in the mouth, somewhere between [k] and [t]. In the course of the Old English period, the difference between the velar and the palatal variants became greater, and the palatal stop has developed into Modern English [tʃ] (as in *church*). Indeed, it had probably reached this stage by the end of the Old English period, so it is convenient to use the [tʃ] pronunciation when reading Old English. The Old English symbol *c*, then, can represent either [k] or [tʃ]. It is not always possible by looking at an Old English word to know which pronunciation to use, because the vowel following the *c* may well have changed since prehistoric times: thus *cēlan* 'to cool' and *cynn* 'kin' both have the velar stop [k], even though they have front vowels, because they derive from prehistoric OE forms **kōljan* and **kunni*. Often, the modern pronunciation can be a guide: thus the velar [k] was used in *cyssan* 'to kiss', *cǣg* 'key', *þancian* 'to thank' and *cæppe* 'cap, hood', while the palatal [tʃ] was used in *cinn* 'chin', *cēosan* 'to choose' and *cīdan* 'to quarrel, chide'. Originally, it is clear, the two sounds were merely variants of a single phoneme: [k] was the allophone used before back vowels and [tʃ] the allophone used before front vowels; but in the course of the Old English period they developed into two separate phonemes. The kind of process by which this happened can be illustrated by two words already given as examples: *cinn* (pronounced [tʃinn]) and *cynn* (pronounced [kynn]) (notice that even in word-final position the double consonant is pronounced [-nn]). Originally, the contrast between the two words was carried by the vowels [i] and [y], and the difference between the two initial consonants had no significance. But in late Old English, in many parts of the country, the [y] of *cynn* lost its lip-rounding and became [i], so that the word was then *cinn*, pronounced [kinn]. At that stage, therefore, there was a pair of words, pronounced [kinn] and [tʃinn], which were distinguished from one another solely by the difference between [k] and [tʃ]; and this suggests that /k/ and /tʃ/ were now separate phonemes.

In most positions, OE [k] also became palatalized when it followed [s], and the combination represented by the OE spelling *sc* normally develops into Modern English [ʃ]. The [ʃ] pronunciation was in existence by the end of the OE period, so it is convenient to use it when reading OE texts. Examples are *scip* 'ship', *scrūd* 'dress, shroud', *fisc* 'fish' and *blyscan* 'to blush'. In some positions, however, [sk] remained unchanged, as in *ascian* 'to ask' and *tusc* 'tooth'.

OE *c* never represents a pronunciation [s], as it does in Modern English *centre*, *city* and *lace*. This spelling-convention was introduced from French after the Norman Conquest, and is unknown in Old English.

The letter *g* was used in Old English to represent two different phonemes. On the one hand there was a /j/ phoneme, similar to the semivowel in Modern English *yes*, as in the words *gēar* 'year', *fæger* 'fair', *cǣg* 'key' and *geoc* 'yoke'. On the other hand there was a /g/ phoneme, similar to the consonant of Modern English *go*, as in the words *gōd* 'good', *gēs* 'geese' and *dogga* 'dog'. When, however, this phoneme occurred undoubled between vowels, a different allophone was used: instead of being a voiced velar stop, it was the voiced velar fricative [ɣ], made by narrowing the passage between the back of the tongue and the soft palate; this pronunciation would have been used, for example, in the words *fugol* 'bird' and *lagu* 'law'. In Middle English this velar fricative developed into the approximant [w], and the words were written *fowel* and *lawe*; in Modern English they have become *fowl* and *law*. Often, the OE scribes did not distinguish in spelling between /g/ and /j/, but when /j/ occurred before a back vowel they tended to spell it *ge*, as in the word *geoc* already quoted; here the *eo* probably does not indicate a diphthong, but the *e* is simply inserted to show the quality of the preceding consonant. Alternatively, the spelling *i* could be used for /j/ in such positions, and in fact the word is also found with the spelling *ioc*.

When the /g/ phoneme was doubled, it was usually spelt *gg*, as in *frogga* 'frog' and *dogga* 'dog', but sometimes the spelling *cg* was used instead, and we find *frocga*, *docga*. The spelling *cg*, however, was also used to represent a /dʒ/ phoneme (resembling that of Modern English *judge*), as in *ecg* 'edge', *brycg* 'bridge' and *secgan* 'to say'.

The spelling *n* represented an /n/ phoneme, as today, but when it occurred before [k] or [g] it was pronounced [ŋ] (like the *ng* of our *sing*). Examples are *þancian* 'to thank' and *finger* 'finger', pronounced ['θaŋkian] and ['fiŋger]. In Old English the spelling *ng* represents the pronunciation [ŋg], never just [ŋ]: so OE *hring* 'a ring' was pronounced [hriŋg], whereas the Modern English equivalent is [rɪŋ]. This means that in Old English [ŋ] was not an independent phoneme, as today, but was simply an allophone of the /n/ phoneme, the variant of /n/ which occurred before [k] and [g]. Indeed, in the standard language it did not become an independent phoneme until about the year 1600.

The letter *h* often represented a more strongly articulated consonant than it does today. At the beginning of a syllable it was probably the glottal fricative [h], much as today; but in other positions it was either [x] (like the *ch* of German *ach*) or [ç] (like the *ch* of German *ich*), according to the preceding vowel. So OE *hætt* 'hat' was [hætt], but *niht* 'night' was [niçt], and *dohtor* 'daughter' was ['doxtor]. The three sounds were allophones of a single phoneme, which we can call /h/.

The letter *r* also represented a more powerfully articulated consonant than it does today: OE /r/ was probably trilled, that is, produced by a rapid succession of taps by the tip of the tongue on the teeth-ridge, whereas the corresponding consonant in Modern English is usually an approximant. Moreover, OE /r/ was pronounced in positions where it does not occur today (at least in most British speech), namely before consonants and before a pause. So you have to pronounce the /r/ in OE words like *bearn* 'child' and *wæter* 'water'.

Indeed, in general, when you read Old English texts, you have to remember that every symbol must be pronounced: the *h* in *niht* 'night', the *c* in *cnēo* 'knee', the *e* at the end of *cwene* 'woman', both the *n* and the *g* in *singan* 'to sing', both *s* sounds in *cyssan* 'to kiss', and so on. Also, you have to try to avoid being misled by relatively recent sound changes in English, which are liable to affect our interpretation of spellings. For example, in Old English the quality of a vowel is not affected by a preceding /w/, or by a following /l/ or /r/, as it often is in Modern English (as in *watch, ball, burn*). Again, the first vowel in OE words like *cwene* 'woman' and *hopa* 'hope' must be pronounced short. And unstressed vowels must be given their full quality, and not all reduced to [ə], so that for example *bera* 'a bear' must be distinguished in pronunciation from *bere* 'barley'. In the matter of stress, be guided in general by Modern English.

It will be seen that some OE spelling symbols are ambiguous, since they can stand for more than one phoneme: this is true of *c, g* and *cg*. Most of the symbols, however, are unambiguous, and in the past it has been common practice for historical philologists to use letter symbols rather than phonetic symbols when discussing the phonology of Old and Middle English. We shall follow this practice.

Sound changes in Old English

Old English shows certain phonological developments of its own compared with the other Germanic languages. The Proto-Germanic diphthongs were changed in Old English. For example, PG *ai* became OE *ā*, so that Old English has *stān* and *hām* where Gothic has *stains* 'stone' and *haims* 'village'. And PG *au* became OE *ēa*, so that Old English has *drēam* where Old Norse has *draumr* 'dream', and *bēam* where German has *Baum* 'tree, pole', and *ēare* where Gothic has *ausō* 'ear'.

In prehistoric Old English a number of combinative sound changes took place. One with far-reaching effects was **front mutation** or **i-umlaut** (also known as *i*-mutation). This was a series of changes to vowels which took place when there was an *i, ī* or *j* in the following syllable. Subsequently, the *i, ī* or *j* disappeared, or changed to *e*, but its original presence can be established by examining the cognate words in other languages. For example, front mutation accounts for the difference in vowel between the related words *dole* and *deal*. In Old English they are *dāl* 'portion' and *dǣlan* 'to divide, distribute', in which the *ǣ* is due to front mutation; this is clear if we look at the cognate Gothic words, which are *dails* and *dailjan* (note that the sound spelt *ai* in the Gothic words regularly becomes *ā* in Old English before front mutation takes place; the *i* in these spellings could not cause front mutation itself).

OE *dǣlan* is a weak verb, and it is normal for the stem-vowels of OE weak verbs to show front mutation. The weak verbs were formed in two main ways: there are denominative verbs (formed from nouns or adjectives), and causative verbs (formed from strong verbs). OE *dǣlan* is an example of a denominative verb, formed from the noun *dāl*. Causative verbs were formed on the past-singular stem of strong verbs. The strong verb *rīsan* meant 'to rise', and the corresponding causative verb is *rǣran* 'to cause to rise, rear'. The Proto-Germanic past-tense singular was **rais-* (OE *rās* 'rose'), and from this was formed the causative verb **raisján*. The accent was on the ending, so by Verner's Law (discussed in chapter 4) it became **raizján*. In West Germanic, PG /z/ became /r/, so the prehistoric OE form was **rārjan*, which by front mutation became *rǣran*. Front mutation is normal in all the forms of weak verbs. Their infinitive was formed with the suffix **-jan*, and their various other inflections also contained *i* or *j*. For example, in prehistoric Old English, the third-person singular ending of the present tense was **-iþ*, so that 'he divides' was **dāliþ*. The *i* caused front mutation of the *ā*, and then itself changed to *e*. This *e* was lost in some varieties of Old English, so that the recorded forms of the word are *dǣleþ* or *dǣlþ*.

The change from *ā* to *ǣ* was a movement to a closer and more frontal vowel, and this is the general direction of the changes caused by front mutation: it was obviously a kind of assimilation, the affected vowels being moved to a place of articulation nearer to that of the following vowel or *j*. Thus *ū* became fronted to *ȳ*, a change which accounts for the different vowels of *mouse* and *mice*, which have developed regularly from OE *mūs*, *mȳs*; the original plural form was **mūsiz*, but the *i* caused the *ū* to change to *ȳ*; then the ending **-iz* was lost, giving the OE plural *mȳs*.

Similarly, front mutation changed short *u* to *y*; this change is reflected in the different vowels of *full* and *fill*, which in Old English are *full* and *fyllan* (from earlier **fulljan*). In some positions, an unmutated *u* developed in prehistoric Old English into *o*; sometimes, therefore, we get a contrast between unmutated *o* and mutated *y*, as in the words *gold* 'gold' and *gyldan* 'to gild'. Other pairs of words illustrating the front mutation of *u* to *y* are OE *fox* 'fox' and *fyxen* 'vixen', *cnotta* 'a knot' and *cnyttan* 'to tie, knit', *lust* 'pleasure, desire' and *lystan* 'to please'.

Front mutation changed *ō* to *ē* (or *ǣ* in non-West-Saxon dialects, indicating the rounded quality of the front vowel thus produced), and this accounts for the different vowel of *food* (OE *fōd*) and *to feed* (OE *fēdan*). Other such pairs in Modern English are *doom* and *deem*, *goose* and *geese*, *tooth* and *teeth*, *blood* and *bleed*, *book* and *beech*. Even where the *ō* has been shortened since OE times, we still often have the spelling with *oo*, which shows that the vowel was once long. Finally, front mutation changed short *a*, *æ* and *o*, which all became *e*; modern pairs illustrating these changes include *man* and *men*, *wander* and *wend*, *Canterbury* and *Kent*, *long* and *length*, *tale* and *tell*, *straight* and *stretch*.

Even from these few examples, you will see that front mutation made considerable changes in the pronunciation of English. But do not confuse pairs like *foot* and *feet*, where the vowel difference is caused by front mutation in prehistoric Old English, with pairs like *sing* and *sang*, where the difference goes right back to the system of vowel-gradation in Proto-Indo-European.

Other combinative changes in prehistoric Old English caused the diphthongization of pure vowels, often with different results in different dialects. One change, called 'breaking' or 'fracture', affected vowels before /l/ plus consonant, /r/ plus consonant, and /h/. So West Saxon and Kentish have the forms *ceald* 'cold', *earm*

'arm' and *eahta* 'eight', compared with Gothic *kalds, arms* and *ahtau*. The Anglian dialects, however, have unbroken vowels in many positions, as in *cald* 'cold' and *æhta* 'eight'. Another prehistoric change was the diphthongization of some front vowels after initial [j] and palatalized [k], as in West Saxon *geaf* 'he gave', *giefan* 'to give', *gēar* 'year', and *gīe* 'ye, you'. The change also took place in Northumbrian in some positions, but not in Kentish or Mercian: the Mercian forms of those four words are *gæf, gefan, gēr* and *gē*. This set of changes is usually known as palatal diphthongization, but the reality of the sound change has been questioned, with critics suggesting that the changes may be purely orthographic changes, intended to signal the palatal quality of the preceding consonants, rather than indicating a change in the pronunciation of the vowels involved. Breaking and palatal diphthongization probably took place earlier than front mutation. At a later date than front mutation there was a third type of diphthongization, called 'velar umlaut' or back mutation, which was caused by an unstressed back vowel in the following syllable, when only a single consonant intervened; this process accounts for the diphthongs in such forms as *heofon* 'heaven'. It occurred extensively in Kentish and Anglian, but in West Saxon is found only before a limited number of consonants. The exact dates of these various sound changes are unknown, but it seems probable that they took place sometime between the middle of the fifth century and the middle of the eighth century.

Old English morphology

In grammar, Old English carried out some simplifications of the Proto-Germanic system. OE nouns usually have only four cases: nominative, accusative, genitive and dative. Moreover, the number of commonly used declensions is reduced, the vast majority of nouns tending to be attracted into three or four large declensions. At the same time, there are fewer distinctive case-endings than in Proto-Germanic, because of the weakening and loss of sounds in unstressed syllables in prehistoric Old English, and the operation of analogy. A few distinctive endings remained: all nouns have the ending *-um* for the dative plural, and most have *-a* for the genitive plural, and many masculine nouns have a genitive singular in *-es* and a nominative and accusative plural in *-as*. But in no nouns is a distinction made between nominative plural and accusative plural, and in many nouns other distinctions are obliterated too. For example, the feminine noun *giefu* 'a gift' has the one form *giefe* for its accusative, genitive and dative singular, and the masculine noun *guma* 'a man' has the one form *guman* for its accusative, genitive and dative singular and its nominative and accusative plural. Old English in fact relied a good deal for its case distinctions on the adjectives, which had preserved more distinctive endings than the nouns, and on the definite article *se*, which still had a large number of forms for different cases and genders. Old English did still, however, make great use of its inflectional system, and to a great extent it still preserved grammatical gender.

In its verbal system, Old English inherited from Proto-Germanic a two-tense system (traditionally called 'present' and 'past'), with different forms for indicative and subjunctive. Proto-Germanic also had inflections for the passive, but these did not survive in Old English. As examples of verb-forms, let us look at the strong verb *helpan* 'to help'. In the present tense, Old English retained the person distinctions in the indicative singular, as in *ic helpe* 'I help', *þū hilpst* 'you (sg) help', and *hē/hēo/hit hilpþ* 'he/she/it helps'. But in the plural it made no person distinctions: *wē/gē/hīe helpaþ* 'we/ you/they help'. In the present subjunctive there was one form for the singular *helpe*, and one for the plural, *helpen*. There were also imperative forms, that is, ones for giving commands: singular *help*, plural *helpaþ*. In the past tense there was a distinctive form for the second-person singular, *þū hulpe* 'you (sg) helped', as against first- and third-person *ic/hēo healp* 'I/she helped'; in the plural there was no distinction of persons, but the one form *hulpon* 'we/you/they helped'. In the past-tense subjunctive there was one form for the singular (*hulpe*) and one for the plural (*hulpen*). There was also a past participle, *holpen*, and a present participle, *helpende*. It will be seen that the verbal system, although simplified compared with Proto-Germanic, still had many more variant forms than Modern English.

In Old English, as in other Germanic languages, we also see the beginnings of a new tense system using auxiliaries, and especially the development of forms for the perfect and for the passive, like Modern English *I have helped* and *I am helped*. The perfect tenses existed in Old English, but were not used as frequently or as consistently as they were later. The perfect tenses of transitive verbs (that is, those that take a direct object) were formed by the use of the verb *habban* 'to have' and the past participle of the verb. Originally, sentences like 'He had broken a leg' meant something like 'He possessed a broken leg'; and in fact in the Old English equivalent of this sentence the word *broken* was sometimes given an inflection to make it agree with *leg*. Thus in the *Anglo-Saxon Chronicle* (Parker MS) in the entry for the year 755 we read *oþ þæt hīe hine ofslægenne hæfdon*, literally 'until they him killed had', where the *-ne* of *ofslægenne* is the inflection for the accusative singular masculine, making it agree with *hine* 'him'. But even in the Old English period this habit of inflecting the past participle was dying out, and in a later manuscript of the *Chronicle* (Laud MS) the same entry reads *oþ þet hig hine ofslægen hæfdon*. The perfect tenses of intransitive verbs (those with no direct object) were formed with the verbs 'to be' (*bēon, wesan*) or 'to become' (*weorþan*). So a translator of King Alfred's time writes *þā wæs þæs folces fela on ān fæsten oþflogen* 'then had (literally 'was') much of that multitude fled into a fortress', in which *wæs oþflogen* translates the Latin pluperfect *confūgerant*.

The passive too was formed with the verbs 'to be' or 'to become' and the past participle. We can take an example of the passive from the same text of King Alfred's time: *þær wearþ Alexander þurhscoten mid ānre flān* 'there was (literally 'became') Alexander pierced by an arrow'. Only transitive verbs can produce passives of this type, since it is the direct object of the active sentence that becomes the subject of the passive one: 'An arrow there pierced Alexander' becomes 'There was Alexander pierced by an arrow.' In Old English, the passive could only be formed with verbs that took an object in the accusative case. Many OE verbs took an object in the dative case, and some an object in the genitive. The verb *helpan*, for example, usually had a dative object, occasionally a genitive one: *þū monegum helpst* 'you help many (people)' (where *monegum* is dative plural); *þonne þū hulpe mīn* 'when you helped me' (where *mīn* is the genitive of the pronoun). Such sentences could not be made passive in Old English; it was only after the dative case of nouns and pronouns had disappeared in Middle English that it became possible to say such things as 'Many people are helped by you.'

Old English syntax

Because of its inflectional system, Old English had greater freedom of word-order than Modern English. In Old English we can say *se cyning hæfde micel geþeaht* 'the king held a great council'; and as a stylistic variant of this we can say *micel geþeaht hæfde se cyning*: this is quite unambiguous, because the nominative article *se* marks the subject of the sentence, but the word-order throws the emphasis on 'a great council'. But in Modern English we cannot use this second word-order, because 'A great council held the king' means something quite different. It is not that Old English lacked rules and preferences about word-order: we have already seen that it favoured three particular types of word-order for the clause: S–V–O, V–S–O and S–O–V. These can be illustrated from a sentence of King Alfred's, which begins as follows:

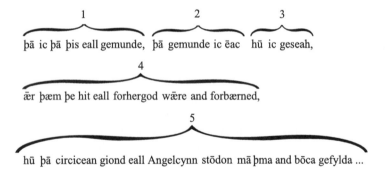

This contains five clauses: (1) 'When I then this all remembered', (2) 'then remembered I also' (3) 'how I saw', (4) 'before it all ravaged was and burnt up', (5) 'how the churches throughout all England stood with treasures and books filled ...'. Clause (1) is a subordinate clause, and has the S–O–V order often (but not invariably) found in such clauses. Clause (2) has V–S–O order (the direct object being the remainder of the whole sentence); this order is common when the clause begins with an adverbial expression, especially *þā* 'then' and *þǣr* 'there'. Clause (3) has the common S–V–O order (the direct object being clause 5). Clause (4) is a subordinate clause in the passive; the verb is in the subjunctive, and is placed *after* the past participle 'ravaged'. Clause (5) has the order S–V, but the verb is intransitive, so there is no direct object; the nouns dependent on the past participle 'filled' (which are in the genitive plural) are placed before it.

The order V–S–O is normal in questions: *Hwȳ didest þū þæt?* 'Why did you that?', *Hæfst þū ǣnigne geféran?* 'Have you any companion?' Negation is achieved by use of the particle *ne*: *Fram ic ne wille* 'Away I do not wish (to go).' If the *ne* was the first word in the sentence, the word-order V–S–O was likely: *ne mihte hē gehealdan heardne mēce* 'he could not hold the hard sword'. The *ne* occurred so frequently before certain words that it often coalesced with them, producing forms like *nis* (*ne* + *is*) 'is not' and *nolde* (*ne* + *wolde*) 'did not want'. Multiple negation was common, that is, *ne* might occur several times in the same sentence. Such repetitions, far from cancelling one another out, in fact made the negation more emphatic, as in line 233 of the poem *Judith*: *nānne ne sparedon* (literally 'they did not spare no one', that is 'they did not spare anyone'). Neither in questions nor in negative sentences does Old English make use of auxiliary *do*: where we say 'Why do you go?' and 'I do not go', Old English has *Hwȳ gāþ gē?* and *ic ne gā*.

The structure of the noun phrase is quite similar to that of Modern English, the normal pattern being determiner–adjective–noun. Exceptions to this pattern are provided by the forms *eall* 'all', *bēgen* 'both' and adjectives ending in *-weard*. These precede the determiner, as in *eal þes middangeard* 'this entire earth', *bēgen þā gebroþru* 'both the brothers' and *on sūþeweardum þǣm lande* 'in the southern part of the land'. It is however perfectly possible for adjectives to follow the noun, or for one to precede it and another to follow it: *Denum eallum* 'to all the Danes', *micle meras fersce* 'big fresh-water meres'. It is even possible for a determiner to follow the noun, especially if it is emphatic: *Ic eom micle yldra þonne ymbhwyrft þes* 'I am much older than this world.' Titles of rank usually follow the name they qualify: *Ælfred cyning* 'King Alfred'.

One big difference from Modern English is in the system of demonstratives. Today we have a threefold system: *the, this, that*. But in Old English there are only two demonstratives, *se* 'the, that' and *þes* 'this'. On the other hand, the ternary modern system comprises only five different forms (*the, this, these, that, those*), whereas each of the OE demonstratives is declined through three genders, five cases (the fifth being the instrumental) and two numbers. In the plural, indeed, there is no distinction of genders, and in the singular there is some overlapping of forms, but even so there are about ten different forms of *se*, and the same number of *þes*. One particular point to note is that the word *þæt* is simply the nominative and accusative singular neuter form of *se*, not a contrasting demonstrative.

The vocabulary of Old English

To enlarge its vocabulary, Old English depended more on its own resources than on borrowings from other languages. From Proto-Indo-European, the Germanic languages had inherited many ways of forming new words, especially by the use of prefixes and suffixes. Thus, in Old English, adjectives could be formed from nouns by means of such suffixes as *-ig*, *-lēas* and *-ful*, giving words like *blōdig* 'bloody', *frēondlēas* 'friendless' and *þancful* 'thankful'. Conversely, nouns could be formed from adjectives: for example, there was a Proto-Germanic suffix *-iþō* (prehistoric OE *-iþa*) which could be added to adjectives to form abstract nouns: on the stem of the adjective *fūl* 'foul, dirty' was formed the prehistoric OE noun *fūliþa*; the *i* caused front-mutation and was later lost, leading to the recorded OE form *fȳlþ* 'impurity, filth'. Similar formations have led to such Modern English pairs as *merry* and *mirth, slow* and *sloth, strong* and *strength, true* and *truth*. Adverbs were commonly formed from adjectives by means of suffixes such as *-e* and *-līce*: so from the adjective *fæst* 'firm' was formed *fæste* 'firmly', and from *blind* was formed *blindlīce* 'blindly'.

There were large numbers of prefixes, many of which could be added to verbs. See King Alfred's sentence on p. 126 above: *forhergod* and *forbærned* are the past participles of the verbs *forhergian* and *forbærnan*, formed by the addition of the prefix *for-* to the verbs *hergian* 'to harry, ravage' and *bærnan* 'to burn'; the prefix *for-* has an intensifying force, and in particular often signifies destruction, so that *forhergian* means 'destroy by harrying' and *forbærnan* 'destroy by burning'. Another common verbal prefix is *ge-*, which often has a perfective force, signifying the achievement or the completion of the action. So *sceran* means 'to cut', and *gesceran* 'to cut right through'; *rīdan* means 'to ride', and *gerīdan* 'to ride up to, conquer, occupy'. There is a well-known example of this perfective use of *ge-* in King Alfred's account of a voyage by the Norwegian Ōhthere:

> þā siglde he þonan sūþryhte be lande swā swā he mehte on fīf dagum gesiglan.

The interesting thing here is the difference between *siglde* 'sailed' and *gesiglan* 'to get somewhere by sailing'. The sentence means 'Then sailed he from there southwards along the land as (far) as he was able to sail in five days.'

As well as using affixation, Old English formed new words by compounding. The difference is that an affix is a bound morpheme, whereas a compound word is formed by the joining of two or more free morphemes. So, for example, literature, arithmetic, grammar and astronomy were called *bōccræft*, *rīmcræft*, *stæfcræft* and *tungolcræft*, that is, book-skill, number-skill, letter-skill and star-skill. Homelier compounds have survived to our own times, like *ēarwicga* 'earwig', *hāmstede* 'homestead', *sunnebēam* 'sunbeam' and *wīfmann* 'woman'.

Old English did however borrow a number of words from other languages, especially for the concepts and institutions of Christianity. OE *cirice* or *cyrce* 'church' is derived from the Greek *kuriakón*, meaning '(house) of the Lord', and was probably borrowed by pre-Christian Germanic-speaking groups; similar forms are found in all the Germanic languages, whereas the Romance languages have words derived from the Latin *ecclesia*, like French *église*. Most of the words connected with Christianity, however, date from after the conversion, and are from Latin (though Latin itself had borrowed many of them from Greek). They include OE *apostol* 'apostle', *biscop* 'bishop' (Latin *episcopus*), *munuc* 'monk' (Latin *monachus*), *mynster* 'monastery, church' (Latin *monastērium*), as well as words for abbot, disciple, nun, pilgrim, pope and school.

But even in this field Old English made considerable use of its native language material. Sometimes existing words were simply transferred to Christian use, as with *Easter*, *hell* and *holy*. Sometimes new words were coined from native elements: thus Latin *evangelium* was rendered as *gōdspell* 'good message', which has become our *gospel*, and *trinitas* 'trinity' was rendered as *þrīnes* 'threeness'.

Specimens of Old English

Let us end this chapter with brief examples of OE prose and verse. We begin with an example of OE prose, taken from a text addressing an individual called Eadweard (Edward). The fact that Eadweard is referred to as 'broðor Eadweard' ('brother Eadweard') might be thought to indicate that Eadweard was a monk, but we cannot be sure of this. Quite a few Old English prose texts are translations of Latin texts, but this can reasonably be supposed to be an original composition in Old English. In the sole extant manuscript (Oxford, Bodleian Library, MS Hatton 115 (5135)) this passage is laid out as the second half of a text that begins with a discussion of biblical prohibitions on eating blood – a topic that bears some relation to the concerns with behaviour at feasts expressed in this passage. The text is also concerned with Englishmen dressing in the Danish manner, presumably as a result of contact between those of Viking and Anglo-Saxon extraction in the Danelaw. The picture this presents of Anglo-Saxons drinking and behaving badly – and apparently wearing Viking-style low-cut tops and long hair – offers a rare insight into the seamier side of life in a period whose textual records are largely the product of individuals in religious orders. This is relatively informal writing (although not without rhetorical embellishments: note, for instance, the tricolon 'bysmorlic dæd and mycel higeleast and huxlic bysmor') and it gives us a glimpse of something like everyday discourse in the late Anglo-Saxon period. We have transcribed the text below from the microfiche of the manuscript available in volume 6 of *Anglo-Saxon Manuscripts in Microfiche Facsimile*, but have silently expanded abbreviations, and capitalized and punctuated according to modern conventions. We have not, however, altered the manuscript reading *stencg*, although it is clear that this represents the word *stenc* ('odour'). It is probable that this is simply a scribal error. The text is glossed above, word by word, and we append a translation into more idiomatic modern English.

I say   also to you, brother Eadweard, now you me of this
Ic secge eac ðe,   broðor Eadweard, nu ðu me þyses

asked, that you do   unrighteously that you the
bæde, þæt ge doð unrihtlice   þæt ge ða

English customs abandon which your fathers held   and
Engliscan þeawas forlætað þe   eowre fæderas heoldon and
heathen men's customs love who
hæðenra manna þeawas lufiað þe

you the life not allow, and with that show   that you
eow ðæs lifes ne unnon, and mid ðam geswuteliað þæt ge
despise your race and your
forseoð eower cynn and eowre

elders with the vices,   when you for them in insult
yldran mid þam unþeawum, þonne ge him   on teonan
dress yourselves in Danish, with uncovered
tysliað eow   on Denisc, ableredum

neck and blinded eyes.   Not say I no more about
hneccan and ablendum eagum. Ne secge ic na mare embe
the shameful   dressing, except that
ða sceandlican tyslunge, buton þæt

us tell   books, that he is   excommunicated who heathen
us secgað bec   þæt se beo amansumod   þe hæðenra
men's customs holds in his life, and his own
manna þeawas hylt on his life, and his agen

race dishonours with them. I ask   also you, brother,
cynn unwurþað mid þam. Ic bidde eac þe, broðor –
because you are in [the] country with
forþamðe þu byst uppan lande   mid

women   oftener than I am,   that you them a thing
wimmannum oftor   þonne ic beo – þæt þu him an þing
tell, if you for shame nevertheless it them
secge, gif ðu for sceame swaþeah   hit him

tell   can; me shames greatly that I it tell you. I it
secgan mæge; me sceamað þearle þæt ic hit secge ðe. Ic hit
heard often told (and it is
gehyrde oft secgan (and hit is

evil-truth) that these rustic women want often
yfelsoð) þæt þas uplendiscan wif wyllað oft

to drink and even to eat foully on toilets
drincan and furþon etan fullice on gangsetlum

at their feasts; but it is shameful deed and great
æt heora gebeorscipum; ac hit is bysmorlic dæd and mycel

folly and outrageous shame that
higeleast and huxlic bysmor þæt

any person ever so dissolute be should that he the
ænig man æfre swa unþeawfæst beon sceole þæt he þone

mouth above with foods fill and at
muð ufan mid mettum afylle and on

other end him goes the filth out from, and drink
oðerne ende him gange þæt meox ut fram, and drince

then both the beer and the
þonne ægðer ge þæt ealu ge þone

odour, that he indeed thus fulfils his wicked greed. I
stencg, þæt he huru swa afylle his fracodan gyfernysse. Ic

not can for shame the
ne mæg for sceame þa

disgraceful deed that any person should eat in going
sceandlican dæde þæt ænig mann sceole etan on gange

as foully tell as it foul is, but
swa fullice secgan swa hit fullic is, ac

that never needs none the men who are good.
þæt næfre nedeð nan ðæra manna ðe deah.

I also say to you, brother Edward, now that you have asked me about this, that you are all behaving unrighteously in abandoning the English customs which your fathers practised and loving the customs of heathen men who do not allow you to live, and in doing so you make clear by those vices that you despise your race and your elders, when, as an insult to them, you dress yourselves in the Danish way, with uncovered neck and blinded eyes. I will say no more about this shameful way of dressing, except that books tell us that he who practises heathen customs

in his life, and dishonours his own race with them, will be excommunicated. I also ask you, brother – because you are in the countryside with
women oftener than I am – that you should say something to them, if
indeed you can say it to them for shame; it shames me greatly that I
should say it to you. I have often heard it said (and it is terrible but true),
that the rustic women will often foully drink and even eat on the toilets
at their feasts; but it is a shameful deed and a great folly and an outrageous shame that anyone should ever be so dissolute that he should
stuff his mouth with foods up above while the filth goes out the other
end, and he drinks both the ale and the stink, so that he thus fulfils his
wicked greed. I cannot, for shame, describe the shameful act of anyone
eating on the toilet as disgustingly as the act itself is disgusting, but no
one who is any good ever ought to do this.

The highlighted forms *secge*, *mæge*, *sceole*, *afylle*, *gange* and *drince*
are subjunctive: the indicative forms would be *segst*, *meaht*, *sceal*,
afylleþ, *gangeþ* and *drinc(e)þ*. The word *wyllað* is from the verb *willan*
'to wish, be willing, intend'; this verb was not originally used, like
present-day *will*, merely to signal futurity or prediction, although
there are some signs of a development in this direction in late Old
English texts. In this case, *wyllað* does not appear to signal futurity, as the women's actions are a continuous pattern of behaviour
from the past through to the present. In referring to the future, Old
English usually uses the so-called present tense: at the start of this
passage, the author writes 'Ne secge ic na mare embe' ('I will say
no more about'), using the form *secge*, usually labelled as present
tense, to express something he will not do in the future. Similar
issues arise with forms such as *sceal* (from the verb *sculan*), which
usually means 'must, has to, is obliged to' rather than expressing
futurity. A slightly different case of a common verb whose meaning has shifted is the verb *magan*: the present-tense singular form
mæg may seem, when one reads it aloud, quite similar to its modern
descendant *may*, but in fact it usually expresses meanings more like
'can' than 'may'. For instance, the refrain of the well-known poem
now known as *Deor* reads (with added modern punctuation) 'þæs
oferēode; þisses swā mæg'. Many have been tempted to translate
'it passed away for that; so it may for this', but the sentiment is
not one of uncertainty whether or not circumstances will improve
with regard to 'this'; rather the narrator is expressing certainty
that it is possible for things to change for the better.

To return to our letter, the author addresses brother Eadweard individually as *þū* (singular), but when he turns to the activities of Eadweard's wider community, he addresses them as *gē* (plural), whereas today we use *you* in both cases. In Old English, *thou* and *thee* were singular, and *ye* and *you* plural, but in Middle English times the custom arose of using *ye/you* as a polite or deferential way of addressing a single person, and this usage spread; *thou* and *thee* gradually dropped out of use in everyday speech, and finally disappeared (except in some dialects, where they persist to this day). The difference between *ye* and *you* was the same as that between *he* and *him*: one was nominative and the other accusative. This distinction was maintained until the sixteenth century: it is regularly observed in the King James Bible of 1611, though in everyday speech at that date *you* was the normal form for both nominative and accusative, and *ye* was dying out.

Originally, *you* was not the accusative form but the dative: OE *ēow* 'to you' (or 'for you', 'by you', 'with you' and so on). The original accusative form was *ēowic*, but during the OE period this was supplanted by *ēow*. The same thing has in fact happened with all the personal pronouns (except *it*): our words *him*, *me*, *us*, *her* and *thee* originally meant 'to him', 'to me', and so on. The early OE accusative forms were *hine*, *mec*, *ūsic*, *hīe* and *þec*, but these fell out of use during the Old and Middle English periods (with *mec*, *ūsic* and *þec* disappearing earliest, and the others in Middle English), and were replaced by the dative forms.

In the phrase 'þas uplendiscan wif wyllað' we have a neat illustration of the various ways in which inflexions can provide important information in OE. The word *wif* itself could be singular or plural, and we have no way of knowing which. Fortunately the inflexional endings of the other words in this phrase let us know that we are dealing with a plural noun: the demonstrative form *þas* is plural (the singular would be *þis*); the adjective *uplendiscan* has a plural inflexion *-an*; and the verb *wyllað* has a plural inflexion *-að*, which indicates that its subject (in this case *wif*) should be plural.

The ways in which relative clauses are introduced in this letter are also of some interest. In the phrase 'se beo[þ] amansumod þe hæðenra manna þeawas hylt' we have the word *þe*, which we have glossed as 'who'. In the phrase 'ge ða Engliscan þeawas forlætað þe eowre fæderas heoldon' we see the same word, *þe*, but here the appropriate gloss is 'which', as it is referring to the *þeawas* ('customs') rather than a person or people. The words *who* and *which* did exist in Old English (*hwā, hwilc*), but were indefinite or interrogative pronouns, not relatives. For the relative function, Old English used the indeclinable particle *þe*, or the declinable pronoun *se* (identical in form with the definite article), or the two together. In Middle English, *which* and *that* were used as relatives, but *who* was not used in this way until Early Modern English, and even then not as frequently as today: in the 1611 Bible, the Lord's Prayer begins 'Our Father, *which* art in heaven'.

Finally, a few lines of OE poetry. Like much early Germanic poetry, this did not use rhyme but alliteration. Each line of verse was divided into two halves, and in each half there had to be two fully stressed syllables, some of which alliterated with one another; in other words, they began with the same letter, which usually (but not always) represented the same phoneme; all vowels, however, were allowed to alliterate together. The first stress of the second half-line had to alliterate with one or both of the stresses of the first half-line. In rare instances the second stress of the second half-line also alliterated. In the passage below, line 1 alliterates on *b*, line 2 has vowel-alliteration (*eald, æsc*), line 3 alliterates on *b*, line 4 on *h*, and so on. There were also quite complicated 'rules' about the permissible patterns of syllable-length and stress in a half-line, though these became laxer in the course of the OE period, as did the 'rules' about alliteration. It is unlikely that Old English poets were aware of a set of rules for versification: the rules are in fact merely our modern attempt to describe the basic patterns which Old English poets used. To the poets themselves, these were probably simply what sounded right. We do not need to think about how many stressed syllables are required in a limerick in order to compose one: once we have heard a few limericks, we quickly internalize the pattern and can produce it without conscious thought. No doubt Old English poets composed just as naturally. We have chosen a famous passage from a late OE poem that commemorates an actual historical event. In 991 the men of Essex, led by Byrhtnoth their *ealdormann* (the king's deputy and chief executive for the county), fought a battle at Maldon against a force of Vikings, who had sailed into the mouth of the River Blackwater. After a bitter struggle, the English were defeated and Byrhtnoth killed, and the end of the poem, from which this extract comes, tells how his companions remained on the battlefield to die with their lord.

> Byrhtwold maþelode,   bord hafenode,
> Se wæs eald genēat   æsc ācwehte;
> hē ful baldlīce   beornas lǣrde:
> 'Hige sceal þē heardra,   heorte þē cēnre,
> mōd sceal þē māre,   þē ūre mægen lȳtlaþ.
> Hēr līþ ūre ealdor   eall forhēawen,
> gōd on grēote.   Ā mæg gnornian
> se þe nū fram þis wīgplegan   wendan þenceþ.
> Ic eom frōd fēores: fram ic ne wille,
> ac ic mē be healfe   mīnum hlāforde
> be swā lēofan men,   licgan þence.'

This can be rendered as follows:

> Byrhtwold spoke, lifted his shield,
> He was an old retainer, shook his ash (spear),
> He full boldly exhorted the warriors:
> 'Mind must be the firmer, heart the more valiant,
> Courage must be the greater, as our strength diminishes.
> Here lies our lord, quite hewn down,
> The noble man in the dust. Ever will he have cause to mourn
> Who now thinks to depart from this battle.
> I am old of life; hence I will not,
> But by the side of my lord,
> By the man so dear, I intend to lie.'

Like much heroic poetry, the passage is highly formal, moving forward with parallel phrases and near-repetitions, and it has a marked diction of its own. It opens, for example, with a formulaic phrase, 'so-and-so spoke'. The stock of conventional poetic diction was very large, because of the need for alliteration: there were numerous words for warrior (like *beorn* in the passage), for weapons (like *æsc*), and for horse, ship, prince, and so on. Some of these are descriptive compounds: in *Beowulf*, for example, the sea is called *swanrād* 'the swan-road'. Some are decorative periphrases: a king can be called *beaga brytta* ('giver of rings') or *sincgiefa* ('giver of treasure'), since he was expected to bestow liberal gifts on his followers in return for their military service. An example of a poetic compound is the word *wīgplega* in the passage; we have glossed this as 'battle', but literally it means 'war-play'.

6 Norsemen and Normans

During the later part of the Old English period, two different groups of non-English speakers invaded the country. Both groups were Scandinavian in origin, but whereas the first had retained its Scandinavian speech, the second had settled in northern France and become French-speaking. Both of their languages, Old Norse (ON) and Old French (OF), had a considerable influence on English.

The Vikings in England

The harrying of Europe by the Scandinavian Vikings, which took place between about 750 and 1050, was the last phase of the expansion of the early Germanic peoples. Its basic cause was perhaps overpopulation in a region of poor natural resources, but there were other contributory causes. The custom of leaving the inheritance to the eldest son meant that there were always younger sons wanting to carve out inheritances for themselves. Political conflicts drove many noblemen into exile. And then, in the late eighth century, Charlemagne destroyed the power of the Frisians, who had hitherto been the greatest maritime power of north-western Europe, and thereby left open the sea-route southward for the Vikings. At about the same date, the ancient craft of boat-building in Scandinavia reached the stage at which it could produce the magnificent ocean-going sailing-ships which served the Vikings for trade, piracy and colonization.

The Vikings were great traders, but it is for their more predatory activities that they are most remembered. Their attacks varied from piratical expeditions by single ships to the invasion of a country by sizeable fleets and armies. The word *viking* (Old Norse *víkingr*) perhaps means 'creek-dweller', and hence 'pirate'; but there are cognate forms in Old English and Old Frisian, and the OE word, *wīcing* 'a pirate', is recorded in the days before the Scandinavian raids, which has led some to argue for alternative etymologies based on an Old English, rather than Old Norse, origin for the word.

The Vikings consisted of Swedes, Norwegians and Danes. The Swedes mostly went eastwards, to the Baltic countries and Russia, while the Norwegians and Danes tended to go westwards and southwards. The Vikings who attacked England were referred to by the Anglo-Saxons as *Dene* 'Danes' (and as pagans), but there were also Norwegians among them. The first attacks took place round about 800, and by 838 they had become serious. At first they were mere piratical raids in search of plunder; then large groups took to spending the winter in England, as happened in 850 and in 854; then large armies stayed for longer periods, like the one that landed in East Anglia in 865 and operated as a single unit for no less than nine years; and finally came conquest and settlement, which began in the last few decades of the ninth century. Viking armies came very near to conquering the whole of England, but King Alfred held the south and the west against them, the turning-point being his defeat of Guthrum at Edington in 878; the boundary between Alfred's territories and the Viking-controlled territories known as the Danelaw ran roughly along a line from London to Chester (see figure 9). In the tenth century, the West Saxon kings reconquered the north and east, but in the meantime the Vikings established kingdoms in those areas, and there was sufficient Scandinavian settlement to influence the English language in significant ways.

This Scandinavian settlement has left its mark on English place-names. Common Scandinavian place-name elements are *by* 'village, homestead', as in *Grimsby* 'Grim's village'; *thorp* 'secondary settlement, outlying farmstead', as in *Grimsthorpe*; *toft* 'building-site, plot of land', as in *Langtoft* (where the first element means 'long'); and *thwaite* 'woodland clearing, meadow', as in *Micklethwaite* 'large clearing'. Some place-names are more distinctively Norwegian, some more Danish: the element *thorp*, for example, was rarely used by the Norwegians in England, and is a

Figure 9 The division of England between King Alfred and the Danes

good sign of Danish settlement (though it also occurs occasionally in Anglo-Saxon place-names as a variant of *throp*). The main areas of Norwegian settlement were in the north-west – in Lancashire and Cumbria; elsewhere in the Danelaw there were Danes, the densest areas of place-name formation being in Derbyshire, Yorkshire, Nottinghamshire, Lincolnshire, Leicestershire and Norfolk.

Scandinavian influence on English went a good deal further than place-names, however. The English were not exterminated by the Scandinavian settlers, but the latter were sufficiently numerous to influence English speech. The actual numbers involved are, however, a matter of some debate, and we must bear in mind that in such cases the number of settlers is not the only factor affecting the impact of settlement on a native language. Old English and Old Norse were still reasonably similar, and Englishmen and Danes could probably understand each other, and pick up each other's language, without too much difficulty. In the later OE period we must visualize various bilingual situations. There would be Englishmen speaking Old Norse, and Danes speaking Old English, and when they didn't know a word in the other language they would use a word from their own, perhaps giving it a pronunciation and inflections that they thought appropriate to the other language. Sometimes they would use a word in the other language but give it the meaning of the corresponding form in their own language. And no doubt there were children of mixed marriages who could speak both languages fluently. Thus great mixing took place between the two languages. In the end, Old Norse died out in England (it was already dying in the time of King Cnut, at whose court English was spoken), while English continued in use, but not before a good deal of Scandinavian had got mixed in with it.

There are various ways of recognizing Scandinavian words in English, though in fact some words were practically identical in Old English and Old Norse, and would give the same result in Modern English. Some words, however, can be identified as of Scandinavian origin because of their phonological form. Thus the word *awe* is certainly of Scandinavian origin: the Old English form is *ege*, pronounced ['eje], the first vowel having been changed by front-mutation and the *g* palatalized to [j] by the following vowel, and it would lead to a modern form *ey (just as OE *legen* has produced our word *lain*). But neither the front-mutation nor the palatalization occurred in Old Norse, where the word was *agi*, and this, if borrowed in late Old English, would develop quite regularly into modern *awe*. Another pair of words with Old English [j] and Old Norse [g] was *ǣg* and *egg*; the OE word became Middle English *ey*, a form found in Chaucer; our word *egg* comes from the Scandinavian. Similarly, Old English sometimes has [tʃ] where Old Norse retains [k], so that *church* is English and *kirk* Scandinavian, *ditch* English and *dike* Scandinavian. Again, Germanic [sk] did not become palatalized in Old Norse as it did in Old English, so that a word of Scandinavian origin will have [sk] where one of English origin has [ʃ]: thus *shirt* is English and *skirt* Scandinavian (both words meaning originally 'a *short* garment'); and similarly with *shrub* and *scrub*.

Among the vowels, one difference is that PG *ai* becomes *ei* in Scandinavian but *ā* in Old English: thus Old Norse *nei* corresponds to OE *nā*, the former giving Modern English *nay*, the second *no*. Other examples include the interjection *hail!* (cognate with OE *hāl*, Modern English *whole*) and *swain* (cognate with OE *swān* 'herdsman'). PG *au* became *ēa* in Old English, but remained *au* in Old Norse, so that *lēas* corresponds to *lauss*; our *loose* comes from the Scandinavian form, but the OE form survives as the suffix *-less*, in words like *homeless* (OE *hāmlēas*). Such phonological tests are not foolproof, for in some cases a dialectal variant in Old English can produce the same result as Scandinavian influence, but on the whole they are a reliable guide.

But even when phonological evidence is lacking or doubtful, we can sometimes be confident that a word comes from the Scandinavian. Often, for example, a word is not recorded in Old English, but is recorded in Old Norse. An example is the verb 'to take', which is from Old Norse *taka*; this is not found in Old English, which uses the verb *niman*. In Middle English we find both verbs, but *take* is found in areas where there was Scandinavian influence, and *nim* in areas free from such influence. The verb *to nim* survived into Early Modern English, in the sense 'to steal', and is responsible for the name of Shakespeare's Corporal Nym, who was adept at *nimming* other people's property; the past participle has survived as the word *numb*, which originally meant 'taken, seized' (OE *numen*). Other examples include *anger, to cast, to die* and *ill*, from Old Norse *angr, kasta, deyja* and *illr*; Old English used instead the words *wrǣþþ, weorpan, steorfan* and *yfel*, which have become *wrath, warp, starve* and *evil*.

Sometimes the Old Norse and Old English words would produce the same Modern English form, but with different meanings. Old Norse *dvelja* meant 'dwell', but OE *dwellan* meant 'lead astray': this suggests that the Modern English word is the result of Scandinavian influence. Our word *gate* is descended regularly from the OE plural form *gatu*, but in northern dialects there is another word *gate*, meaning 'way, road, street', from Old Norse *gata*. In London, places such as Aldgate and Newgate really were at gates in the city wall; but in cities such as Leeds and York, *-gate* is the Scandinavian form: Briggate and Kirkgate are 'Bridge Street' and 'Church Street'.

In other cases the form of the modern word may come from one language and the meaning from the other: thus the OE word for 'bread' was *hlāf*, which has become our *loaf*, while OE *brēad* usually meant 'fragment'; but ON *brauð* did mean 'bread', so the modern word has its form from Old English but its meaning from Old Norse. The word *dream* is more peculiar. Old English *drēam* means 'noise, sound, joy, mirth, revelry', and is commonly used in descriptions of the pleasures of the warriors relaxing in the hall over their ale or mead, and of the music accompanying those pleasures; it is never used in Old English texts to mean 'dream', for which the word is *swefn*. This, however, was the meaning of the Old Norse *draumr*, and it might seem that here again the modern word has the English form and the Scandinavian meaning. This is by no means certain, however, because the early examples of *dream* in its modern sense (recorded from the thirteenth century) appear not to be confined to areas subject to strong Scandinavian influence. Perhaps the true explanation is that there was an OE word *drēam* meaning 'dream', but that it occurred only in everyday speech, not in the literary language; it is noteworthy that the corresponding Old Saxon form, *drōm*, means both 'joy' and 'dream'.

Most of the Scandinavian loanwords first appear in writing in the Middle English period, but their form shows that they had been taken into English in the late OE period, for they have undergone the sound changes that mark the transition from Old to Middle English. They do not appear earlier in writing because at that time there was no literary tradition in the Danelaw, and most surviving texts are in the West Saxon dialect, which was the one least influenced by Old Norse. A few loans, however, do occur in OE texts. In the early days of the Viking raids there was probably not much opportunity for conversation between Englishmen and Vikings; the only loans from this period are a few words for Viking ships and weapons, which have not survived into the modern language.

Later, when the Vikings had begun to settle in England, a number of words were borrowed relating to law and administration, such as *thrall* (with its original sense 'slave'), and the word *law* itself.

But what is most striking about the Scandinavian loanwords as a whole is that they are such *ordinary* words. The English and the Scandinavians had very similar cultures, and the fusion of the two peoples was a close one; many of the words taken over, in consequence, were homely everyday ones, words belonging to the central core of the vocabulary. Thus the word *sister* is Scandinavian (the Old English is *sweostor*), and the names of such close family relationships are part of the central core of vocabulary (on which see also chapter 3). So are the names of parts of the body, yet the words *leg* and *neck* are Scandinavian. Other common nouns include *bag, cake, dirt, fellow, fog, knife, skill, skin, sky* and *window.* Everyday adjectives include *flat, loose, low, odd, ugly* and *wrong*, and among everyday verbs are *call, drag, get, give, raise, smile, take* and *want*. Moreover, some grammatical words are from Scandinavian, namely the conjunctions *though, till* and *until*, and the pronouns *they, them* and *their,* which in Old English were *hīe, him* and *hiera*. The Scandinavian pronouns no doubt had an advantage because they were less likely to be confused with the words for *him* and *her*. They were first used in the northern dialects, and spread southwards during the Middle English period; *they* spread faster than the other two, and Chaucer and his contemporaries in south-east England in the fourteenth century used *they* for the nominative but English forms like *hem* and *hire* for 'them' and 'their'. The form *hem* meaning 'them' still survives as *'em* (initial /h/ being regularly lost in unstressed words). The borrowing of such central grammatical words as personal pronouns shows the strength of the Scandinavian influence.

When the Scandinavian words appear in English texts they are given English inflections. Occasionally, however, a Scandinavian inflection was mistakenly apprehended as part of the stem, and incorporated in the English word. Thus there was an Old Norse ending -*t* which was added to adjectives to mark the neuter gender, and also to form adverbs. So the adjective *þverr* 'adverse, contrary' had the neuter form *þvert*, and this has been taken over into English as *thwart*; the same ending has survived in *want* and *scant*. The Old

Norse reflexive ending -*sk* (which usually imparts to verbs the sense 'doing to/for oneself', or a passive sense) has been preserved in *bask* 'to bathe oneself' and the archaic *busk* 'to prepare oneself'.

The total number of Scandinavian loans is in fact rather small, compared with the number of words later borrowed from French and Latin; on the other hand, many of them are words in very frequent use, and there is a Scandinavian enclave in the very central regions of the English vocabulary. In the main areas of Viking settlement, a larger vocabulary of Scandinavian loanwords is preserved in regional dialects, so that there are still parts of England and Scotland where you can hear good Scandinavian words like *big* 'to build', *hoast* 'cough', *laik* 'to play', *lait* 'to search', *lathe* 'barn' and *lie* 'scythe'.

The Norman Conquest

The Norman Conquest of 1066 was not such a violent break in English history as people sometimes imagine. There was already strong French influence in England before the Conquest, at any rate at the higher levels of society: Edward the Confessor was half Norman, and his court had close relations with France. It is certainly true, however, that the Conquest, and the centuries that followed, had a profound influence on the English language. For some centuries, English ceased to be the language of government, and there was no such thing as a national, standard literary English; and when English did once again become a major literary language across the whole country it had changed a good deal under the influence of the conquerors.

The rulers of Normandy had originally been Scandinavian Vikings, who occupied parts of northern France and were eventually recognized by the French crown: in 912, Rollo became the first duke of Normandy, and accepted the king of France as his overlord. By the middle of the eleventh century, however, the Normans had long lost their Scandinavian speech: they spoke French, and were essentially French in culture. People sometimes talk, therefore, as though the Norman Conquest were the coming of a higher civilization to the backward and barbaric Anglo-Saxons. This, however, is a misapprehension. Six hundred years had passed since the

Anglo-Saxon invasion of Britain, and in that time the English had developed a sophisticated civilization.

The Anglo-Saxons had a fine literature, both in verse and in prose. They had traditions of scholarship which went back to the seventh century, and when Charlemagne, at the end of the eighth century, wanted to reform his educational system, he imported an Englishman to do it for him. This tradition had been badly disrupted by the Viking invasions, but there was a revival under West Saxon leadership in the second half of the tenth century. The Anglo-Saxons were also fine artists and craftsmen: they produced beautiful carved crosses, and jewellers' work, and illuminated manuscripts to compare with any in the world. They were also famous for their needlework, and the celebrated Bayeux Tapestry was probably made in England.

These people did not need William of Normandy and his adventurers to bring them civilization. French became the language of the upper classes in England simply because it was the language of the conquerors, not because of any cultural superiority on their part. What happened was that the native aristocracy were largely destroyed, and their lands were distributed to William's Norman followers, who became the new ruling class. Many key ecclesiastical positions, such as bishoprics and abbacies, were also given to Normans in the years following the Conquest, so that the church and education were dominated by them. French, therefore, was the language of the aristocracy and the court, and it remained so for over two hundred years, although there are signs that English became the day-to-day language of even aristocrats within a generation or two: the literary and courtly French employed in England (known as Anglo-Norman) was probably essentially a second language for many of its speakers within a few generations. Nevertheless, anybody whose native tongue was English, and who wanted to get on in the world, had to learn French. The following comment on the situation was made in the late thirteenth century in a long history of England written in verse, usually known as the *Chronicle of Robert of Gloucester*:

> þus com, lo, Engelond in-to Normandies hond:
> And þe Normans ne couþe speke þo bote hor owe speche,

> And speke French as hii dude atom, and hor children dude also
>   teche,
> So þat heiemen of þis lond, þat of hor blod come,
> Holdeþ alle þulke speche þat hii of hom nom;
> Vor bote a man conne Frenss me telþ of him lute.
>
> Ac lowe men holdeþ to Engliss, and to hor owe speche ʒute.
> Ich wene þer ne beþ in al þe world contreyes none
> þat ne holdeþ to hor owe speche, bote Engelond one.
> Ac wel me wote uor to conne boþe wel it is,
> Vor þe more þat a mon can, þe more wurþe he is.

This can be translated as follows:

> Thus came, lo, England into Normandy's hand: and the Normans then
> knew how to speak only their own language, and spoke French as they
> did at home, and also had their children taught (it), so that noblemen of
> this land, that come of their stock, all keep to the same speech that they
> received from them; for unless a man knows French, people make little
> account of him. But low men keep to English, and to their own lan-
> guage still. I think that in the whole world there are no countries that
> do not keep to their own language, except England alone. But people
> know well that it is good to master both, because the more a man knows
> the more honoured he is.

This bears witness to the prestige of French, but also to the fact
that English was still spoken by the majority ('lowe men'). Now,
however, that English was no longer the language of upper-class
culture and administration, West Saxon gradually lost its place as
a standard literary language, although efforts at working with this
system continued in some ecclesiastical centres into the twelfth
century. For at least three centuries there was no single form of
English recognized as a norm across most of the country, and people wrote in the language of their own region. Early Middle English
texts give the impression of a variety of dialects, without many
common conventions in pronunciation or spelling, and with considerable divergences in grammar and phonology.

Middle English dialects

Figure 10 shows the approximate boundaries of the main dialects
of Middle English. You must remember, however, that a map of this

Figure 10 The main dialect areas of Middle English

kind, with sharply defined dialect boundaries, is a great simplification. A more accurate map would show numerous isoglosses marking the boundaries of various dialect features, and obviously these
would not all run together along the dialect boundaries shown on
our map. A team at the University of Edinburgh has indeed produced
a dialect atlas of Late Middle English, showing the regional distribution of the spelling-variants of nearly three hundred items, and this
gives a much more refined picture of the Middle English dialects.

Nevertheless, our map is a useful one, since there are a number
of major dialect features which are typical of the regions shown,
and it does make sense to talk (for example) about an East Midland

type of dialect, or a northern type of dialect. The regions shown are northern (divisible into Scots and northern English), East Midland, West Midland, south-eastern and southern. The separation of the Northumbrian dialect of Old English into the Scottish and northern English dialects of Middle English is in part due to the political separation of the two regions, which led to the emergence of a Scots literary language in the course of the Middle English period. The marked difference between the East Midland and West Midland dialects of Middle English, which are both descended from the Mercian dialect of Old English, is due in part to the fact that the East Midlands were in the Danelaw, whereas the West Midlands were in the part of England held by King Alfred, so that the two areas were subjected to different influences. We cannot, however, rule out the possibility that there were already divergent subvarieties of Mercian in the Old English period, since our evidence for the Mercian dialect(s) of Old English is very scanty. The south-eastern dialect is descended from the Kentish dialect of Old English, and the southern dialect (which can be subdivided into south-western and central-southern) is descended from West Saxon.

There are many differences between these Middle English dialects, and we shall look at just a few examples of various kinds. First, a few differences in phonology. OE *ā* remained north of the Humber, but south of the Humber it changed in the twelfth century into the half-open rounded vowel [ɔː] (like that of present-day *law*); this phoneme is usually called Middle English ǭ (long open o). In Modern English, ME ǭ has developed into /əʊ/, as in *home* and *boat*, whereas the northern [aː] has developed into [ɛː] or [eː], giving forms like Scots *haim*. The southern forms are normal in Modern English, both British and American, but there are a few words where a northern form has entered the standard language, the phoneme then being realized as /eɪ/. Thus the word *raid* is a northern dialectal variant of the word *road*: both come from OE *rād*, which originally meant 'a riding, a journey'; it is a telling comment on life in the turbulent north during the Middle Ages that a riding of Scots into England or of Englishmen into Scotland should come to mean a *raid*. Another such doublet is the pair *whole* and *hale*, both from OE *hāl*. The word *hail* (as a greeting) is from the Scandinavian version of the same word.

Another example of dialectal variation is the ME treatment of the OE front rounded vowel *y*, as in the word *cynn* 'kin'. In the north, in the East Midlands, and in Devon, Dorset and Wiltshire, this word appears as ME *kinn*. In Kent, and in parts of Essex, Middlesex, Sussex and Suffolk, it appears as *kenn*. While elsewhere (mainly, that is, in the old West Saxon areas) it appears as *kunn*. These probably represented the pronunciations [kɪn], [kɛn], and [kyn] respectively.

Similarly, OE long *ȳ* became ME *ī* or *ē*, or remained *ȳ*, in the same areas: OE *brȳd* 'bride' appears in ME in such forms as *brid*, *bred* and *bruid*, probably representing the pronunciations [briːd] [breːd] and [bryːd]. Standard Modern English is descended from a dialect where OE *y* and *ȳ* normally developed into ME *i* and *ī*, the latter having developed into Modern English /aɪ/; so OE *cynn* and *mȳs* have become our *kin* /kɪn/ and *mice* /maɪs/. But we have inherited stray forms from other dialects: *merry* and *left* (opposite of *right*) come from the south-eastern dialect, for the West Saxon forms are *myrige* and *lyft*; and *bury* (OE *byrgan*) has its pronunciation from Kentish but its spelling from the old West Saxon area; while *busy* (OE *bysig*) also has the southern spelling, but has its pronunciation from the East Midlands or the north.

A characteristic of the dialects of the West Midlands and of the south-east is the treatment of OE short *æ*. In the West Midlands and the south-east this appears as *e*, but elsewhere as *a*: so OE *æppel* 'apple' is ME *eppel* in the West Midlands and the south-east, but *appel* elsewhere; this development had in fact already taken place in Old English. Another characteristic of the West Midland dialect is its treatment of OE short *a* before nasal consonants: West Midland has *mon* 'man' and *thonc* '(kindly) thought, gratitude, thanks', where the other dialects have *man* and *thanc*. A characteristic of the southern dialects is the voicing of word-initial /f-/, /θ-/ and /s-/, which become /v-/, /ð-/ and /z-/; this is not always shown in the spellings (though you may be able to spot examples in the passage on pp. 145–6 above), but it probably happened everywhere south of the Thames and the Severn, that is, in the south-eastern and southern dialects and in part of the South-West Midlands. The forms *vat* and *vixen* (OE *fæt* and *fyxen*) have come into the modern standard language from one of these southern dialects.

The grammatical differences between the ME dialects include differences in inflections, and in the forms of the personal pronouns. During the ME period, there was a tendency for northern forms to permeate southwards. The following examples show the kinds of difference that were typical in the late thirteenth century:

	'she comes'	'they come'
Northern	scho comis	thai come/comis
East Midland	sche comes/cometh	thei comen
West Midland	hue cometh/comes	hi comen
South-eastern	hi cometh	hi cometh
Southern	heo cometh	he cometh

It will be apparent that the Modern English third-person singular and plural verb inflections (*he/she/it comes* and *they come*) derive ultimately from northern and/or Midlands forms. Likewise *they* is a form originating in the north and the East Midlands, reflecting its Scandinavian derivation. The pronoun form *she* is a well-known linguistic puzzle that has yet to be solved definitively. The geographical distribution of the form in Middle English, however, suggests that claims for the influence of Old Norse on its development deserve serious consideration.

The differences in vocabulary between the regions are most striking in the matter of loanwords. In the northern and East Midland dialects there are numerous Scandinavian words; some of these permeated into the other dialects during the ME period, but many never became accepted outside the old Danelaw. French loanwords, on the contrary, first appeared most densely around London, the centre of fashion and administration, and spread northwards and westwards from there; by the fourteenth century, they were being used freely all over the country.

English versus French

While English was thus left without a standard literary dialect, the prestige-languages in England were Latin and French. Latin was the language of the church, of scholarship, and of international communication; after the Conquest it was also important in administration, but here it gradually gave way to French. The invaders of 1066 spoke Norman French, a northern dialect of the language, and in England this developed characteristics of its own, and is then called Anglo-Norman. In the thirteenth century, however, when the Central French dialect of Paris had begun to exert a strong influence on the rest of France, the Anglo-Norman dialect lost some of its prestige in England: it was regarded as rather old-fashioned and rustic, and the courtly language was Central French.

In the thirteenth century, French was still being spoken at the English court, and literature was being written in French for the nobility of England; but it is this century that sees the tipping of the balance away from French and back to English. Although French was for a long time the prestige-language in England, it was never the mother tongue of the majority of the population. A considerable number of Normans settled in England after the Conquest, but they were few in comparison to the existing population, and ultimately French died out in England. An event that contributed to the demise of Anglo-Norman was King John's loss of Normandy to the French crown in the opening years of the thirteenth century. Many of the English nobility had estates in Normandy as well as in England, and now had to decide which of the two they belonged to. A common solution was for one son to inherit the English estates, and another son the Norman estates, and this can be seen going on in the first half of the thirteenth century. Thus the ties with Normandy were severed, and the ex-Norman nobility gradually became English. The English crown, indeed, continued to hold lands in France, especially in southern Aquitaine, and went on importing Frenchmen to its court, but the English nobility were jealous of such royal favourites, and in the Barons' Wars against Henry III in the middle of the century there was a good deal of anti-foreigner propaganda. National feeling was beginning to arise in England, as in other countries of western Europe, and this must have raised the prestige of the English language.

The fourteenth century sees a great increase in the use of English as a literary language. French was no longer the mother tongue even of the nobility, and those who wanted to speak French had to learn it. Literature, even the most courtly literature, was written more and more in English, and in the second half of the century there was a great literary upsurge, with Chaucer as one of its major figures. English was also used more and more in administration. In 1362 the king's speech at the opening of Parliament was made in English, and in the same year an Act was passed making English the official language of the law courts instead of French, though their records were to be kept in Latin.

The fourteenth century also saw the switch from French to English as the medium of grammar-school education. Here we have an interesting piece of contemporary evidence. During the first half of the century a monk of Chester called Ranulf Higden wrote in Latin a long work called *Polychronicon*; this was a universal history (a favourite medieval form), beginning at the Creation and coming down to Higden's own time. In 1385–7 this work was translated into English by John of Trevisa, writing in a south-western dialect. In book I of the work, Higden gives an account of the languages of Britain; the English, he says, have had Danes and Normans mixed in with them, and this has led to a corruption of the native language. He then continues (in Trevisa's translation):

> þis apeyring of þe burþtonge ys bycause of twey þinges. On ys for chyldern in scole, aȝenes þe vsage and manere of al oþer nacions, buþ compelled for to leue here oune longage, and for to construe here lessons and here þinges a Freynsh, and habbeþ suþthe þe Normans come furst into Engelond. Also gentil men children buþ ytauȝt for to speke Freynsh fram tyme þat a buþ yrokked in here cradel, and conneþ speke and playe wiþ a child hys brouch; and oplondysch men wol lykne hamsylf to gentil men, and fondeþ wiþ gret bysynes for to speke Freynsh, for to be more ytold of.

This can be translated as follows:

> This corruption of the mother tongue is because of two things. One is because children in school, contrary to the usage and customs of all other nations, are compelled to abandon their own language, and to construe their lessons and their tasks in French, and have since the Normans first came to England. Moreover, gentlemen's children are taught to speak French from the time that they are rocked in their cradle and are able to speak and play with a child's trinket; and rustic

men want to make themselves like gentlemen, and strive with great industry to speak French, in order to be more highly thought of.

This passage testifies to the high prestige that French still enjoyed when it was written (perhaps around 1330), and to the continued use of French in education (though it is no doubt significant that Higden protests against this). But when John of Trevisa translated this passage in 1385, he added a piece of his own, which was not in the original. It begins as follows:

> þys manere was moche y-used tofore þe furste moreyn, and ys seþthe somdel ychaunged. For Iohan Cornwal, a mayster of gramere, chayngede þe lore in gramerscole and construction of Freynsh into Englysch; and Richard Pencrych lurnede þat manere techyng of hym, and oþer men of Pencrych, so þat now, þe ȝer of oure Lord a þousond þre hondred foure score and fyue, of the secunde kyng Richard after þe Conquest nyne, in al þe gramerscoles of Engelond childern leueþ Frensch, and construeþ and lurneþ an Englysch.

This can be rendered:

> This custom was much in use before the first plague [that is, the Black Death of 1349], and since then has somewhat changed. For John Cornwall, a licensed teacher of grammar, changed the teaching in grammar school and the construing from French into English; and Richard Pencrich learnt that method of teaching from him, and other men from Pencrich, so that now, in the year of Our Lord 1385, in the ninth year of King Richard II, in all the grammar schools of England children are abandoning French, and are construing and learning in English.

Trevisa goes on to say that this has the advantage that the children learn more quickly, but the disadvantage that they know no more French than their left heel, which is bad for them if they have to go abroad. He adds that to a great extent gentlemen have now given up teaching their children French.

The greatest stronghold of French in England was perhaps the king's court, but when Henry IV seized the throne in 1399, England, for the first time since the Norman Conquest, acquired a king whose mother tongue was English. In the fifteenth century the decline in the use of French in England became more pronounced.

Not only was it no longer a native language in England, but now there were actually members of the nobility who could not speak French at all. Henceforth, a fluent command of French was to be regarded as an accomplishment.

The new standard English

With the re-establishment of English as the language of administration and culture came the re-establishment of an English literary language, a standard form of the language that could be regarded as a norm. In fact, there were *two* standard forms of English, that of England and that of Scotland, the latter now usually being called Middle Scots. Scotland was an independent kingdom, and the language of the lowlands and of the royal court, which they called 'Inglis', became its dominant language; the Highlands were Gaelic-speaking, and there were also Norse speakers in the Western Isles and in the far north; but it was 'Inglis', descended from a Northumbrian dialect of Old English, that gradually spread and came to be used alongside Gaelic. The Norse-derived dialects of mainland Scotland, unlike Gaelic, had probably fallen out of use by around the end of the Middle Ages. Of Middle Scots, more will be said later.

In England, as we have already seen, the new standard language which arose in the late Middle Ages was not descended from the West Saxon literary language. It was in fact based on the East Midland dialect of Middle English. This was probably due to the importance of the East Midlands in English cultural, economic and administrative life. One of the two universities, Cambridge, was in this area. It was an extremely important commercial area, as well as being a rich agricultural region; we have to remember that, before the Industrial Revolution, the north of England lacked the economic importance that it has today: it was a primitive region, economically and socially backward compared with the south; and Norwich was one of the great cities of England at a time when Leeds, Liverpool, Manchester and Sheffield were comparatively insignificant. Above all, an East Midland dialect was the basis of London speech, and London was the seat of government and the cultural centre of the nation, besides being by far the largest city in the country. The London dialect was in fact rather a mixed one, but in the fourteenth century it seems to have been basically East Midland in type, with influences from the neighbouring south-eastern and southern dialects. These border influences on London speech explain some of the non-East-Midland forms in modern standard English, like the south-eastern *merry* and *left* which we have already noticed. In the main, however, Modern English has forms descended from the East Midland dialect of Middle English, itself mainly descended from the Mercian dialect of Old English.

The establishment of a standard language did not take place overnight. In the fourteenth century, while Chaucer was writing in London English, Langland was writing his *Piers Plowman* in a South-West Midland dialect, while in the North-West Midlands an individual, or perhaps a close-knit group, produced the virtuosic poetry of the *Pearl* manuscript (*Pearl, Sir Gawain and the Green Knight, Cleanness* and *Patience*) in a local dialect. But gradually the prestige of the London language grew, and in the fifteenth century its influence was increased by the introduction of printing. In the sixteenth century there was wide recognition of the language of the court at Westminster as the 'best' English, but even then it was no disgrace for a gentleman to speak with a regional accent. Nevertheless, the *literary* language had been largely standardized by the end of the fifteenth century, and in the Modern English period you cannot always tell what part of the country people come from by examining their writings, as you often could in the Middle English period.

French loanwords in Middle English

Although French died out in England, it left its mark on English. Its main effect was on the vocabulary, and an enormous number of French loanwords came into the language during the Middle English period. We have to treat the datings of these loans with some caution: there are fewer texts in Early Middle English than in Late Middle English, and some of the loans first recorded in the fourteenth century may have entered the language much earlier. Nevertheless, even allowing for this bias in the evidence, it seems that they came in fastest when French was dying out. In the eleventh and twelfth centuries, when French was the language of the upper classes, the number of words borrowed by English was not great, but in the thirteenth, and still more the fourteenth century, there were numerous loanwords. This is not surprising: when bilingual speakers were changing over to English for such purposes as government and literature, they felt the need for the specialized terms that they were accustomed to in those fields, and brought them over from French. It was not that English was deficient in such vocabulary: in almost every case there was already an English word for the concept; this is one of the reasons why so much of the vocabulary of Old English and Early Middle English now seems so unfamiliar to us.

The influx of French words differed in several ways from the influx of Scandinavian words. We have already seen that Scandinavian words spread down from the Danelaw, whereas French words may have tended to spread from London and the court, and locally from the lord's castle. Moreover, the French words were on the whole not such homely ones as the Scandinavian words: the Vikings had mixed in with the English on more or less equal terms, but the Normans formed a separate caste that imposed much of their culture on their subordinates. Many of the French loanwords reflect this cultural and political dominance: they are often words to do with war, ecclesiastical matters, the law, hunting, heraldry, the arts and fashion. For the same reason, French words tended to penetrate downwards in society, whereas the Scandinavian words came in on the ground floor. Finally, the French words were entirely new ones, with no obvious resemblance to anything in English, whereas many of the Scandinavian loans were merely dialectal variants of their English counterparts.

As might be expected, titles of rank tended to be taken from French. These include (in their modern spellings) *baron, count, duke, marquess, peer, prince* and *sovereign*; we did however retain the English words *earl, king, knight, lady, lord* and *queen*. Words to do with administration include *chancellor, council, country, crown, government, nation, parliament, people* and *state*. The law courts were long conducted in French, and we have borrowed the words *accuse, attorney, court, crime, judge, justice, prison, punish, sentence* and *verdict*. French dominance of ecclesiastical life is reflected in such loans as *abbey, clergy, friar, parish, prayer, relic, religion, saint, saviour, sermon, service* and *virgin*. Many of the military terms that were borrowed are now obsolete, but there are also *armour, battle, castle, tower* and *war* (itself originally taken into French from Germanic). Words reflecting French dominance in the arts and fashion include *apparel, costume, dress, fashion*; and *art, beauty, chant, colour, column, music, paint, poem* and *romance*. Also borrowed were many abstract nouns, especially the names of mental and moral qualities, such as *charity, courtesy, cruelty, mercy* and *obedience*.

There are other indications of the aristocratic stamp of medieval French loanwords. Things connected with ordinary people tend to retain their English names, whereas upper-class objects often have French names. Thus we have English *home* and *house* but French *manor* and *palace*; English *child, daughter* and *son*, but French *heir* and *nurse*; English *maid, man* and *woman*, but French *butler* and *servant*; English *calf, ox, sheep* and *swine*, but French *veal, beef, mutton* and *pork*. In Modern English we often have French and Germanic words surviving side-by-side with similar meanings; in such cases the Germanic word tends to be more popular, and perhaps more emotionally charged, while the French word is often more formal, refined, or official. Thus we have such pairs as *doom* and *judgement*, *folk* and *nation*, *hearty* and *cordial*, *holy man* and *saint*, *stench* and *odour*.

If you know Modern French, you may sometimes be puzzled by the difference between an English word and the corresponding French word. Sometimes these differences are due to changes that have taken place in the pronunciation of both languages since medieval times. Thus our word *age* was borrowed from Old French *age*; our pronunciation retains the original [dʒ], while in Modern French it has become [ʒ]; on the other hand, Modern French retains the original vowel [aː], whereas in English it has developed into [eɪ]. Our word *chief*, similarly, is a Middle English borrowing from Old French *chef*; the initial consonant [tʃ] in our word is akin to the Old French one, whereas in Modern French this has developed into [ʃ]; on the other hand, Modern French has retained the original short vowel, whereas *chief* has developed a long vowel. Our word *chef* is a more recent borrowing of the same word, and so has a pronunciation resembling the Modern French one.

Some of the discrepancies between ME loanwords and Modern French words have other explanations, however. One cause is dialectal variation in Old French itself. Standard Modern French is descended from a Central French dialect of Old French, but the Normans spoke a Northern French dialect, which differed from it in a number of ways. For example, the Old French diphthong *ei* became *oi* in Central French, but remained *ei* in Anglo-Norman. Hence we have English *prey, strait* and *veil* (from Anglo-Norman *preie, estreit, veile*), where Modern French has *proie, étroit* and *voile*. (In Modern French, of course, the *oi* has remained in the spelling, but the pronunciation has become [wa].) In Central French, the groups [ga] and [ka] in word-initial position became [dʒa] and [tʃa], but this change did not take place in Norman French: this accounts for English *garden* and *catch* beside French *jardin* and *chasser*. This last word illustrates another difference: in Normandy, Old French *s* became *ch*, so that Norman had *cachier* 'to chase' and *lanchier* 'to throw' where Central French had *chacier* and *lancier* (Modern French *chasser, lancer*); the Norman words have given our *catch* and *launch*. As a final example, there was a difference in the treatment of [w] in Old French loanwords from Germanic: the [w] was retained in Norman, but changed to [g] in Central French, so that we have *wage, war* and *wardrobe*, while Modern French has *gage, guerre* and *garderobe*.

On the whole, however, only the early French loanwords were taken from Norman; in the thirteenth and fourteenth centuries, when the great bulk of the borrowings were made, it was Central French that was fashionable, and it was from this dialect that words were taken. But the borrowings from Norman are very thoroughly assimilated into English, and include more ordinary everyday words than the later borrowings from Central French, perhaps because in many cases they were introduced by the Norman rank and file who came over at the Conquest. Thus the early loans include such words as *garden, hour, market, people* and *wage*. In some cases, a word was borrowed in its Norman form, and then later borrowed again in its Central French form, so that we have both forms in Modern English, usually with different meanings. Such doublets include *catch* and *chase, cattle* and *chattel, warden* and *guardian*, and *wage* and *gage* 'pledge'.

When the words were first borrowed, they may have been given a French pronunciation, especially among bilingual speakers. But very soon they were adapted to the English phonological system, and given the English sounds which to the speakers seemed nearest to the French ones. This is normal when a word is borrowed from a foreign language. In recent times, for example, the word *garage* has been borrowed into English from French, but even speakers who know French pronounce the word in an English way: they do not, for example, use a French uvular [r], or a French [a]. Moreover, the word *garage* (at any rate in British speech) is now given an English kind of stress pattern, being stressed on the first syllable. The same kind of thing happened with many French loanwords in Middle English: at first, a word like *nature* was stressed on the second syllable, as this seemed most like the French way of saying it, but after a time the stress was moved to the first syllable, as this was more in conformity with English speech habits. In Chaucer's poetry, such words can often be seen to fluctuate, being sometimes stressed one way, sometimes the other. In polysyllabic words, the stress was not always moved all the way to the first syllable, and the final stressing arrived at has been influenced by several different factors: compare *melody* with *melodious*, *advertise* with *advertisement*. Moreover, there are sometimes variant stressings in Modern English, as in *controversy*.

The early French loanwords were so well assimilated into English that they were soon felt as not in any way foreign. This made it easier for the language to accept later Romance and Latin loans; indeed, English seems, in the course of the late Old English and early Middle English period, to have become more hospitable to foreign words and less prone to use its own resources for word-creation. Where Old English invented words like *tungolcræft* 'star-skill' or *prīnes* 'threeness', Middle and Modern English often borrow or adapt a word from abroad, like *astronomy* (from French which had borrowed it from Latin, which had itself borrowed it from Greek) and *trinity* (from French and Latin). But once they have been taken into English, such loanwords can be combined with native elements to form further words. French–English hybrids appear quite soon after the Conquest, the earliest types being French stems with English prefixes or suffixes, like *beautiful, faithless, gentleness, preaching* and *ungracious*.

Co-existence with French for so many centuries naturally had a great influence too on English literary traditions. Some of these were quite disrupted. The tradition of Old English historical writing in prose was lost, and when people like Robert of Gloucester begin writing history in English again, they write verse chronicles in the French manner. There must have been places, however, where some English literary traditions were preserved, and in the second half of the fourteenth century there was a flourishing school of poets using the alliterative line descended from Old English poetry. Chaucer, however, employs systems of syllable-counted rhyming verse based on continental models. Here, as in so many fields, the centuries of contact with Anglo-Norman and Central French literary modes made a deep impression on English culture.

7 Middle English

Old English did not disappear overnight at the Norman Conquest, nor did it immediately stop being written, for the West Saxon literary tradition was continued for a time in some of the great monasteries. But, in the years following the Conquest, changes which had already begun to show themselves in pre-Conquest Old English continued, and in less than a century we can say that the Old English period is over, and that Middle English has begun.

The Conquest, in fact, made the change from Old English to Middle English look more sudden than it really was, by introducing new spelling conventions. An established literary language like late West Saxon tends to be conservative in its spelling: changes occur in pronunciation, but the scribes often go on writing the words in the traditional way. But the Norman scribes disregarded traditional English spelling, and simply spelt the language as they heard it, using many of the conventions of Norman French. Consequently, many changes that had not been reflected in OE spelling, or which had appeared only in occasional spellings, now emerged clearly.

New spelling conventions

Quite apart from revealing hidden changes, the new orthography gave English writings quite a new look. A number of new consonant symbols were introduced. A new symbol *g* was introduced for the stops represented by OE ӡ, and the OE symbol was retained only for the fricatives. Where Old English had used *f* to represent both [f] and [v], ME scribes used *u* or *v* (which were allographs at this period) for the voiced sound. Similarly, *z* was introduced besides *s*, though

Table 7.1 Old and Middle English spelling conventions

Pronunciation	OE Spelling	ME Spelling	Examples in ME
[kw]	cw	qu	queen, quick
[ʃ]	sc	ss, sch, sh	fiss, fisch, fish
[dʒ]	cʒ	i, j, g	iuge, juge 'judge'; egge 'edge'
[k]	c	k, c	kinn, cool
[tʃ]	c	ch	chinn 'chin'
[s]	s	s, c	cyndre, sindir 'cinder', centre
[g]	ʒ	g	god, good 'good'
[j]	ʒ	ʒ, y	ʒer, yer, yeer 'year'
[x,ç]	ʒ	h, ʒ, gh	liht, liʒt, light
[ɪ]	i	i, y	king, kyng
[iː]	ī	i, y	fir, fyr 'fire'
[eː]	ē	e, ee	quen, queen
[oː]	ō	o, oo	fod, food
[uː]	ū	ou, ow	hous, hows 'house'

not consistently. The digraph *th* gradually replaced *ð* and *þ*, but *ð* is found up to about 1300, and *þ* remained quite common until about 1400; indeed, a debased form of *þ* survives even today in the initial *Y* of expressions like 'Ye Olde Tea Shoppe', in which *Ye* is simply a late medieval way of writing *þe*. It is to be noted that in Middle English there were separate phonemes /f/ and /v/, /s/ and /z/, and /θ/ and /ð/, where in Old English there had been pairs of allophones. In the spelling, however, this fact was only fully recognized for /f/ and /v/, and this still remains the case today, as can be seen from pairs such as *cloth/clothe* and *close* (adjective) / *close* (verb).

Some of the remaining differences in orthography between Old and Middle English are shown in table 7.1. Remember that we are not here discussing changes in *pronunciation*, but changes in *spelling*. The changes shown are *typical* ones: there is a great deal of variation from text to text, and, in Early Middle English, changes take place in what can sometimes seem a sporadic and haphazard way.

The letter *y* was no longer used to represent a front rounded vowel, but was simply used as an alternative to *i*, so that ME *king* and *kyng* represent exactly the same pronunciation, as do ME *fir* and *fyr* 'fire'. The ME dialects that preserved the front rounded vowels [y] and [y:] from OE *y* and *ȳ* usually spelt them *u* or *ui*: OE *cynn* became *kunn*, and OE *fȳr* 'fire' became *fur* or *fuir*. OE [dʒ] never occurred in word-initial position, only medially and finally, but ME loanwords from French, like *judge*, have [dʒ] in initial position. Not all these changes were improvements: both *q* and *y* were superfluous, and *ou* was not a very satisfactory spelling for [u:], because it was also used to represent two different ME diphthongs.

One oddity of ME spelling that is still with us was the result of a change of script. In place of the insular script of Old English, the Norman scribes introduced a continental style of handwriting. In this style, it was difficult to tell how many strokes had been made when letters like *m*, *n* and *u* occurred together, and groups like *un*, *uu* and *um* were difficult to distinguish from one another. For this reason, scribes took to writing *o* instead of *u* when it occurred in groups of this kind. So for OE *sunu*, *cuman* and *lufu*, we often find ME *sone*, *comen* and *loue* (=*love*). But this was a change in spelling, not in pronunciation: the word *sun* (OE *sunne*) has always had the same vowel-sound as the word *son* (OE *sunu*), and the modern difference in spelling is a matter of chance.

Changes in pronunciation

We have already noticed some of the changes in pronunciation that took place in the transition from Old to Middle English: the development of OE *y* and *ȳ* in different areas, and the change of OE *ā* to *ǭ* (long open *o*) south of the Humber. Alongside this ME *ǭ* (pronounced [ɔ:]), there was a phoneme usually called ME *ō* (long close *o*), pronounced [o:] (as in Modern German *wo* 'where'), which was descended from OE *ō*. The two phonemes have been kept distinct to the present day: for example, OE *gāt* has became *goat*, while OE *gōs* has become *goose*. In Middle English texts, however, the two phonemes are not usually distinguished in the spelling, and it was not until early modern times that one came to be spelt *oa* and the other *oo*. Another similar awkward pair in Middle English are the phonemes usually called ME *ę̄* (long open *e*) and ME *ē* (long close *e*). ME *ę̄* was descended from OE *ǣ* and *ēa*, and was pronounced [ɛ:], a half-open vowel similar to that of Modern French *faire*. ME *ē* was descended from OE *ē* and *ēo*, and was pronounced [eː], a half-close vowel similar to that of Modern German *zehn*. Once again, however, the two phonemes were not usually distinguished in ME spelling, and it was not until early modern times that it became common to spell the first as *ea* or *ei* and the second as *ee* or *ie*. The two phonemes were still kept distinct in the English of Shakespeare's day, but have fallen together in present-day English, so that we use the same vowel in *sea* (from OE *sǣ*) as in *see* (from OE *sēon*).

Other phonological changes which mark the transition from Old English to Middle English include the disappearance of OE *æ*, which in most dialects fell together with *a*; the monophthongization of all the Old English diphthongs, both long and short; the development of new ME diphthongs, especially by the fusion of a vowel with a following [j] or [w]; and the weakening of the vowels in unstressed syllables, all of them appearing as ME *e* (perhaps representing [ə]). For example, the OE words *fæder* 'father', *heorte* 'heart', *strēam* 'stream', *mægden* 'girl', *fugol* 'bird' and *lagu* 'law' appear in Middle English with such spellings as *fader* or *feder, herte, strem, meiden, fowel* and *lawe*, though with much regional variation.

Late OE and Early ME vowel-lengthening

A sound change which took place in Late Old English, but which did not become apparent until the ME period, was the lengthening of short vowels before certain consonant groups. In many cases the vowels were shortened again during the ME period, but long vowels remained in some dialects, especially before the groups *ld, mb* and *nd*. Lengthening before these groups accounts for the modern forms of words like *old, bold, cold, told*. In Old English (Anglian) these had short *a* (*ald*, etc.); this was lengthened to *ā* during the ninth century, and in the twelfth century this *ā* regularly became *ǭ* south of the Humber, giving ME pronunciations like [ɔːld]. Other examples of lengthening before these three groups are provided by the words *field, child, comb, climb, blind* and *ground* (OE *feld, cild, camb, climban, blind* and *grund*). This lengthening did not take place, however, if the consonant group in question was immediately followed by a third consonant. This accounts for the difference in vowel between *child* and *children*. In most such cases, however, either the long or the short vowel has been generalized in Modern English: thus our *lamb* is from the plural form (OE *lambru*, ME *lambre*), not from the singular (OE *lamb*), which had its vowel lengthened. The word *wind* 'moving air' probably has its short vowel by analogy with words like *windmill*, where the third consonant prevented the lengthening from taking place. In Middle English, *wind* normally had a long vowel, and as late as Shakespeare's time it rhymed with *kind*: thus when Shakespeare writes 'Blow, blow, thou winter wind / Thou art not so unkind' he is not using an eye rhyme, but a genuine rhyme that no longer exists today.

Another vowel-lengthening process, which has had far-reaching effects on both pronunciation and spelling, took place in Middle English itself, during the thirteenth century. This was the lengthening of short vowels in open syllables in two-syllable words (this is often termed Middle English open syllable lengthening). An open syllable is one that ends with a vowel. Where a single consonant occurs between vowels in an English word, the consonant normally belongs to the second syllable, and the first syllable is therefore open. Thus in the OE verb *bacan* 'to bake' the syllable division is *ba-can*, and the first syllable is an open one. This word became early ME *baken* (still with short [a]), and then the vowel in the open syllable was lengthened to [aː] (like the vowel of French *tard*), which in Modern English has regularly developed into the [eɪ] of *bake*. When, however, there are two consonants between the vowels, the first consonant normally belongs to the first syllable, which is therefore a closed one. Thus in ME *thanken*, from OE *þancian*, the syllable division was *than-ken*, and no lengthening took place.

The vowels which were regularly subject to this kind of lengthening were *a*, *o* and *e*. When *o* was lengthened it became a long open vowel, and in the standard language it became identical with ME $\bar{\rho}$, so that today we have the same vowel in *boat* and *home* (from OE *bāt* and *hām*) as in *hope* and *throat* (from OE *hopa* and *þrote*). When *e* was lengthened it too became a long open vowel, and in the standard language it fell together with ME $\bar{e}$, so that today we have the same vowel in *sea* and *to lead* (from OE *sǣ* and *lǣdan*) as in *meat* and *steal* (from OE *mete* and *stelan*).

In some parts of northern England and of East Anglia, the vowels *i* and *u* were also lengthened under the same conditions, and then became ME *ī* and *ū*. A few of these lengthened forms have found their way into the modern standard language, for example *week* (OE *wicu*) and *evil* (early ME *ivel* from OE *yfel*).

Because of the inflectional system of English, the conditions for lengthening were sometimes fulfilled in one form of a word, but not in another. For example, OE *cradol* 'a cradle' became ME *cradel*, and here lengthening of the *a* would occur. But the plural 'cradles' was OE *cradelas* (Early ME *cradeles*), and 'in a cradle' was *on cradole* (Early ME *on cradele*), and no lengthening would take place in these, because they were three-syllable forms. Similarly, OE *cran* 'a crane' would not have its vowel lengthened in Middle English, but the inflected forms, like *cranas* 'cranes' would do. In such cases Modern English has usually generalized one form or the other for each word: in the two examples given, it is the lengthened vowel that has been generalized, leading to our *cradle* and *crane*. In some cases, however, it is the short vowel that has been generalized: we use a short vowel in *vat, vats*, from the OE nominative singular *fæt*, not the long vowel which would have arisen from OE inflected forms like *fatu* 'vats'. Occasionally, both long and short forms have been retained, so that Modern English has two words where Old English had only one. OE *stæf* 'a staff' became ME *staf*, while the plural *stafas* became ME *staves*. From *staves* has been formed a new singular *stave*, and from *staff* a new plural *staffs*. In present-day Received Pronunciation, *staff* in fact has a long vowel, but this is a more recent development, dating from the seventeenth century.

This ME lengthening of vowels in open syllables of dissyllabic words has affected our spelling conventions. In Early Middle English, words like *bake* had two syllables. After the first vowel had been lengthened, the final *-e* was lost, and such words became monosyllables. But the *-e* was often retained in the spelling, and so we tend in Modern English to regard a final *-e* as a mark of a preceding long vowel or a diphthong, provided there is only one consonant symbol in between. Thus we use spellings like *home* and *stone*, where the final *-e* has no etymological justification, but is simply inserted to show that the *o* represents a long vowel or a diphthong. The Old English forms, of course, were *hām* and *stān*, and the modern words might well be spelt *hoam* and *stoan* (like *oak* and *road* and other such words that had *ā* in Old English). Moreover, because of the lengthening in open syllables, we often insert two consonant symbols in the spelling to show that the vowel is short: we write *backer* and *copper*, as distinct from *baker* and *coper*.

Middle English morphology

The Middle English period is marked by a great reduction in the inflectional system inherited from Old English, so that Middle English is often referred to as the period of weakened inflections. There were a number of causes for this. One was the mixing of Old English with Old Norse. Frequently, the English and Scandinavian words were sufficiently similar to be recognizable, but had decidedly different sets of inflections. In these circumstances, doubt and confusion would arise about the correct form of ending to use, and speakers in bilingual situations would tend to rely on other grammatical devices where these lay to hand. The existence and growth of such other devices must itself have contributed to the decay of the inflectional system, while itself being stimulated by this decay.

Another cause was phonological: the loss and weakening of unstressed syllables (which had already begun in Late Old English, although the standard West Saxon spelling system often hides these changes) at the ends of words destroyed many of the distinctive inflections of Old English. As a result of these changes, OE word-final *-a, -u* and *-e* all became ME *-e*. The endings *-an, -on, -un* and *-um* all became *-en*, which was later reduced to *-e*. The endings *-as* and *-es* both became *-es*, while *-aþ* and *-eþ* both became *-eþ*. Moreover, the final *-e*, which was all that was left of some of these endings, itself disappeared during the ME period: in the north, where the changes first took place, it was no longer pronounced by the mid-thirteenth century, and in the south it had disappeared by about 1400.

These changes had significant effects on the inflectional system, since many endings now became identical. For example, the OE noun *sunu* 'son' would become ME *sone* in all cases except the dative plural, which would become *sonen*, and even that would also later become *sone*. The same would be true of the differently declined nouns *giefu* 'gift' and *wine* 'friend'. As a result, the whole inflectional system became simplified. Among nouns, for example, the two declensions with the most distinctive of the remaining inflections tended to attract all the other nouns to themselves. At the same time, the number of different cases was reduced, especially in the declension of the adjective and of the definite article.

Among the nouns, two main declensions were generalized. One was the declension which in Old English had its nominative plural in -*as* (*stānas* 'stones') and its genitive singular in -*es* (*stānes* 'of a stone'). Both these endings became ME -*es*, so that both the nominative plural and the genitive singular were *stones*. The other declension was the one which in Old English formed both its nominative plural and its genitive singular in -*an*, which in Middle English became -*en*. Thus *ēage* was 'eye', and *ēagan* 'eyes' and 'of an eye'; in Middle English these became *eye* and *eyen*. Of these two declensions, the first became dominant in the northern dialects, in which all nouns tended to form the nominative plural and the genitive singular with -*es*, and forms like *eyes* are normal by about 1200. In the south, on the other hand, it was the -*en* declension that became dominant by the middle of the period, and many nouns that in Old English belonged to other declensions came to use the -*en* plural (though -*es* was common for the genitive singular). So we find forms like *devlen* 'devils' and *englen* 'angels', where Old English had *dēoflas* and *englas*. But in the course of the ME period the -*es* plural spread southwards and displaced -*en*, and by the fifteenth century it was almost universal, and of course our normal modern plural ending is directly descended from it. In Shakespeare's time we still find a few plurals in -*en* which have since disappeared, like *eyen, shoon, hosen, housen* and *peasen* (the singular of which was *pease*, as still in *pease pudding*). And today we still have *oxen, children* and *brethren*.

We still have a few relics of other declensions: there are the mutated plurals like *feet, geese, mice* and *men*, where the vowel of the plural was changed by front mutation, and there is no plural ending; and there are uninflected plurals like *deer* and *sheep* which are descended from Old English neuter nouns in which the nominative and accusative plural had no ending (*dēor* 'wild animal', plural *dēor* 'wild animals'). We have also complicated things a little in Modern English by introducing a few learned plurals in words borrowed from Latin and Greek, like *formulae* and *nuclei* and *phenomena*, but on the whole we have pretty thoroughly generalized the Old English -*as* ending for the noun plural. We now spell it -*s* or -*es*, and (at any rate in south-eastern England) pronounce it /-s/ or /-z/ or /-ɪz/ according to the preceding phoneme (compare *caps, cabs, matches*).

In Early Middle English we find all four of the OE noun cases still preserved in both singular and plural, but in the course of the period there is a tendency to reduce the total number of forms to three: one for the nominative and accusative singular (like *eye*), one for the genitive singular (like *eyes* 'of an eye'), and one for all plural uses (like *eyen* 'eyes'). In the north, and later elsewhere, the plural and the genitive singular were identical, and there were only two forms, *eye* and *eyes*. A dative singular with the ending *-e* persisted for quite a time, especially in the south, but as the final unstressed *-e* was lost in all dialects by the fifteenth century this too disappeared. Occasionally, too, there are genitive plural forms in *-e* or *-ene* even in Late Middle English, as in *kingene king* 'king of kings'. But such forms disappear by the end of the ME period, and we reach the modern situation, where for most nouns we have only two different forms (*boy, boys*). We now recognize a further two forms in our spellings, though not in pronunciation (*boy's, boys'*), and in fact a few nouns do have four distinct forms (*man, man's, men, men's*). We still have a few relics of the old case system preserved as fossils in modern words and expressions. The word *alive* comes from OE *on līfe* where *līfe* is the dative singular of *līf* 'life'. The final *-e* has been lost, of course, but we have retained the voiced [v], not the [f] of the nominative. In Lady Day and Lady Chapel, *Lady* represents an old genitive form (compare 'Lady Day' with 'the Lord's Day'). And the archaic word *whilom* comes from OE *hwīlum*, the dative plural of *hwīl* 'time, while', meaning 'at times'.

The same process of loss of case distinctions took place in adjectives and demonstratives. In adjectives, the trend was towards the use of only two forms: the base-form (for example, *fair*), and a form with the ending *-e* (such as *faire*) which was used both for the plural and as the weak form. This stage has been reached in Chaucer, who writes 'the weder is fair' and 'she hadde a fair forheed', but 'faire wives' (where we have the plural form) and 'this faire Pertelote' (where the weak form is used after the demonstrative *this*). When the final *-e* was lost towards the end of the ME period, these two forms became the same, and the adjective became indeclinable, as it is today.

In Old English the definite article showed three genders (*se* masculine, *sēo* feminine, *þæt* neuter), and was declined through all four cases, singular and plural, and in fact in the singular had a fifth case, the instrumental, *þȳ* or *þon*. The form *the* arose as Late Old English *þe*, which supplanted *se* and *sēo*; it had its initial thorn from the influence of the other case-forms, which all began with *þ*. In the course of Middle English, the other forms disappeared, and *the* became used for all of them: Chaucer nearly always uses *the*, though he also has a plural form *tho* (from OE *þā*). By the end of the Middle English period we have reached the modern position, in which *the* is the only form of the definite article, and *that* (originally the nominative/accusative singular neuter form of the definite article) has become a contrasting demonstrative with its own distinct meaning.

We have seen that the definite article and the adjective played a large part in Old English in marking out distinctions of case and number. The loss of this function by the end of the Middle English period (when both the adjective and the definite article had become indeclinable) represented a major change in the structure of the language. It also meant that grammatical gender disappeared, and was replaced by 'natural gender'. That is, we now tend to refer to female creatures as *she*, male creatures as *he*, and inanimate objects as *it*. Things are indeed a bit more complicated than that: a ship for example can be *she*, and a dog (or even a human baby) can be *it*. But still we are a long way from the system of Early Old English, where *wīfmann* 'woman' was masculine, *lār* 'learning' was feminine, and *wīf* 'woman' was neuter, and the forms of the pronoun, the adjective and the definite article had to be chosen accordingly. Even in Late Old English, however, there is a strong tendency for women to be referred to as 'she' and men as 'he', whatever the gender of the noun that has been used.

Middle English syntax

As the inflectional system decayed, other devices were increasingly used to replace it. For one thing, word-order became more important: inflections were increasingly incapable of showing which noun was the subject of the sentence, and which the object, and this function was taken over by the use of the S–V–O word-order, which became the dominant one in the ME period. The S–O–V word-order found in some subordinate clauses disappeared in Early Middle English. The use of V–S–O order, especially after certain adverbs, persisted throughout the period, and is not uncommon as late as the seventeenth century. Indeed, the use of V–S order (but without an object) is still occasionally found today. But it was in the Middle English period that S–V–O was established as the normal type, as it still is. In the passage from Wycliffe (late fourteenth century) that we looked at in chapter 2, every single clause has the S–V type of word-order.

Another device encouraged by the decay of the inflectional system was the use of separate words to perform the functions formerly carried out by word-endings. For example, prepositions like *in, with* and *by* came to be used more frequently than in Old English. A few OE phrases with their modern equivalents will illustrate this: *hungre ācwelan* 'to die of hunger'; *meahtum spēdig* 'abundant in might'; *dæges and nihtes* 'by day and by night'; *mildheortnysse Drihtnes full is eorþe* 'the earth is filled with the mercy of God'. There are no prepositions at all in the original OE expressions, and the prepositions in the present-day glosses translate OE inflectional endings.

The Middle English verb system

A similar tendency for inflections to be replaced by more analytic devices is also seen in the verb system of Middle English. As we have seen, the OE verb had many inflections, but basically only two simple tenses, present and past. In Middle English and Modern English the system of inflections becomes much reduced, but a complicated system of tenses is built up by means of the primary auxiliaries (*be, have* and later *do*) and the modal auxiliaries (*shall, should, will,* etc.). The future tense with *shall* and *will* is established in Middle English, although there are signs of its development beginning in Late Old English. Phrasal past tenses formed with auxiliaries and the past participle also begin to appear in Late Old English. In Old English, as we have seen, *ic sceal* usually meant 'I am obliged to', and *ic wille* normally meant 'I wish to'. Indeed, *shall* and *will* have never entirely lost the connotation of obligation and desire respectively, but today their main function is to signal prediction or futurity, and this function (already hinted at in some late OE usages) developed in the ME period. Thus a character in one of Chaucer's poems says 'I shal myself to herbes techen yow / That shul been for youre heele and for youre prow'. Here *shal* is singular (from OE *sceal*) and *shul* is plural (from OE *sculon*), and the sentence means 'I shall myself direct you to herbs that will be for your health and for your benefit.'

As we have seen, the perfect tenses with *habban* or *bēon* and the passive forms with *bēon* or *weorþan* already existed in Old English, but they came to be used more frequently in Middle English. In the perfect, *have* spread at the expense of *be*, but *be* was common with verbs of motion and verbs of change of state, and this continued to be the case even in Early Modern English: 'Worcester *is stolne* away by Night: thy Fathers Beard *is turn'd* white with the Newes' (Shakespeare, *Henry IV Part 1*). In the passive, *be* supplanted *weorþan* (ME *werþe, worþe*), which had fallen out of use by the end of the ME period.

The continuous tenses, formed with *be* and the present participle ('He is coming', 'We were eating'), also arise in Middle English, but are not at all common until the Modern English period. There is indeed an OE construction using *be* and the present participle. Thus in the *Anglo-Saxon Chronicle* entry for the year AD 755 we read *Ond hīe þā ymb þā gatu feohtende wǣron, oþ þæt* ..., which is probably to be translated 'And then they went on fighting around the gates, until ...'. The construction is here used for a continuous action with limited duration, and so is very similar to our continuous tenses. These continuous tenses, however, are probably not descended from the OE usage. It is more likely that they arose from ME sentences like *he was areading*, where *areading* has developed from *on reading*, and the sentence means 'he was engaged in the act of reading'. Later *areading* lost its first syllable, and we arrived at the modern sentence *he was reading*. Originally this *reading* was not part of the verb, but was a noun (OE *rǣdung*), meaning 'the act of reading'. Many nouns of this kind originally ended in *-ung*, like OE *leornung* 'learning', but this changed to *-ing* in Middle English.

By the end of the Middle English period, therefore, the perfect, passive and continuous markings of the verb were all well established, though much less frequently used than today. The ways in which they could be combined were also limited: as we shall see later, it was not until the eighteenth century that it became possible to use all possible combinations of them.

Specimens of Middle English

We can illustrate some of these points by looking at a couple more examples of ME writing, one early and one late. First an extract from the *Peterborough Chronicle*, which was a continuation of the *Anglo-Saxon Chronicle*, kept going at the monastery at Peterborough until 1154. Under the year 1137 there is a long annal describing the anarchy and miseries of King Stephen's reign, and we have taken an extract from this. The chronicler has been describing how all the great magnates disregarded Stephen, and used forced labour to build themselves castles. The word *me*, which occurs several times in the passage, is the unstressed form of *man*, used as in Old English as an impersonal 'one'. Punctuation is modernized, and abbreviations are silently expanded.

> þa þe castles uuaren maked, þa fylden hi mid deoules and yuele men. þa namen hi þa men þe hi wenden ðat ani god hefden, bathe be nihtes and be dæies, carlmen and wimmen, and diden heom in prisun, and pined heom efter gold and syluer untellendlice pining, for ne uuæren næure nan martyrs swa pined alse hi wæron. Me henged up bi the fet and smoked heom mid ful smoke. Me henged bi the þumbes other bi the hefed, and hengen bryniges on her fet. Me dide cnotted strenges abuton here hæued and uurythen it ðat it gæde to the hærnes. Hi diden heom in quarterne þar nadres and snakes and pades wæron inne, and drapen heom swa. Sume hi diden in crucethur, ðat is in an ceste þat was scort and nareu and undep, and dide scærpe stanes þerinne, and þrengde þe man þærinne, ðat him bræcon alle þe limes ... Warsæ me tilede, þe erthe ne bar nan corn, for þe land was al fordon mid suilce dædes, and hi sæden openlice ðat Crist slep, and his halechen. Suilc and mare þanne we cunnen sæin we þoleden xix wintre for ure sinnes.

This is very early Middle English, and not very easy for the modern reader. A fairly close translation is as follows:

> When the castles were made, then filled they (them) with devils and evil men. Then seized they the people that they believed possessed any property, both by day and by night, both men and women, and put them

in prison, and tortured them (with) indescribable torments in order to get gold and silver, for never were martyrs so tortured as they were. They ('One') hanged (them) up by the feet and smoked them with foul smoke. They hanged (them) by the thumbs or by the head, and hung mail-coats on their feet. They put knotted cord about their heads and tightened it so that it entered the brains. They put them in a cell in which were adders and snakes and toads, and killed them so. Some they put in a 'torturer', that is, in a chest which was short and narrow and shallow, and put sharp stones in it, and crushed the man in it so that all his limbs broke ... Wherever people tilled, the earth bore no corn, for the land was completely ruined with such deeds, and they said openly that Christ slept, and his saints. Such, and more than we are able to tell, we suffered nineteen years for our sins.

The orthography of the passage still shows the influence of the OE scribal tradition, for instance in the use of *æ* and of the spelling *sc* for [ʃ] (for example, *scort* 'short'). For [w], too, it sometimes uses wynn (here represented by <w>, as in *wæron* 'were'), but often instead uses *uu* (*uuaren* 'were'), and for [v] it most often uses *u*, not *f* (for example, *deoules* 'devils'). It uses both thorn and eth, but alongside these is now found *th* (*bathe* 'both'), and instead of *cw* we see the French spelling *qu* (*quarterne* 'cell, dungeon', from OE *cweartern*). OE *ā* is still represented by *a*, not *o* (for example, *þa* 'when', *mare* 'more, greater'), presumably because the change of *ā* to *ǭ* had not yet taken place in the part of the East Midland area where the text was written.

There are also points of grammar which remind us of Old English. The pronouns of the third-person plural are the English forms *hi, heom* and *her(e)*, not the Scandinavian *they, them, their*. There is a verb which is strong (as in Old English) which is now weak (*slep* 'slept', from OE *slēp*). This is one of the verbs which changed from strong to weak during the ME period, and Chaucer uses both *he slepte* and *he sleep*. There is one example of S–O–V word-order in a subordinate clause ('the people that they believed any property possessed'), and a few examples of V–S–O order (such as, 'then seized they the people').

Despite these resemblances to Old English, however, there are also decided differences. This is especially seen in the inflections, which are very much reduced compared to Old English. The adjectives have lost almost all their endings: there is a plural *-e* on some of them (such as *yuele*), but otherwise nothing. For example, *mid ful smoke* would in Old English have been *mid fūlum smocan*, with inflections for the dative singular. The definite article is almost invariably *þe* or *the*, as in *þe castles* and *bi the fet*, though there is one example of the plural *þa* (in *þa men*). In Old English, of course, the definite article was fully declined, and the equivalent of *bi the fet* would have been *be þǣm fōtum*, the preposition *be* governing the dative. For the nouns, the normal plural in the passage is *-(e)s* (*castles, bryniges*), and in several words this is used where in Old English there was a different one, for example *þumbes* and *snakes*, which had the OE plural forms *þuman* and *snacan*. There is however one plural ending *-en*, in the word *halechen* 'saints', from OE *hālgan*. Apart from these plural endings, the nouns have practically no inflections, except for one dative singular, the *-e* of *quarterne*. An interesting case is the phrase *be nihtes and be dæies*: this is a kind of halfway house between the Old English *nihtes and dæges*, in which the genitive inflection *-es* has an adverbial force, and the modern *by night and day*. The ME writer has introduced the preposition *by*, but has also retained the OE *-es* ending (perhaps apprehended as a plural).

In vocabulary, the passage shows very little French influence, having only *castles* and *prisun*. These are from Norman French, the former having initial [ka-] where Central French had [tʃa-] (Old French *chastel* from Late Latin *castellum*, Modern French *château*). In several places where Modern English would use a French loanword, the passage has an English word which is no longer used, like *halechen* 'saints' and *pining* 'torments'. Nor are there many Greek or Latin loans in the passage: the two words from Greek (*martyrs* and *devils*) are not new loans, but had been borrowed in Old English, and the only new Latin loan in the passage is *crucethur* 'torture-box', probably from Latin *crūciātor*; and since the writer feels the need to explain what this term refers to, it was probably not firmly established as an English word.

As we might expect from a text from the old Danelaw, however, there are more Scandinavian words, though fewer than in some later texts: *bathe* 'both', *bryniges* 'mail-coats', *carlmen* 'men', *drapen* 'killed' and *hærnes* 'brains'. Only one of these has survived in modern literary English, namely, *both*, from Old Norse *báðir*.

In reading the passage you may have been struck by the word *nadres* 'adders'. The OE word is *nǣdre*, and there are similar words in other Germanic languages (such as Gothic *nadrs*, German *Natter*). Why has the initial /-n-/ been lost in Modern English? As we have already seen, word-final /-n/ in unstressed syllables was lost in Middle English, early in the north and later in the south; an example of this in the passage is the use of *me* as the unstressed form of *man*, meaning 'one, people' (like French *on* or German *man*). This final /-n/, however, was not lost under all circumstances: it was retained when it occurred immediately before a vowel, but lost when it occurred before a consonant or a pause. Because of this, double forms arose for many words, one form with final /-n/ and one without. For example, the unstressed form of OE *ān* 'one' led to the modern indefinite article: the vowel was shortened in Old English, because of the absence of stress, and then in Middle English the final /-n/ was lost before consonants but not before vowels, giving the two forms *a* and *an*, as in *a father* and *an uncle*. Similarly the unstressed form of OE *mīn* led to ME *my* and *mine* (*my father* but *mine uncle*). But when there are pairs in the language like *my nephew* and *mine uncle*, mistakes sometimes occur about the point of division between the two words, and there appear forms like *my nuncle*. The word *nuncle* did in fact exist, and is found in Shakespeare (for example, *King Lear* I.iv.117). The word *adder* is of this type, the expression *a nadder* having been apprehended as *an adder*. Other words that owe their modern forms to this kind of change are *apron* (Old French *naperon*), *newt* (OE *efete*), *nickname* (formerly *ekename* 'additional name') and *umpire* (Old French *nompere*). Similarly, the pet-names Nan, Ned and Nell are derived from 'mine Anne', 'mine Edward' and 'mine Ellen'.

It is also clear that in many words a final /-n/ would be retained in the inflected forms, while being lost (except before vowels) in the base-form. So OE *mægden* 'a girl' became ME *maide* while *mægdenes* 'of a girl' became *maidenes*. In such cases analogy has generally operated to generalize one or other form: thus forms with final /-n/ have been generalized in *iron* and *seven*, and those without final /-n/ in *holly* (OE *holegn*) and *haughty* (Old French *hautein*). In a few cases, both forms have been preserved, so that in Modern English we have doublets like *broke/broken*, *eve/even(ing)*, *maid/maiden*, *morrow/morn, no/none* and *ope/open* (in some of these pairs, one of the forms would now be considered archaic or marked). Moreover, because of the example of such pairs, we have even added final /-n/ to words which did not originally have it. An example is *often*, which in Old English was *oft*: in Middle English the common adverbial ending *-e* was added, to make it *ofte*, and in the fourteenth century the analogical /-n/ was tagged on.

For our example of later Middle English we can take a few lines from Chaucer's *Canterbury Tales*, dating from the late fourteenth century. As mentioned at the end of the preceding chapter, Chaucer did not employ the traditional English alliterative style of verse, and used instead French and Italian models. He uses rhyme, in stanzas or couplets, and verse lines with a fixed number of syllables.

In Chaucer's verse, many words have a final *-e* in the spelling. In many cases, but not all, this has to be pronounced, probably as [-ə]. In speech, word-final unstressed *-e* was dead or dying in Chaucer's time, but it continued to be used in poetry. In Chaucer's verse, it is elided (and so not pronounced) if it occurs immediately before a vowel. But remember that in many words with initial *h* in the spelling, the *h* was not pronounced, so that in fact the word began with a vowel. This applied to many French loanwords, such as *harlot, hazard, heritage, host* and *humble*. These had already lost their initial [h-] before they were borrowed into English, and the modern pronunciations are due to the spelling and to Latin influence. Moreover, in the thirteenth century, word-initial /h-/ had been lost in unstressed words in English, so that words like *hit* 'it' and *hire* 'her' developed double forms, a strong form with initial /h-/ and a weak form without it; word-final *-e* would be elided before the weak form, but not before the strong. As a further complication, there were a considerable number of words where the final *-e* in the spelling was purely orthographical, and was never pronounced: this is certainly the case, for example, with the pronoun-determiners *hire* 'her', *hise* 'his', *oure* 'our' and *youre* 'your'. In the following passage, which is in ten-syllable rhymed couplets, we have put a dot over *e* in cases where we think it should be pronounced.

The passage is an excerpt from the delightful animal fable, 'The Nun's Priest's Tale'. Chauntecleer, the cock, has disturbed his favourite wife, Pertelote, by groaning in his sleep, and explains to her that he has had a nightmare:

Me mette / how that I romed vp and doun
With Inne oure yeerd / wheer as I saugh a beest
Was lyk an hound / and wolde han maad areest
Vp on my body / and han had me deed
His colour / was bitwixė yelow and reed
And tippėd was his tayl / and bothe hise eeris
With blak / vnlyk the remenant of hise heeris
His snowtė smal / with glowynge eyėn tweyė
Yet of his look / for feere almost I deyė
This causėd me / my gronyng doutėlees
Avoy quod she / fy on yow hertėlees
Allas quod she / for by that god abouė
Now han ye lost / myn herte and al my louė
I kan nat loue a Coward / by my faith
For certes / what so any woman seith
We alle desiren / if it myghtė bee
To han housbondės / hardy wise and free
And secree / and no Nygard ne no fool
Ne hym / þat is agast of euery tool
Ne noon auantour / by that god abouė
How dorste ye seyn for shame / vn to youre louė
That any thyng myghte makė yow aferd
Haue ye no mannės herte / and han a berd

This is not too difficult to understand, but there are things in it that may mislead a modern reader, so we had better have a modern version:

'I dreamt that I was strolling up and down in our yard, where I saw an animal [which] was like a dog, and [which] wished to seize my body and to kill me. Its colour was between yellow and red, and its tail and both its ears were tipped with black, unlike the rest of its hairs; its muzzle (was) slender, with two glowing eyes; I still almost die of fear at its look. This caused me my groaning, undoubtedly.' 'Really!' she said, 'Fie on you, spiritless. Alas,' she said, 'for, by God above, now have you lost my heart and all my love. I cannot love a coward, by my faith. For assuredly, whatever any woman may say, we all wish, if possible, to have husbands that are brave, wise, and generous, and discreet, and no miser and no fool, nor one that is frightened of every weapon, nor a boaster. By God above, how did you dare, for shame, to say to your love that anything could make you frightened? Do you lack the courage of a man, and have a beard?'

For the modern reader, the tricky things here are familiar-looking words which have changed slightly in meaning since Chaucer's time, like *smal* 'narrow, slender' and *tool* 'weapon'. But it is not difficult with a little practice to acquire a reasonable facility in reading Chaucer.

Unlike the Peterborough scribe, the scribe here often uses double letters to indicate a long vowel, as in *maad* and *eeris*. In some such words the vowel has since been shortened, for example, *deed* 'dead' and *look* 'look', but in Chaucer we must pronounce it long: [dɛːd], [loːk]. The passage contains one example of thorn, but none of eth, the normal spelling being *th* (for example, *that*). There are no examples of either wynn or yogh, the scribe instead using w (as in *wolde*) and either *gh* (as in *mighte*) or *y* (as in *yeerd*).

In vocabulary, the striking thing about the passage, compared with the Peterborough one, is the large number of French loanwords, such as *areest, beest, caused, colour* and *feith*. Several of them are words relating to moral qualities, especially the kind that would be discussed in courtly circles, such as *avauntour, coward, hardy, secree*. The passage contains fewer Scandinavian loanwords: *bothe, deye* 'die' and *housbondes* (already recorded in Late Old English), and possibly *nygard* and *tipped*. Scandinavian influence may also have reinforced the northern English pronunciation of the adjective and preposition *lyk* 'like', which in southern English would probably have had final [-tʃ].

Chauntecleer and Pertelote are a courtly pair of birds, and address one another by the polite pronouns *ye* and *you*, not by the familiar *thou* and *thee*. Chaucer consistently maintains the distinction between nominative *ye* and accusative *you* ('fy on yow', but 'Now han ye lost'). Notice, too, that *ye* still takes a plural verb (*han*), even though used as a polite singular.

A personal pronoun that we have not met in any earlier passage, but which is normal in Chaucer, is *she*. The origin of this word is disputed. The OE form was *hēo*, and forms like *she* are not found until the twelfth century, the earliest recorded example being *scae* in the

Peterborough Chronicle under the year 1140. It seems that *she* arose in the East Midlands and spread from there, becoming the normal form in literary English by the middle of the fourteenth century, though forms like *heo* and *hue* persisted in the south and the South-West Midlands until the mid-fifteenth century. The northern variant *sho* is recorded from the thirteenth century onwards. There are basically two possible ways of accounting for the forms *she* and *sho*: they could have developed from OE *hēo*, or from the feminine of the OE definite article, *sēo*. By a stress change, which could have been prompted by Old Norse influence in the Danelaw area (compare Old English *lēoð* 'song' with its Old Norse cognate *ljōð*), the falling diphthongs in these words could become rising diphthongs, leading to such forms as [sjoː] (< *sēo*) and [hjoː] (< *hēo*). The idea that such a stress change was possible is supported by our word *choose*, which is descended from OE *cēosan*. The OE word would regularly lead to present-day *cheese*, and forms of this kind are found throughout the ME period, while *choose* probably resulted from a change of the diphthong *ēo* to [joː]. In the case of *hēo* or *sēo*, the resulting initial [sj] or [hj] might have been assimilated to the phonetically similar, but much more common, sound [ʃ], producing [ʃoː]. Such an assimilation of [hj] to [ʃ] can be observed in some place-names originating in, or influenced by, Old Norse; most famously Shetland (< Old Norse *Hjaltland*). Such a development satisfactorily accounts for the northern *sho* forms, but we are left with a puzzle as to how the *she* forms arose. Proponents of the derivation from *sēo* point to an alternative form <sie> in some Old English texts of Mercian origin as a possible source, but this form is very rare, and could even be the result of scribes miscopying the very common variant form <sio>. Many scholars prefer a derivation from *hēo*, which avoids positing a demonstrative form moving into the personal pronoun pattern. The origins of the vowel of the *she* forms, however, remain uncertain. Whatever their origin, the forms with initial [ʃ] probably spread so successfully because they provided a clear distinction between 'he' and 'she'.

The passage has the southern plural form *eyen* 'eyes', but also the non-southern plural *eeris* 'ears' (where Old English had *ēaran*), an example of the gradual displacement of the *-en* plural ending by *-es* spreading from the north. The form *tweye* is from the OE

masculine *twēgen* (whence also our *twain*); the form *two*, which is
also found in Chaucer, is from the OE feminine *twā*. In the verbs,
there is an infinitive ending *-n* ('wolde han maad', 'How dorste
ye seyn'). There is also a present-plural ending *-(e)n* ('Now han ye
lost', 'We alle desiren'). The third-person present singular ending
is regularly *-(e)th* ('any woman seith'). This inflection was normal
in the south all through the Middle English period, and we regularly find forms like *he saith* or *he sayeth, he walketh*, and so on. The
forms with *-(e)s* ('he says', 'he walkes', etc.) spread from the north,
and were not predominant in the standard literary language until
the later sixteenth century. There are no examples of continuous
tenses in the passage: Chauntecleer says 'I *romed* vp and doun',
where today it would be more natural to say 'I *was strolling* up and
down'. Perfect tenses, on the other hand, are common in Chaucer,
as in 'Now han ye lost myn herte'. The opening words of the passage, *me mette*, have been translated 'I dreamed'. Literally, however,
they mean something like '(it) dreamed to me', *me* being a dative.
Such impersonal constructions are not uncommon in Old and
Middle English, giving expressions like *him hungreth* 'he is hungry'
and *mē lyst rǣdan* 'it is pleasing to me to read' (that is, 'I like to
read'). They were rare by the sixteenth century, but one survival is
methinks, from OE *mē þync(e)þ* 'it seems to me'.

The syntax of the passage is clearly much more modern than
that of the Peterborough passage. There are no examples of S–O–V
word-order, and the predominant pattern is S–V, with just one
example of the auxiliary preceding the subject when the clause
begins with an adverb ('Now han ye lost myn herte'). Striking,
however, is the complete absence from the passage of auxiliary *do*,
as is normal in Chaucer. Moreover, a relative pronoun is omitted in
a beest Was lyk an hound 'an animal which was like a dog'. The missing relative is the subject of the relative clause, and in present-day
English it is impossible to omit it in such a case.

Middle Scots

The earliest substantial records of the Scots literary language
date from the second half of the fourteenth century, the first really
big work being John Barbour's long narrative poem *The Bruce*

(c. 1375). Thereafter, however, there is a well-documented literary tradition, culminating in the poetry of Robert Henryson and William Dunbar in the late fifteenth and early sixteenth centuries. As in the south, spelling was somewhat variable, but Scots had certain distinctive spelling-conventions of its own. For example, in spellings like *ai*, *ei* and *oi*, the *i* is inserted to show that the vowel is long, not that it is a diphthong: so the spellings *haim* 'home', *grein* 'green', and *rois* 'rose (the flower)' represented [haːm] (later [hɛːm]), [greːn] (later [griːn]) and [roːz]. The spelling *ch* corresponded to southern *gh* (*nicht* 'night'), and *quh-* to southern *wh-* (*quhen* 'when'). In phonology, we have already seen that OE *ā* became northern [aː] (later [ɛː]), whereas south of the Humber it became [ɔː]: Scots *haim*, *bain*, *sair*, compared with southern *home*, *bone*, *sore*. OE *ō*, which in the south became ME [oː], in the north became the front rounded vowel [yː], spelt *u* or *ui* (as in *fud* or *fuid* 'food'). In the north, final unstressed *-e* was lost very early, and in consequence short vowels were retained in many words that in the south underwent lengthening as a result of Middle English open syllable lengthening (on which, see above). In the north, OE *macan* 'to make' had already lost its final *-n* in Late Old English; this gave Early Middle English *make*, and the final *-e* was lost before the lengthening of vowels in open syllables of two-syllable words, so that the word appears as northern *mak* or *mek*, with a short vowel.

Distinctive Scots grammatical features include the use of *-it* for the ending of the past tense and past participle of weak verbs (*closit* 'closed'); the use of *-and* for the present participle (*dansand* 'dancing'), where elsewhere the ending is *-ende* or *-inde*; and the use of the inflection *-is* for noun plurals (*knychtis* 'knights'), for noun genitives (*the moderis breist* 'the mother's breast'), for the third-person singular present of verbs (*he takis* 'he takes'), and for the present plural of verbs (*makaris ... playis heir ther pageant* 'poets play here their pageant').

In vocabulary, one striking thing is the paucity of loanwords from Gaelic. There are numerous French loans, for Scotland maintained close relations with France, and also Scandinavian loans, but most of these are also found south of the border.

As an example of Middle Scots, we can look at a brief extract from Robert Henryson's 'Morall Fabillis of Esope the Phrygian', written in the second half of the fifteenth century: two stanzas from 'The Taill of Schir Chantecleir and the Foxe':

> This wylie tod, quhen that the lark couth sing,
> Full sair hungrie vnto the toun him drest,
> Qhuair Chantecleir, in to the gray dawing,
> Werie for nicht, wes flowen fra his nest.
> Lowrence this saw, and in his mynd he kest
> The ieperdies, the wayis, and the wyle,
> Be quhat menis he micht this cok begyle.
>
> Dissimuland in to countenance and cheir,
> On kneis fell, and simuland thus he said:
> 'Gude morne, my maister, gentill Chantencleir!'
> With that the cok start backwart in ane braid.
> 'Schir, be my saull, ꝫe neid not be effraid,
> Nor ꝫit for me to start nor fle abak;
> I come bot heir seruice to ꝫow to mak.'

This wily fox, when the lark sang, quite bitterly hungry betook himself to the village, where Chantecleer, weary of night, had flown from his nest at the grey dawn. Lawrence [the fox] saw this, and pondered in his mind the tricks, the methods, and the stratagem, by what means he might beguile this cock. Dissimulating in countenance and manner, he fell on his knees, and feigning thus said: 'Good morning, my master, noble Chantecleer!' At that the cock at once started backward, 'Sir, by my soul, you do not need to be afraid, nor to jump or start back because of me; I only come here to do you service.'

The auxiliary *couth*, literally 'could', is used to form the past tense, rather like later 'do': *couth sing* means 'did sing', 'sang'. The phrase *wes flowen* 'had flown' illustrates the continued use of auxiliary *be* to form the perfect tense with verbs of motion. The word *fra* 'from' is from Old Norse *frā*, the corresponding OE word being *fram*. The southern form of *fra* is *fro*, which survives in the expression 'to and fro'.

During the sixteenth century, Scots was increasingly influenced by the southern language. One reason for this was the prestige of the English poets, such as Chaucer, Gower and Lydgate. Another was the influence of biblical translations: the Reformation was marked by a whole series of such translations in England, but not in Scotland. The Geneva Bible of 1560, with its Calvinistic marginal comments, was especially influential. By the later sixteenth century, books in the southern language were being printed in Scotland. And when in 1603 James VI of Scotland became James I of England, southern influence increased, for London became the centre from which patronage radiated, for Englishmen and Scots alike. The Scots literary language became increasingly permeated by southern forms, and by the end of the seventeenth century had practically ceased to exist. The distinguished eighteenth-century Scots thinkers and men of letters, David Hume, Adam Smith and William Robertson, were all born in Scotland, and educated at Scottish schools and universities, but all three wrote in the southern literary language, not in Scots.

This does not mean that people in Scotland stopped speaking Scots, but simply that in writing they adopted the conventions of the south. But since the southern literary language was based on a dialect extremely different from Scots, there was quite a discrepancy for a Scot between the spoken and the written language. This, combined with Scots national feeling, led to the creation of a Scots dialect literature, which attempts in its spellings and its grammar to represent actual Scottish speech. The father of the Scots dialect movement was Allan Ramsay (1686–1758), and its most famous figure was Robert Burns (1759–96). This literary movement continues today, but having a dialect literature of this kind is not the same as having a standard literary language: when Middle Scots was a standard literary language, all written transactions (if not in Latin) were carried out in it. But since the eighteenth century this has not been so: there have been works of literature in Scots, but the history books and the contracts and the chemistry textbooks have been written in what is essentially the southern literary language, though with a few specifically Scottish variations. Today, however, the Scottish Parliament encourages the use of Scots, and some of its proceedings are conducted in Gaelic and Scots and recorded in these languages as well as standard written English.

8 Early Modern English

The late Middle Ages had seen the restoration of English as a major literary language in England, and the beginnings of the establishment of a standard form of written English. This did not mean, however, that English was the only language used in England: Latin still had great prestige as the language of international learning, and it was a long time before English replaced it in all fields. Under the influence of the humanists, the grammar-school syllabus was centred on Classical Latin from the early sixteenth century onwards: pupils learned the Latin language, and studied Latin literature, history and rhetoric. In the universities, Latin was the medium of instruction. Even the natural scientists, the proponents of the New Philosophy, often wrote in Latin. The philosopher of the new science, Francis Bacon, wrote his *Advancement of Learning* (1605) in English, but the book that he intended as his major contribution to scientific method, the *Novum Organum* (1620), was in Latin. And the three greatest scientific works published by Englishmen between 1600 and 1700 were all in Latin: Gilbert's book on magnetism (1600), Harvey's on the circulation of the blood (1628) and Newton's *Principia* (1689), which propounded the theory of gravitation and the laws of motion. Even in Newton's time, however, Latin was falling into disuse, and his *Opticks* (1704) was in English.

English versus Latin

In the supplanting of Latin and the final establishment of English as the sole literary medium in England, a considerable part was played by the religious disputes that raged from the fifteenth to the seventeenth century. During the Reformation, people engaged in controversy wanted to be read by as large a public as possible. Many of the people attracted by Protestantism were of humble origins, and lacked a classical education; this meant that controversial books and pamphlets tended to be written in English. When Sir Thomas More wrote for the entertainment of the learned men of Europe, as in the *Utopia* (1516), he wrote in Latin, but when he was drawn into the domestic religious argument against the Reformers he wrote books and pamphlets in English. Milton, similarly, over a century later, wrote defences of the English republic which were intended for the learned men of Europe, and these were in Latin; but the bulk of his controversial prose (on episcopacy, divorce, the freedom of the press and so on) was intended to have an immediate impact on English politics, and was written in English. The translation of the Bible into English, moreover, and the changeover from Latin to English in church services, raised the prestige of English. The more extreme Protestants, indeed, regarded Latin as a 'popish' language, designed to keep ordinary people in ignorance and to maintain the power of priests.

Another factor in favour of English was the increase in national feeling which accompanied the rise of the modern nation-state in the fifteenth and sixteenth centuries. This national feeling led to a greater interest and pride in the national languages, while the language of international Christendom, Latin, slowly fell into the background. Nationalism led to conscious efforts to create a vernacular literature to vie with that of Greece and Rome, and both Spenser's *Faerie Queene* (1590) and Milton's *Paradise Lost* (1667) were conscious attempts to do for English what Homer and Virgil had done for Greek and Latin.

A third factor in favour of English was the rise of social and occupational groups which had little or no Latin, but which were eager to read and to learn, and wanted books in English. Such were many of the practical men of sixteenth- and seventeenth-century England – skilled craftsmen, instrument makers, explorers, navigators, soldiers – often from the citizen or yeomen classes. A gentleman-scientist like Gilbert wrote in Latin, but there were plenty of Elizabethan treatises on practical subjects like navigational instruments, geometry and warfare, which were written in

English for the plain man, and sometimes by him. Here an important part was played by the spread of literacy and the expansion of
the reading-public which followed the introduction of printing in
the late fifteenth century. The use of masculine terms in the preceding paragraph is deliberate, for literacy was much higher amongst
men than women in this period. Whilst upper-class women such as
Queen Elizabeth I could be very highly educated, and female writers such as Aphra Behn and Margaret Cavendish began to appear
in print towards the end of this period, the level of female literacy
around 1500 has been calculated at 1%, as opposed to 10% of the
male population.

On the other hand, there were social groups which fought hard
for the retention of Latin, because their professional monopoly
depended on excluding ordinary people from the mysteries of their
art; physicians appear to have been particularly bitter in their
attacks on medical works published in English. This led to fierce
controversy about the suitability of English for works of science
and scholarship, which raged especially in the second half of the
sixteenth century. This controversy was gradually won by the sup-
porters of English, as more and more fields of study were successfully invaded by it.

But, while English was thus replacing Latin as a medium of literary and scholarly discourse, it was at the same time more under its
influence than at any other time in its history. The Renaissance was
the period of the rediscovery of the classics in Europe. In England
there was quite a revival of Greek scholarship, symbolic of which
was the foundation of St Paul's School by Dean Colet in 1509. But
always it was Latin that was of major importance, and we see the
constant influence of Latin literature, Latin rhetorical theories, the
Latin language.

Loanwords from Latin

One result of this Latin influence on English was the introduction of a large number of Latin loanwords into the language. We
have already seen that the influx of French words in the Middle
English period had predisposed English speakers to borrow words
from abroad. In Renaissance England this predisposition was given

full scope, and there was a flood of Latin loans, the peak period being between about 1580 and 1660. The introduction of loans was encouraged by the large number of translations made from Latin. When English invaded a field of discourse (for example, rhetoric, logic, geometry, classical history, warfare), the first stage usually took the form of translations of standard Latin works; in the second stage, there were original English works deeply indebted to Latin originals; and in the third stage there were entirely independent English works. In this process, there was a strong tendency for writers to invent English technical terms by adapting those of the Latin originals. It must be added, however, that there was also a 'purist' movement (another manifestation of English nationalism) which attacked the use of loanwords, and advocated the coining of new technical terms from native elements. Such a purist was Ralph Lever, who in a textbook of logic published in 1573 invented such words as *endsay* 'conclusion', *foresays* 'premisses', *saywhat* 'definition', *witcraft* 'logic' and *yeasay* 'affirmation'. It is striking, however, that none of these coinages caught on, and that we use words derived from the Latin expressions that Lever rejected (*affirmation*, *conclusion*, etc.).

The Renaissance loans were not, of course, the first Latin words to be borrowed by English. We have already seen how words like *mint*, *street* and *wine* were borrowed while the English were still on the continent, and words like *bishop* and *minster* during the OE period. A few Latin words were borrowed, too, into Middle English: they include religious terms, like *gloria* and *requiem*; words from the law courts, like *client*, *conviction* and *memorandum*; medical and scientific words, like *dissolve*, *distillation*, *equator* and *recipe*; and numbers of abstract words, like *conflict*, *dissent*, *imaginary* and *implication*.

There are a number of Latin loans in Old and Middle English, but in Early Modern English this increases considerably, and by 1600 Latin is the greatest source of loanwords in English. Some of the words were taken over bodily in their Latin form, with their Latin spelling, like *genius* (1513), *species* (1551), *cerebellum* (1565), *militia* (1590), *radius* (1597), *torpor* (1607), *specimen* (1610), *squalor* (1621), *apparatus* (1628), *focus* (1644), *tedium* (1662) and *lens* (1693). Not, indeed, that they were always taken over with their original Latin meaning: in Latin, for example, *focus* meant 'hearth, fireplace' (whence French *feu*), while *lens* was the Latin for 'lentil', and was applied to pieces of optical glass because a double-convex lens is shaped like a lentil-seed.

Some of the loans, however, were adapted, and given an English form. For example, the Latin ending *-ātus* is often replaced by *-ate*, as in *desperate*. In some cases the Latin inflection is simply omitted, as in *complex* (Latin *complexus*). This reshaping is often influenced by the form of French words derived from Latin; for example, the Latin ending *-itas* sometimes becomes English *-ity* (as in *immaturity*), and Latin *-entia* and *-antia* can appear as English *-ence, -ency* and *-ance, -ancy* (as in *transcendence, delinquency, relevancy*). Indeed, it is sometimes difficult to be sure whether a word has come into English direct from Latin or via French.

These Latin loans tend to be learned words. Some are scientific words, like *equilibrium*, *momentum* and *vacuum*. Some are mathematical, like *area*, *calculus*, *radius* and *series*. Some are legal terms, like *affidavit*, *alias* and *caveat*. Not surprisingly, quite a few have to do with the liberal arts (grammar, rhetoric, logic, philosophy, etc.) or with classical civilization. Many of the Latin loans, however, are less specialized, and belong to the general vocabulary – nouns like *relaxation* and *relegation*, adjectives like *offensive* and *relevant*, verbs like *investigate* and *imbue*. There are a few everyday words, like *album*, *circus* and *miser*, but the vast majority are the kind of words that are introduced into a language through the medium of writing rather than in speech.

Inkhorn terms

The Elizabethan headmaster Richard Mulcaster commented in 1582 on the large number of foreign words being borrowed daily by the English language, 'either of pure necessitie in new matters, or of mere brauerie, to garnish it self withall'. This points to two different motives for the loans: a utilitarian one ('necessity'), because the language needs new words to say new things; and 'mere brauerie', which means 'sheer ostentation'. Because of the prestige of Latin, the use of Latin loanwords was taken by some people to be a sign of education or of social superiority, marking them off from the common herd. Thus arose a lunatic fringe, which used strange and pompous Latinate words out of 'mere brauerie', where perfectly good English expressions already existed. Such pompous words were called 'inkhorn terms', and were frequently ridiculed, as for example by Thomas Wilson in his influential *Arte of Rhetorique* (1553). Absurd affecters of Latinisms are also depicted in the drama, for example Holofernes in Shakespeare's *Love's Labour's Lost* and Crispinus in Ben Jonson's *Poetaster*. To the modern reader, however, some of the 'inkhorn terms' seem quite unexceptionable, having since been fully accepted. The ridiculous words used by Crispinus in *Poetaster* include nice specimens like *furibund* 'furious', *lubrical* 'smooth, slippery, wanton', *oblatrant* 'carping, reviling' and *turgidous* 'swollen, puffed up'; but they also include *defunct, reciprocal, retrograde, spurious* and *strenuous*. In any case, the attacks on inkhorn terms were not necessarily attacks on Latin loans in general: Wilson admits that some Latin loans are acceptable, and Shakespeare may make fun of Holofernes and his pedantry, but he himself is no purist, and is a great user of new words.

The remodelling of words

Not only did Latin influence bring in new words; it also caused existing words to be reshaped in accordance with their real or supposed Latin etymology. We owe the *b* in our modern spelling of *debt* and *doubt* to Renaissance etymologizing, for the earlier spellings were *dette* and *doute*, which were their forms in Old French; the *b* was inserted through the influence of Latin *debitum* and *dubitāre*. Here the change was merely one of spelling, for the *b* has never been pronounced in English (except by Holofernes); and the same is true of the *p* inserted in *receipt* and the *c* in *indict*. But there are cases where the actual pronunciation of a word was altered under Latin influence. Thus in Middle English we find the words *assaut*, *aventure*, *descrive*, *parfit* and *verdit*, which in the Renaissance were remodelled under Latin influence to *assault, adventure, describe, perfect* and *verdict*. An odd survival of ME *aventure* is seen in the phrase 'to draw a bow at a venture' (from I Kings XXII.34), where *at a venture* is a misdivision of *at aventure*, meaning 'at random'.

Some of these Renaissance remodellings are based on false etymologies, thus combining pedantry with inadequate scholarship.
Such is the case with *advance* and *advantage*, remodelled from ME
avance and *avantage*. The modern forms obviously arose from the
belief that the initial *a-* represented the Latin prefix *ad-*, but in fact
both words derive from French *avant*, which comes from Latin *ab
ante*. A similar case is the word *admiral*, a reshaping of earlier *ami-
ral*. This word came into English from French, but the French had it
from Arabic, where it occurred as the first two words of such titles
as *amir al bahr* 'commander of the sea'. In this case the form with
ad- is found already in Middle English, and conversely *ammiral* is
found as late as Milton. The change in this instance may have been
encouraged by the resemblance to *admirable*.

Loanwords from other languages

Although Latin was by far the main source of loanwords in
the early modern period, a number were borrowed from other
languages too. The next largest source after Latin was French;
the French loans included military words (such as *bayonet, feint*)
and words from the life-sciences (such as *anatomy, muscle*), but
also many words from the general vocabulary (for example, *docil-
ity, entrance, invite*). There were a few words from Classical Greek,
though most of these came via Latin or French. They tended to be
learned words, and many of them are technical terms of literary
criticism, rhetoric, theology, or the natural sciences; words which
were probably borrowed direct from Greek include *anathema, cos-
mos, larynx* and *pathos*.

A few words were borrowed from Italian and Spanish. Part of
a young gentleman's education was the grand tour of the continent, and in the sixteenth century there are frequent sarcastic references to the gallant who comes back to England affecting foreign
clothes, customs and morals, and larding his speech with foreign
words. The Italian loans include words to do with warfare (*fuse,
salvo, squadron*), with commerce (*argosy, artichoke, felucca*) and
with the arts (*cupola, fresco, madrigal, opera*). Spanish loans, too,
are often concerned with commerce or warfare (*anchovy, armada,
cargo, sherry*). Since the early European exploration of America

was largely carried out by the Spaniards and the Portuguese, many early words for specifically American things came into English via Spanish or Portuguese. From Spanish came *cannibal, cockroach* and *potato*, and from Portuguese *flamingo* and *molasses*, while *mosquito* could have come equally well from either language. The word *cannibal* comes from the Spanish *Canibales*, a variant of *Caribales* or *Caribes*, the name of a people of the southern West Indies.

The only other sizeable source of loanwords in the period was Dutch. The Netherlands had had close commercial contacts with England ever since the Norman Conquest, and many of the words borrowed by English have to do with seafaring and trade. Middle English examples include *deck, firkin* and *skipper*. Sixteenth-century loans include *cambric, dock, splice* and *yacht*, while in the seventeenth century we find *brandy, cruise, keelhaul, sloop, smack* and *yawl*. The Dutch were also famous for oil-painting (seventeenth-century *easel, sketch*) and for drinking (ME *booze*).

Word-formation

While large numbers of loanwords entered the language in the early modern period, especially from Latin, words nevertheless continued to be coined from existing English language-material by traditional methods of word-formation, especially affixation, compounding and conversion. Indeed, it is probable that more words were produced in this way than were borrowed from foreign languages, though this fact was not noticed by contemporaries, who were obsessed with inkhorn terms. In fact, any loanword entering the language is soon likely to have other words derived from it by the normal native processes of word-formation. For example, in the fourteenth century the adjective *comfortable* was borrowed from French; by the end of the century the adverb *comfortably* had been derived from it, followed by the adjective *uncomfortable* (1592).

By far the commonest method of word-formation in the early modern period was affixation, that is, the coining of new words by the use of prefixes and suffixes. Most of the words thus formed were nouns or adjectives, though there were also some adverbs and a few verbs. The two suffixes most frequently used for forming nouns were *-ness* and *-er*, the former being added to adjectives (*bawdiness, briskness*) and the latter to verbs (*feeler, murmurer*). Adjectives were often formed by the use of *-ed* (*latticed*) or of *-y* (*batty, briny*). Adverbs were normally formed from adjectives with the suffix *-ly* (*bawdily*), but occasionally the ending *-wise* is found (*sporting-wise*). The usual suffix for forming verbs was *-ize* (*anathematize*). There were also many prefixes, of which by far the commonest was *un-*, which was used freely with nouns, adjectives, participles, verbs and adverbs (*uncivility, unclimbable, unavailing, unclasp, uncircumspectly*).

A considerable number of words were formed by compounding, that is, the combination of two or more free morphemes. They are nearly all nouns, and the commonest type is Noun + Noun (*sheep-brand, waterdock*). There are also a fair number of the type Adjective + Noun (*Frenchwoman, freshman*), and of the type Verb + Object (*scrape-penny* 'miser').

The third reasonably common type of word-formation was conversion, the process by which one word is derived from another with no change of form. Three types were especially common: the formation of verbs from nouns (*to bayonet, to gossip, to invoice*); the formation of nouns from adjectives (*an ancient* 'an old man', *a brisk* 'a fop'); and the formation of nouns from verbs (*an invite, a laugh*).

The words formed by affixation, compounding and conversion are often ordinary everyday words, or words to do with practical affairs like farming, fishing and handicrafts. By contrast, as we have seen, Latin loanwords tend to be more formal and literary, and often concern specialized fields of discourse like science, medicine, religion, classical culture and the liberal arts.

Early Modern English grammar

Speakers and writers of Early Modern English often had a choice of forms or of constructions where today we have no choice – for example, in verb-inflections, personal pronouns, relative pronouns, and the formation of negative and interrogative sentences. Some of the grammatical features of the period can be illustrated by an excerpt from Shakespeare's *Henry IV Part 1*, written in about 1597. The text is taken from the Quarto of 1598. After the robbery on Gadshill, Falstaff and Prince Hal have been performing an extempore play in their favourite tavern in Eastcheap, but are interrupted by the arrival of the sheriff:

Hostesse. O Iesu, my Lord, my Lord.

Falst. Heigh, heigh, the Deuil rides vpon a fiddle sticke: whats the matter?

Hostesse. The Sheriffe and al the watch are at the doore, they are come to search the house, shall I let them in?

Falst. Doest thou heare Hal? neuer call a true piece of golde a counterfet, thou art essentially made without seeming so.

Prince. And thou a naturall coward without instinct.

Falst. I deny your Maior, if you will deny the Sheriffe so, if not, let him enter. If I become not a Cart as well as another man, a plague on my bringing vp, I hope I shall as soone bee strangled with a halter as another.

Prince. Go hide thee behind the Arras, the rest walke vp aboue, now my masters for a true face, and good conscience.

Falst. Both which I haue had, but their date is out, and therefore ile hide me.

Enter Sheriffe and the Carrier.

Prince. Now Master Sheriffe, what is your wil with me?

Sher. First pardon me my Lord. A hue and crie hath followed certaine men vnto this house.

Prince. What men?

Sher. One of them is well known my gratious Lorde, a grosse fat man.

Car. As fat as Butter.

Prince. The man I do assure you is not here,
For I my selfe at this time haue emploid him:
And Sheriffe I will ingage my word to thee,
That I will by to morrow dinner time
Send him to answere thee or any man,
For any thing he shall be charg'd withal,
And so let me intreat you leaue the house.

Sher. I will my Lord: there are two gentlemen
Haue in this robbery lost 300 markes.

Prince. It may be so: if he haue robd these men
He shal be answerable, and so farewell.

There the present-plural of the verb has a zero inflection, as today: whereas Chaucer wrote *han* and *desiren*, Shakespeare writes 'two gentlemen *Haue* ... lost', and this is the normal usage of the time. Occasionally, the *-en* plural ending is used in the sixteenth century as an archaism, notably in the poetry of Spenser, or to indicate rustic speech; now and then a plural *-eth* is found, especially with *hath* and *doth*; and occasionally we find the old northern *-es* plural ending, as in Shakespeare's 'my old bones *akes*' (*The Tempest*). But these are minority usages, and disappear from Standard English during the seventeenth century.

In the third-person singular, the passage has *-es* ('rides'), but also the *-eth* morpheme ('hath'). As we have seen, Chaucer regularly uses *-eth*, but during the sixteenth century this is increasingly displaced in the standard language by *-es*, which is the normal form in speech by the end of the century. The *-eth* forms continued to appear in writing, however, especially in formal styles, and of course are found in poetry right up to the twentieth century, long after they had disappeared from speech. Some *-eth* forms persisted longer than others: the contracted forms *doth*, *hath* and *saith* are common throughout the seventeenth century, and so are words like *judgeth*, *passeth* and *teacheth*, in which the *-es* ending would constitute a syllable.

However, the passage also contains the third-person singular form *haue* ('if he haue robd these men'), with the base-form of the verb and no inflection. This is an example of the subjunctive. In Early Modern English, the subjunctive is found in the second- and third-person singular present, for example, *he go*, *thou go*, alongside the non-subjunctive forms, *he goes*, *thou goest/goes*. The verb *to be* has more subjunctive forms, such as *I be*, *thou were*, *it were*. The subjunctive is used to signal doubt, hypothesis, or uncertainty, and so is common after such conjunctions as *if* and *though*. There are a few vestiges of the subjunctive today ('if it be so', 'if he were here'), but they sound somewhat literary and formal. By contrast, the use of the subjunctive in Early Modern English was normal even in colloquial styles.

For noun-plurals, the passage uses the *-es* morpheme (*masters*, *markes*), but also the mutated plural *men*. The *-es* plural was the normal one in Shakespeare's time, and moreover had by then developed the three allomorphs /-s/, /-z/ and /-ız/ (or /-əz/), which were distributed as today (as in *cats, dogs, horses*). In Early Middle English, the ending was /-əs/, but a series of sound changes in Late Middle English, and a process of grammatical regulation in the fifteenth and sixteenth centuries, led to the modern situation.

The adjectives in the passage are invariable, as today, and so is the definite article *the*. In Shakespeare's time, too, the demonstratives *this/these* and *that/those* were used as today, but alongside them was a demonstrative *yon*, or *yond*(*er*), of obscure origin. When used in the basic local sense, *this* implies 'near the speaker', *that* implies 'remote from the speaker' and *yon* implies 'remote from both speaker and hearer'. Moreover, *yon* carries the additional implication 'visible, in sight', and so almost invariably accompanies (or replaces) a pointing gesture, as when, in the first scene of *Hamlet*, Barnardo says 'When yond same Starre that's Westward from the Pole …'.

The passage uses the forms *they, them* and *their*, as against Chaucer's *they, hem, hire*. The weak form *'em* is however quite common in the drama. The form *you* is used for both nominative and accusative ('if you wil deny', 'let me intreat you'). By Shakespeare's time, *you* was the normal form, and the original nominative *ye* was a less common variant; both of them could be either nominative or accusative. Alongside *you*, however, the passage also has *thou*. In the plural, only *you* could be used, but in the singular there was a choice between *you* and *thou*. This had been introduced in the Middle English period, when, probably under the influence of French (where *vous* is used in a similar way today), the plural pronoun *you* began to be used as a 'polite' term of address to one person. The difference between *thou* and *you* was somewhat like the present-day difference between addressing somebody by their first name, 'John', 'Mary' (='thou'), and addressing them by their title and surname, 'Mr Jones', 'Mrs Smith' (='you'). Children and animals were addressed as *thou*, as were people of a decidedly lower social class, but in this case the higher-class speaker might fluctuate between *thou* and *you*, sometimes being more patronizing, sometimes more complaisant; for the lower-class speaker, however, *you* was compulsory, for it was insulting to say *thou* to somebody of decidedly higher rank. People of the lower classes normally used

thou to one another. Among the 'polite' classes, *thou* was the emotionally charged form: it could be used to express intimacy and
affection, but also to express anger and contempt. In the scene from
which the passage is taken (II.iv), the Prince is addressed as *you* by
everybody except Falstaff, and it will be noticed that Falstaff calls
him 'Hal', whereas everybody else says 'my Lord': Falstaff is pre-
suming on his intimacy with the Prince. The Prince himself is enti-
tled to say *thou* to anybody else in the scene, because of his rank,
but sometimes changes to the politer *you*. It was also normal to use
thou when addressing the deity, or abstractions, or material objects.
During the seventeenth century, *you* gradually supplanted *thou* in
the speech of the gentry and the citizenry, and by the end of the
century was the normal form; *thou*, however, continued to be used
in the literary language, especially in poetry. The lower classes, too,
continued to use *thou*, and it survives in some modern dialects in
northern and western England.

An innovation of the early modern period was the pronoun-
determiner *its*. The traditional possessive form of *it* was *his*, and not
until the end of the sixteenth century do we encounter *its*. It is very
rare in Shakespeare, occurring only in works published late; and it
does not occur at all in the King James Bible of 1611, which invariably uses *his*, as in 'if the salt haue lost his sauour, wherewith shall
it be salted' (Matthew V.13). But *its* spread very rapidly, and was
in common use by the 1620s, presumably because people found it
inconvenient to have the same form *his* for the possessive of both
he and *it*.

In the passage, Falstaff says 'ile hide me', where we say 'I'll
hide myself': for the reflexive use, Early Modern English used the
ordinary pronouns, not forms with *-self*; these were reserved for the
intensive or emphatic use, as in the Prince's 'I my selfe . . . haue
emploid him'. There are no relative pronouns in the passage, but
there is one place where today we should insert one: 'there are
two gentlemen [who] Haue in this robbery lost 300 markes'. This
is another example like the one in the Chaucer passage, with the
zero relative in subject position. The common relative pronouns
in Shakespeare's time were *who*, *which* and *that*, but their use was
not yet restricted as it is today. *Which* was freely used with personal
antecedents, as in 'The Mistris which I serue' (*The Tempest*). More

rarely, *who* could be used with non-personal antecedents: 'her lips, Who … Still blush' (*Romeo and Juliet*). Today, *that* is used almost exclusively in defining relative clauses; in Early Modern English it is commonly used in such clauses, but not infrequently appears in non-defining ones: in Bacon's *Advancement of Learning*, there are examples like the following: 'Midas, that being chosen judge between Apollo … and Pan, … judged for plenty.' In the course of the seventeenth century, relative *that* became increasingly confined to defining clauses, while relative *who* and relative *which* became increasingly restricted to personal and non-personal antecedents respectively in Standard English. The present-day position is reached by the end of the century.

The passage contains several examples of the perfect tense formed with *have*, like 'if he haue robd these men'. There is, however, one example of the perfect formed with *be*: 'they are come to search the house'. Perfects with *be* are common with verbs of motion (*come, enter, run,* etc.) and verbs denoting change of state (*become, grow, turn,* etc.). Even with such verbs, however, we also find perfects with *have*, as in *I haue gone* ('*walked*') *all night* (Shakespeare, *Cymbeline*). There is a difference between the two types: in perfects with *have*, the concern of the sentence is with the action of the verb as a continuing process; in perfects with *be*, the concern is rather with the situation that has arisen as a result of the action of the verb.

The passage contains no examples of Verb–Subject word-order, only Subject–Verb. In fact V–S order, including V–S–O, was not uncommon in the sixteenth century, especially in sentences which began with such adverbs as *now, so, then, there* and *thus*: in Tyndale's translation of the New Testament (1534) we read 'For so persecuted they the Prophetes'. V–S word-order declined sharply in frequency during the seventeenth century, although it has never completely disappeared: we can still use this word-order after negative adverbs such as *never, rarely, scarcely,* etc., as in 'Never before have I tasted such unappetizing food.'

The dummy auxiliary

The passage differs from present-day usage in one way which is more important than it may appear. Falstaff says 'If I become not', where we should use the auxiliary *do* and say 'If I do not become'. On the other hand, Hal uses an auxiliary *do* where we should omit it: 'I do assure you.' Here *do* is not emphatic, and 'I do assure' is merely a stylistic variant of 'I assure'. The use of *do* was in fact optional: Shakespeare could equally well say 'I know' or 'I do know', 'I know not' or 'I do not know', 'Know you?' or 'Do you know?' So auxiliary *do* was used in Early Modern English, but its use was not restricted as it is today.

In present-day English, auxiliary *do* is used in much the same way as the other auxiliaries (*be, have, can, could, will*, etc.). They have four key uses: (1) They are used immediately before *not* (or its weak variants *n't* and *'t*) when a sentence is made negative: 'He may not come', 'I can't remember', 'They wouldn't know', 'He isn't coming'. (2) They are used before the subject of a sentence to form questions: 'May John come?', 'Can you remember?', 'Would they know?', 'Is he coming?' The use of this construction keeps the subject of the sentence in front of the lexical verb, thus preserving an important feature of Modern English word-order. (3) They are used in echo-repetitions: 'John will come, won't he?', 'You can't remember, can you?', 'He isn't coming, is he?' (4) When stressed, they are used to assert emphatically the truth of the sentence as a whole: 'John *will* come', 'They *wouldn't* know', 'He *is* coming.' This gives a different effect from stressing any other word in the sentence, which produces only a partial contrast. If we say '*John* will come', we mean 'John and not somebody else'; if we say 'John will *come*', we mean 'come but not do something else'; but if we say 'John *will* come' we are underlining our belief in the truth of the whole sentence.

These four ways of using auxiliaries are a central feature of the syntax of present-day English. In the passages of Middle English that we have looked at, we have seen negative sentences of the form 'I ween there ne beeth in all the world countries none that ne holdeth to their own speech' and 'Ne never were martyrs so tortured'. These typical ME methods of negating sentences are no longer possible – we have to use an auxiliary followed by *not*.

The importance of auxiliary *do* in our present-day scheme is that it is the *dummy* auxiliary: it performs the four main functions of an auxiliary but is empty of meaning. So we use it when we want to ask a question, or negate a sentence, or have an echo-repetition, or achieve sentence-emphasis, but when none of the other auxiliaries has an appropriate meaning: 'Do you know him?', 'We didn't go', 'She likes Mozart, doesn't she?', 'But John *does* live here.' Notice, however, that questions in which the subject of the sentence is an interrogative word like *who* or *what* (so called '*wh*- questions') do not need auxiliary *do*: 'Who lives there?', 'What gave you that idea?' It is significant that, in *wh*- questions, normal S-V word-order is preserved.

The widespread use of *do* as a dummy auxiliary dates from early modern times, but the present-day restriction in its use had not been reached in Shakespeare's time. Its origins are disputed, but one plausible theory is that it arose from causative *do*. The use of *do* as an auxiliary of some kind goes back to Old English (although there it is mainly found in close translations from the Latin) and is not uncommon in Middle English. Originally, however, it was not a dummy auxiliary, but had a *causative* sense. Thus we find ME sentences with the structure *He did them build a castle*, which meant 'He caused them to build a castle.' In the south-western dialects there was a variant of this construction, with nothing corresponding to *them*, as in *a kastelle he did reyse*, meaning 'he caused a castle to be built' (it is in fact a translation of the French *Chastel fet lever*). But sentences of this second type are potentially equivocal. If we say 'He built a castle' there is already a causative element in the meaning of *built*, since we do not necessarily mean that he built it with his own hands. So ME sentences like *He did build a castle* could be identical in meaning with ones like *He built a castle*. Speakers would thus equate *did build* with *built*, and it is only a small step for this equation to be transferred to non-causative contexts. At that point *did* becomes semantically empty, and 'He did build' is merely a stylistic variant of 'He built'.

The development of this non-causative use of *do* took place in the south-western dialects in the late thirteenth century, and spread from there. At first it was mainly used in poetry, because it was a convenient device for putting a verb into rhyme-position at the end of a line. For example, a fifteenth-century author, in the poem *London Lyckpeny*, writes the line 'Then I hyed me into Est-Chepe', which he rhymes with 'heape'; but elsewhere in the same poem he has the line 'Then vnto London I did me hye', which he rhymes with 'crye'. Here the choice of *hyed* or *did hye* is clearly just a matter of metrical and rhyming convenience. From verse the usage spread to prose, where it is first found about 1400. It spread slowly in the fifteenth century, and rapidly in the sixteenth, and at the same time the old causative use of *do* died out, its place being taken by *make* and *cause*. So, by the sixteenth century, *do* is used as a semantically empty auxiliary, simply as a stylistic variant. The restriction in its use takes place during the seventeenth century: *do* gradually drops out of affirmative declarative sentences (except for the emphatic use), and comes to be used more and more regularly in negative and interrogative ones. The present-day situation is reached by about 1700.

In the fifteenth and earlier sixteenth centuries, the use of auxiliary *do*, in whatever kind of sentence, tends to be the mark of a rather literary style. But from the later sixteenth century onwards, when the process of restriction is under way, it is the non-modern use of *do* which is rather literary, while the modern restricted use is more colloquial: 'I wish' and 'Do you wish?' are more colloquial than 'I do wish' and 'Wish you?' Different verbs, however, varied in their resistance to the process of restriction, and even in the late seventeenth century it is common to find such expressions as 'I know not', 'if I mistake not', 'Say you so?' and 'What think you?'

Changes in pronunciation

In pronunciation, great changes took place in the fifteenth and sixteenth centuries, so that Shakespeare's pronunciation differed considerably from Chaucer's, but differed only in small ways from present-day Received Pronunciation. The biggest changes were in the vowel system, and the main series of changes is often called the Great Vowel Shift. This was a change in the quality of all the long vowels, which began early in the fifteenth century and was not fully completed until late in the seventeenth. The essentials of the Great Vowel Shift are shown in figure 11. The arrows show the direction of change. All vowels became closer in quality, except for the two which were already as close as they could be. These two became diphthongized, and the dotted arrows show the probable change in position of the starting-point of the diphthongs in question.

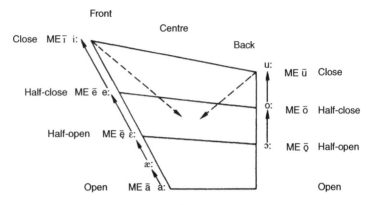

Figure 11 The Great Vowel Shift

The change began early in the fifteenth century with the diphthongization of the two close vowels, ME *ī* and ME *ū*. The other
long vowels then moved up into the space thus made available.
ME *ū*, often spelt *ou* or *ow* (*house, how*), changed from [u:] to the
diphthong [ʊu]. This diphthong gradually became wider, and in
Shakespeare's time it was probably [əu], starting from a central
position (like the vowel of present-day *go*). During the seventeenth
century it reached its present-day quality of [ɑʊ].

When ME *ū* had been diphthongized, ME *ō*, used in words like
food, took its place, moving from [o:] to [u:], where it remained. This
had happened by 1500. During the sixteenth and seventeenth centuries, ME *ǭ*, used in words like *boat* and *hope*, moved from [ɔ:] to [o:].
In about 1800, this developed in south-eastern England into the
diphthong [oʊ], which in the early twentieth century became [əʊ].

A similar development occurred with the long front vowels.
Early in the fifteenth century, ME *ī* (used in words like *mice and fly*)
changed from [i:] to the diphthong [ɪi]. This diphthong gradually
became wider, and in Shakespeare's time was probably [əi], starting
from a central position. During the seventeenth century it became
[aɪ], where it has remained. When ME *ī* had been diphthongized,
ME *ē* (used in words like *green* and *field*) took its place, moving up
from [e:] to [i:], where it remained. This had happened by 1500.
During the sixteenth century, ME *ę* (used in words like *meat, con-
ceive* and *complete*) moved from [ɛ:] to [e:]. Throughout the early

modern period, the vowels descended from ME *ē* and ME *ę̄* were kept distinct: in Shakespeare's time *see* was [siː], but *sea* was [seː].

During the sixteenth century, ME *ā* (used in words like *dame* and *bake*) also became closer. It moved from [aː] to [æː], and then to [ɛː], which it reached by about 1600. It did not stop at that point, however, but continued to get closer, and in the second half of the seventeenth century it was [eː]. But at that time, ME *ę̄* was also [eː], and in the later seventeenth century the two phonemes merged: there is evidence to show that, in the standard language, the same vowel was then used in *sea*, *seize*, *dame* and *mate*. This is no longer the case today, of course, for in the present-day standard language, it is ME *ę̄* and *ē* that have coalesced, not ME *ę̄* and *ā*: we have the same vowel in *meet* and *meat*, not in *meat* and *mate*. This can be explained if we suppose that there were two different styles of speech, perhaps belonging to two different social groups, and that one of them supplanted the other as the standard form. There is evidence, in fact, that there was a non-standard variant pronunciation going right back to Middle English, in which *ę̄* had changed into, or been replaced by, *ē*. In the later seventeenth century the two styles of pronunciation were in competition, and in the eighteenth century the variant pronunciation replaced the other in educated speech. It is likely that this change reflected social changes of the period: the rising middle classes were permeating the gentry, and may have brought some of their pronunciations with them. We still have a few relics of the older style of pronunciation: *break*, *great*, *steak* and *yea*, as their spelling suggests, all had ME *ę̄*, and their pronunciation is presumably retained from the style of speech in which ME *ę̄* became identical with ME *ā*. In about 1800, the [eː] from ME *ā* was diphthongized to the [eɪ] which we use today.

The Great Vowel Shift was asymmetrical, in that there were four long front vowels, but only three long back vowels: in figure 11, there is nothing in the bottom right-hand corner of the vowel diagram. In fact this space became filled: during the sixteenth century, the ME diphthong *au* (used in words like *cause* and *law*) changed from [aʊ] to the long pure vowel [ɒː] (like the vowel of present-day *dog*, but lengthened). This later followed the pattern of the Great Vowel Shift by moving closer, to [ɔː]. Most of the other ME diphthongs also became pure vowels during the early modern period.

ME *ai*, in words such as *maid* and *day*, changed from late ME [ai] to early sixteenth-century [ɛi], which by the end of the century had become [ɛː]. At this stage it merged with ME *ā*, so that in the standard language we have the same vowel in *maid* as in *made*. In some varieties of English, however, the merger did not take place, and many Welsh speakers still distinguish *made* from *maid*. The ME diphthong *ou*, used in words like *soul* and *know*, changed during the early modern period from [ɔu] to [ɔː]. at which point it merged with ME *ǭ*, so that we now have the same vowel in *know* as in *boat*. The ME diphthong *iu*, used in words like *new* and *use*, developed in about 1600 from [iʊ] to [juː]. After certain consonants, however, it simply became [uː], as in *chew, June* and *rude*. In either case, the [uː] merged with ME *ǭ*, so that we have the same vowel in *rude* and *rood*. Alone among the diphthongs inherited by Early Modern English, ME *oi*, in such words as *noise* and *royal*, remained relatively unchanged: its present realization [ɔi] is probably very similar to that used by Shakespeare and indeed Chaucer, though there is evidence that, at one stage, words such as *loin* and *line* were pronounced alike. This was because, as we have described above, the Middle English [iː] in words like *line* was pronounced as [əi] in Shakespeare's time. As the diphthong in *loin* was probably pronounced in a similar way at the time, pairs of words such as *loin: line, oil: isle, toil: tile* would sound like homophones.

In both Middle English and Early Modern English, there was sporadic shortening of long vowels in words of one syllable, especially those ending in a single consonant. There were often long and short variants in circulation side-by-side, one of which has since been standardized. If the shortening took place in the early modern period, the spelling shows us that the vowel was originally long, for our spellings, to a great extent, reflect early modern pronunciations. The vowels especially prone to shortening were ME *ę̄* and ME *ō*. When ME *ę̄* was shortened, it became [ɛ], as in *breath, bread, sweat, spread*. When ME *ǭ* was shortened it became [ʊ]; if the shortening took place in the sixteenth century, this [ʊ] later developed into [ʌ], as in *blood, flood* in southern varieties of English; but if the shortening took place later, the [ʊ] remained, as in *look, foot*.

By contrast, there was relatively little change in the short vowels. Round about 1600, ME *a* (used in *hat, man*) and ME *e* (used in *bed, men*) both became closer: the former moved from [a] to [æ], and the latter from [ɛ] to the rather closer position it has today. The older pronunciations are still heard in much regional English speech. ME *o* (used in *dog, fox*) became more open during the seventeenth century, moving from [ɔ] to the almost fully open position [ɒ], where it has remained. There was a more substantial change in ME *u*, which in the course of the early modern period split into two distinct phonemes, which have become present-day /ʌ/ (as in *cut, son*) and present-day /ʊ/ (as in *pull, wolf*). This split only affected varieties spoken in the south of England: to this day, the difference in pronunciation of words such as *cut* is one of the best-recognized distinctions between 'southern' and 'northern' accents in England. Originally, the phoneme was realized as [ʊ], but in the seventeenth century it became unrounded in most phonetic contexts, and probably also lowered, giving some kind of [ʌ]. But in some phonetic contexts it remained [ʊ], especially when followed by /l/ or preceded by /w/, /p/, /b/ or /f/, as in *bull, bush, full, put, wolf*. At this stage [ʌ] and [ʊ] were merely contextual variants, allophones of a single phoneme, but during the seventeenth century they became independent phonemes. One way in which this happened is illustrated by the words *luck* and *look*. In *luck*, ME *u* underwent the normal change to [ʌ] in the early seventeenth century. The word *look*, as its spelling suggests, originally had a long vowel, ME *ọ̄*, which regularly became [uː] in Early Modern English, giving the form [luːk] (still heard in some regional English varieties); in the seventeenth century, vowel-shortening took place, leading to [lʊk]. But by this time the change of [ʊ] to [ʌ] had already been completed, so that the vowel of [lʊk] did not share in it. At this stage, therefore, there were two words, *luck* and *look*, which were distinguished from one another solely by the difference between /ʌ/ and /ʊ/, which must therefore constitute different phonemes.

Two new consonant phonemes, /ŋ/ and /ʒ/, arose during the course of the period. It will be remembered that, in Old English and Middle English, [ŋ] was simply an allophone of the /n/ phoneme, in words like *sink* [siŋk] and *sing* [siŋg]. But round about 1600 (and earlier in some non-standard varieties of English) word-final [g] was lost after [ŋ], so that *sing* became [siŋ]. There were then pairs of words like *sing* and *sin*, distinguished from one another solely by the difference between /n/ and /ŋ/, which therefore constituted separate phonemes. In other positions, [ŋg] was retained, as in the word *finger*; the pronunciation of words like *singing* and *singer* is due to the influence of the base-form *sing*.

The /ʒ/ phoneme arose in the seventeenth century from the group /zj/. In the sixteenth century, *vision* was pronounced ['vɪzjən]. In the middle of the seventeenth century, the group /-zj-/ coalesced into /ʒ/, giving the pronunciation ['vɪʒən]. The group /zj/ could occur only medially, so the new phoneme was restricted to this position. Subsequently, it appeared in word-final position in loans from French, like *rouge* and *massage*.

In some positions, consonants were lost. Until about 1600, initial /k-/ was pronounced in words like *knee* and *knight*, initial /g-/ in words like *gnat*, and initial /w-/ in words like *write*. In Late Middle English or Early Modern English, /w/ was lost before some back rounded vowels (*sword*, *who*) and at the beginning of unstressed syllables (*answer*, *conquer*), though in some words it was subsequently restored under the influence of the spelling (*swoon*, *awkward*). In the sixteenth century, [ç] was still pronounced in words like *night*, which was [nɪçt]. But in some speech groups, [iç] had become [iː] in Late Middle English, so that the word was [niːt], which became sixteenth-century [nəit], and by about 1600 this pronunciation displaced [nɪçt]. Similarly, [x] was still pronounced in the sixteenth century in words like *though*, *drought*, *daughter* and *rough*, but was lost round about 1600. In some eastern dialects, the [x] did not disappear, but became [f], and some of these forms entered the standard language in the early seventeenth century, leading to the present-day pronunciation of words like *draught* and *rough*.

Table 8.1 gives a summary of the major differences of pronunciation between Middle English and Modern English, by showing the pronunciation of a number of words in Chaucer's time, in Shakespeare's time, and today. The pronunciations are those in conservative standard speech at the times in question. We do not intend to imply, of course, that the pronunciations were necessarily those of Chaucer and Shakespeare themselves.

Some of the earlier pronunciations are still heard in regional varieties in Britain: for example, [gɔːt] is heard in Yorkshire, [huːs] in the far north of England and in Scotland, [təid] and [həus] in

Table 8.1 Some major changes in pronunciation
since Late Middle English

Chaucer	Shakespeare	Today	Modern spelling
tiːd	təid	taɪd	tide
greːn	griːn	griːn	green
mɛːt	meːt	miːt	meat
maːk(ə)	mɛːk	meɪk	make
gɔːt	goːt	gəʊt	goat
foːd	fuːd	fuːd	food
huːs	həus	haʊs	house
kʊt	kʊt	kʌt	cut
riŋg	rɪŋg	rɪŋ	ring
niçt, niːt	niçt, nəit	naɪt	night
kneː	kniː	niː	knee

Wales, [niːt] in many parts of northern England, and [riŋg] in a quadrilateral area whose corners lie roughly at Sheffield, Coventry, Shrewsbury and Preston (Lancs). Moreover, everywhere in England north of a line running just south of Birmingham there is still only one phoneme descended from ME *u*, so that the same vowel is used in *put* and in *cut*, though the precise vowel used varies a good deal from place to place.

Strong and weak forms

These phonological changes of Middle English and Early Modern English apply to stressed syllables. In unstressed syllables, the changes were often different: long vowels were shortened, short vowels reduced to /ə/ or /ɪ/ and consonants lost or, in initial or final position, voiced. There are some words, however, which occur sometimes in stressed position and sometimes in unstressed position, for example personal pronouns. Such words therefore develop double forms, which are usually called strong and weak forms. This kind of development has gone on throughout the history of the language, and today there are numerous English words with such alternative forms. If you ask somebody how to pronounce the word spelt *a-n-d*, the answer (unless you have asked a professional linguist) will almost certainly be '/ænd/'. This, however, is just the strong form. More often, in normal speech, we use a weak form, /ənd/, [ən], or even just /n/.

During the Middle English period, word-initial [h] was lost in unstressed syllables, while word-final [θ], [f] and [s] were voiced to [ð], [v] and [z], and word-initial [θ] was also voiced. The voiced initial consonants of words like *that, the* and *them* go back to ME weak forms, as do the voiced final consonants of *with, of* and *is*. The phonological history of such words can be complicated, however, because it is quite common for a weak form to be restressed and made into a new strong form, from which in due course a fresh weak form can develop. The OE word for 'it' was *hit*, from which arose the weak form *it*. Subsequently this has been restressed and made also into a strong form. In Late ME the strong form of the word *you* was [juː]. This would regularly develop into present-day /jaʊ/, and indeed in the sixteenth century it is occasionally found rhyming with words like *vow*. In Late Middle English, however, there was a weak form [jʊ], and in the sixteenth century this was restressed, and the vowel relengthened to [uː], giving the present-day form.

The fact that many earlier strong forms have disappeared from the language can be illustrated from rhymes. In Shakespeare's time, it is common to find rhymes like *are/spare, have/grave, is/miss, shall/fall, was/pass* and *were/bear*. These were all exact rhymes, depending on old strong forms of *are, have, is, shall, was* and *were*.

Regional variation

As we stated at the beginning of this chapter, by the beginning of the early modern period, the standard written variety of English that had emerged in the fifteenth century was used for printed texts in England. In Scotland, printed texts still had some features of Scots, such as the use of *quh-* where English texts would have *wh-* (*quhilk* for *which*); *-it* rather than *-ed* in past-tense endings; and present participle *-and* for English *-ing*. After the Union of the Crowns in 1603, texts printed in Scotland were increasingly anglicized. Although written English had thus been standardized, the spoken language was much more variable. In the sixteenth century, many authors comment on the different national regional accents and dialects of English. There is a consensus emerging that the English spoken by educated people around London is more prestigious than any other variety, but, as yet, no notion that people born at a distance from the capital should learn to speak 'better'. In *The Arte of English Poesie* (1589), George Puttenham recommended the poet to use 'the usual speech of the Court, and that of London and the shires lying about London within lx miles, and not much above'. He warns the reader not to use 'the terms of Northernmen... nor in effect any speech used beyond the river of Trent' or 'the far Western man's speech', since neither are 'so courtly nor so current as our Southern English is'. Puttenham is not suggesting here that speakers from the north or the west should change their ways: he implies that 'noblemen or gentlemen' in these areas spoke with regional accents. Nevertheless, the prestige model being recommended to the aspiring poet is that of London and the Home Counties. We shall see in the next chapter how regional pronunciations became increasingly stigmatized during the late modern period and middle-class speakers outside London began to aspire to speak 'properly', but in the sixteenth and seventeenth centuries, whilst differences were noticed, and educated London English was viewed as superior, it was still possible for upper-class speakers from the north and the west to use their regional accents: for instance, Sir Walter Raleigh is said to have used his native Devonshire accent at the court of Queen Elizabeth.

There was also awareness of different national varieties of English in this period. Shakespeare's *Henry V* includes a scene in which a Scot, a Welshman and an Irishman, all soldiers serving Henry against the French, converse with each other and with an Englishman. Shakespeare represents their speech as 'different' from the English used by the rest of the characters in the play, which is thus portrayed as the 'norm'. Here is an extract from this scene (Gower is the Englishman):

> **Gower.** How now Captaine Mackmorrice, haue you quit the Mynes? haue the Pioners giuen o're?
> **Irish. By Chrish Law** tish ill done: the Worke **ish** giue ouer, the Trompet sound the Retreat. By my Hand I sweare, and

> my fathers Soule, the Worke **ish** ill done: it **ish** giue ouer: I would haue blowed vp the Towne, **so Chrish saue me law**, in an houre. O **tish** ill done, **tish** ill done: by my Hand **tish** ill done.

> **Welch.** Captaine Mackmorrice, I beseech you now, will you voutsafe me, looke you, a few disputations with you, as partly touching or concerning the disciplines of the Warre, the Roman Warres, in the way of Argument, looke you, and friendly communication: partly to satisfie my Opinion, and partly for the satisfaction, looke you, of my Mind: as touching the direction of the Militarie discipline, that is the Point.

> **Scot.** It **sall** be vary gud, gud feith, gud Captens **bath**, and I **sall** quit you with gud leue, as I may pick occasion: that **sall** I mary.

Here, Shakespeare uses a few stereotypical features to give the impression of Irish, Welsh and Scottish speech. The Irishman's speech has <sh> where we would expect <s>; the Welshman repeats the phrase *look you* and the Scotsman has <s> where we would expect <sh> in *sall*, and <a> rather than <o> in *bath*. Although the scene is humorous, and the language is a source of humour, the Irish, Welsh and Scottish soldiers are not portrayed as inferior to their English comrades, but their English is represented as different from the norm. As we shall see in the next chapter, their eighteenth-century compatriots would be 'helped' to conform to the model of London English by writers who would specifically point out the 'faults' of Irish, Scottish and Welsh pronunciation.

9 Late Modern English

By about 1700, the main changes in pronunciation that made up the Great Vowel Shift were all completed, at least in the south of England. Third-person forms like *loveth* had disappeared from ordinary educated speech. The pronouns *thou* and *thee* and the corresponding verb-forms like *lovest* had disappeared from standard usage, except in special registers, such as religious usage. Auxiliary *do* had come to be used as we use it today. And, all in all, the language differed only slightly from present-day English. This can be seen if we look at a piece of writing from the early eighteenth century. The following is an extract from one of the numbers of *The Spectator* for the year 1711. It was written by Joseph Addison, who was fond of ridiculing the Italian opera, which was then in vogue in London:

> The next Step to our Refinement, was the introducing of *Italian* Actors into our Opera; who sung their Parts in their own Language, at the same Time that our Countrymen perform'd theirs in our native Tongue. The King or Hero of the Play generally spoke in *Italian*, and his Slaves answer'd him in *English*: the Lover frequently made his Court, and gain'd the Heart of his Princess in a Language which she did not understand. One would have thought it very difficult to have carry'd on Dialogues after this Manner, without an Interpreter between the Persons that convers'd together; but this was the State of the *English* Stage for about three Years.
>
> At length the Audience grew tir'd of understanding Half the Opera, and therefore to ease themselves intirely of the Fatigue of Thinking, have so order'd it at Present that the whole Opera is perform'd in an unknown Tongue. We no longer understand the Language of our own

Stage; insomuch that I have often been afraid, when I have seen our *Italian* Performers chattering in the Vehemence of Action, that they have been calling us Names, and abusing us among themselves; but I hope, since we do put such an entire Confidence in them, they will not talk against us before our Faces, though they may do it with the same Safety as if it were behind our Backs. In the mean Time I cannot forbear thinking how naturally an Historian, who writes Two or Three hundred Years hence, and does not know the Taste of his wise Forefathers, will make the following Reflection, *In the Beginning of the Eighteenth Century, the* Italian *Tongue was so well understood in* England, *that Opera's were acted on the publick Stage in that Language.*

If we feel that that piece of writing is very typical of its age, this is largely a matter of tone and style and outlook; there is very little in morphology, syntax or vocabulary that would not be acceptable in present-day English. The biggest difference is perhaps that Addison writes *sung* where we use *sang*. In Old English, the strong verbs had two different stems in the past tense, as in *ic healp* 'I helped' but *we hulpon* 'we helped', and very often yet another vowel in the past participle, as in *holpen* 'helped'. During Late Middle English, the distinction between the past singular and the past plural disappeared; in some verbs, the singular form was used also for the plural, as in *I rode, we rode*; in others, the plural form was used for the singular, as in *I found, we found*; in yet other verbs, a new past tense was formed from the past participle, as in *I bore, we bore*. By 1500, the distinction between the past singular and the past plural had completely disappeared (except for *was/were*), but there was a good deal of variation in the forms used, and large numbers of new past tenses were formed from the past participle, like *bore* and *got*. By the early eighteenth century, a single past-tense form had been pretty-well standardized for each of the strong verbs. To a great extent these are the same as the ones we use in Standard English today, but there are small differences: there are past tenses like *sung, swum* and *writ* ('they writ', etc.), and past participles like *arose, ran, shook* and *spoke* ('he had spoke', etc.). Some of these forms persisted into the nineteenth century in Standard English, and are still used today in regional and non-standard varieties.

At one point we should perhaps write *At* rather than *In* ('In the beginning of the Eighteenth Century'), and there is one example of *do* used in an older way ('since we do put'), though this may perhaps be an example of the emphatic use.

The standardization of spelling

There are a few differences between Addison's punctuation and what would be considered correct today. His use of capital letters is noticeable, as is the apostrophe in the plural *Opera's*. The latter may surprise readers who have been led to believe that the so-called 'greengrocer's apostrophe' in plurals such as *potato's, tomato's* is a recent innovation and a consequence of declining educational standards. Since Addison was often held up as an example of good style in the eighteenth century, the use of an apostrophe in the plurals of nouns ending in a vowel was clearly acceptable at the time. Addison's spelling is almost identical with ours. There are minor differences, like *carry'd* and *publick*, but essentially the system of orthography is the one we use now. In Middle English and Early Modern English, there had been no standard spelling: spellings varied from writer to writer, and even within the work of one writer. Even proper names were not fixed: Shakespeare, in the three signatures on his will, uses two different spellings of his own surname (*Shakspere* and *Shakspeare*), and other variants of the time include *Shagspere*, *Shackespere* and *Shakespeare*. A powerful force for standardization was the introduction of printing, and by the middle of the sixteenth century, although there was still no standard system, there were quite a number of widely accepted conventions. By the end of the early modern period, spelling had become standardized in printed books, though there was still considerable variation in people's private writings.

However, the standard spelling system which became established by the end of the seventeenth century was already an archaic one, and, broadly speaking, represents the pronunciation of English before the Great Vowel Shift. This explains many of the oddities of present-day English spelling. We still preserve letters in our spelling which represent sounds which long ago ceased to be pronounced, like the *k* and *gh* of *knight*, the *t* in *castle*, the *w* in *wrong*. Distinctions are made in spelling where, in most varieties of English, there is no longer any distinction in pronunciation, as in *meat/meet* and *sea/see.* Conversely, in RP and many other varieties, new distinctions have arisen without being recognized in the spelling, so that we use the same letter to represent the vowels of *put* and *putt*, and the same *ng* spelling in *singer* and *finger*. Diphthongs, like the vowel of *mice*, are often represented by a single letter, because the phoneme was a pure vowel in Middle English, and, conversely, modern monophthongs are sometimes represented by digraphs, like the *au* of *author* or the *ou* of *cough*. Superimposed on all this are the effects of Renaissance etymologizing, which accounts for such things as the *b* in *subtle* and the *p* in *receipt*. Such things have introduced considerable inconsistencies into our spelling system.

One result of these inconsistencies is the prevalence of **spelling-pronunciations**, which arise when a word is given a new pronunciation through the influence of its spelling. This is especially likely to happen when universal education and the wide dissemination of books and newspapers introduce people to words in printed form which they have never heard pronounced in their home environment. Thus the word *schedule* originally began with /s-/, and was commonly spelt *sedule* or *cedul*; the spelling with *sch* dates from the mid-seventeenth century, and has led to the present-day pronunciations, /ʃ-/ and /sk-/. The word *schism* also has an unhistorical spelling: the traditional pronunciation is /sɪzm/, but in recent years the spelling-pronunciation /skɪzm/ has appeared. We have already seen that, under Latin influence, initial *h-* was introduced into the spelling of many words where no /h/ was pronounced – such words as *habit, harmony, hemisphere, herb, heritage, host, humble* and *humour*; the spelling-pronunciations with /h-/ are not common until the nineteenth century. Spelling-pronunciations are encouraged by the commonly held view that the written form of a word is the primary or 'right' one, to which the spoken word should be made to conform; this attitude was long strengthened by the predominance in upper-class English education of classical studies, centred on the written texts of two dead languages. The prestige accorded to the written forms explains the fact that even ordinary everyday words may be given spelling-pronunciations: the influence of the spelling has led, in many people's speech, to the reintroduction of the /t/ in *often* and *waistcoat*, [ð] in *clothes*, /h/ in *forehead*, /l/ in *Ralph* and /w/ in *towards*. These consonants had been lost in the traditional standard pronunciations, which would be better represented by such spellings as *offen, weskit, cloze, forrid, Rafe* and *tords*. In these six words the spelling-pronunciation is now fully accepted in educated speech in England, although the older pronunciation of *Ralph* in particular has a certain upper-class cachet.

Standardization and codification

The standardization of spelling was just one aspect of a more general attempt to regulate the language, an attempt which was especially prominent in the second half of the eighteenth century. From the seventeenth century onwards, there was a growing feeling that English needed to be 'ruled' or 'regulated', as Classical Greek and Classical Latin were believed to have been. A ruled language is one in which acceptable usage is explicitly laid down, for example by grammars and dictionaries, or by the rulings of an academy. Some people believed that a properly ruled language would also be unchanging. The great classical scholar Richard Bentley observed in 1699 that every language 'is in perpetual motion and alteration', but nevertheless believed that 'it were no difficult contrivance, if the Publick had any regard to it, to make the *English* tongue immutable'. He is perhaps thinking of the possibility of an official body to fix the language, for between about 1650 and 1760 there was quite a strong movement in favour of the establishment of an English academy, on the lines of the *Académie française*. Its functions would be to 'refine' or 'correct' the English language, to lay down correct usage, and perhaps to freeze the language in the desirable state thus attained. This last ambition is delusive: no language which is being used can be prevented from changing. But it is from this period that we inherit the prescriptive attitudes towards language which have been so influential in the last couple of centuries.

Proposals for an academy came to nothing, but the seventeenth century saw the publication of the first grammars and dictionaries of English. The eighteenth century brought the first really comprehensive dictionaries of English, and an enormous number of English grammars, especially in the second half of the century. It is important not to suppose that all eighteenth-century grammars were equally 'prescriptive' in intent, nor that all the authors of these works slavishly followed Latin models in their accounts of English grammar. Close reading of these texts reveals that their motivations and approaches were varied, but whatever the authors of these works may have intended, the dictionaries and grammars were seized on as authorities: they were commonly regarded, not as records of usage, but as prescriptions for correct usage. Moreover, alongside them sprang up a host of handbooks of correct or 'polite' usage, which were entirely prescriptive in intent.

English dictionaries did not exist until the seventeenth century. Before then, there were two-language dictionaries (for example, English–French and Latin–English), but no dictionaries devoted to English alone. The earliest surviving English dictionary, published in 1604, was a dictionary of 'hard words', as were all subsequent ones in that century. Because of the great vocabulary expansion in the later sixteenth century, and the prevalence of 'inkhorn terms', a need was felt for works which would explain the meaning of obscure words. The history of the dictionary in the seventeenth century is mainly one of expansion: Robert Cawdrey's dictionary of 1604 contained about 2,500 words, while that of Elisha Cole in 1676 contained about 25,000.

At the same time, the dictionaries included progressively more information, such as etymology, and differences of style or acceptability (elegant words distinguished from vulgar ones, dialect words from general educated usage, archaisms from current words). Not until the eighteenth century, however, did dictionaries attempt to record the ordinary everyday words of the language, the first being *A New English Dictionary* of 1702, perhaps by John Kersey. This was followed by the outstanding dictionaries of Nathan Bailey (1721) and of Samuel Johnson (1755). Johnson's monumental work includes extensive quotations from earlier authors to illustrate word-meanings. These dictionaries helped to stabilize spellings and word-meanings, and inevitably came to be treated as authorities.

Grammars of English also date largely from the seventeenth century. In the sixteenth century, and even later, a book called a *Grammar* was normally a grammar of Latin (just as a grammar school was one where Latin was taught). A couple of short grammars of English appeared in the late sixteenth century. Five were

published in the first half of the seventeenth century, and nine in the
second half, while in the eighteenth century there was an absolute
flood of them, with about fifty appearing between 1700 and 1750
and over two hundred in the second half of the century. One reason
why grammars of English began to appear in large numbers in the
late modern period is that schools were beginning to teach English
as well as, or instead of, the classical languages, so that textbooks
were needed. The vast majority of authors of English grammars in
this period were schoolteachers: Joseph Priestley is better known
to posterity as a scientist, but he wrote his *Rudiments of English
Grammar* (1761) whilst teaching at the Academy in Warrington,
and Ann Fisher, the first female English grammarian, opened a
school for 'young ladies who chuse to learn the English Grammar'
in Newcastle upon Tyne, where her highly successful and influential grammar was first published in 1745. When authors first
attempted to produce grammars of English, the models to which
they would turn and by which they would be influenced were Latin
grammars and textbooks. This does not mean that all grammars
of English written in this period attempted to force the language
to conform to classical patterns and paradigms. John Wallis, in
his *Grammatica* of 1653, argued strongly that an analysis suitable
for the classical languages is not necessarily suitable for English,
and Gildon and Brightland, in their *Grammar of the English Tongue*
(1711), accused Ben Jonson of having 'extended and tortur'd our
Tongue to confess the Latin Declensions, Conjugations, and ev'n
Construction, whereas there is nothing more different'. Joseph
Priestley objected to the application of the term 'future tense' to
English 'because we have no modification of our verbs to correspond to it', pointing out that the construction of auxiliary and verb
with *shall* and *will* is exactly the same as with '*do, have, can, must*
or any other'. Nevertheless, most seventeenth- and eighteenth-
century English grammars were influenced by classical grammars,
if only in the terminology used to describe categories such as 'parts
of speech'. In one case, the adoption of classical terminology led to
the invention of a 'rule' which to this day is more honoured in the
breach than the observance. The term 'preposition', applied to the
category including words such as *at, by, from, on, with*, derives from
a Latin word which implies that they are placed before the nouns

and pronouns with which they are associated. In English, this is not necessarily the case: the last five words of the previous sentence could have been ordered as 'which they are associated with' and still have been grammatical. However, most grammarians in the eighteenth and nineteenth centuries defined prepositions as words placed before nouns and pronouns: Robert Lowth, for instance, writes in 1762 that they are 'so called because they are commonly put *before* the words to which they are applied' and William Cobbett in 1823 writes, 'they are called *Prepositions* from two Latin words, meaning *before* and *place*; and this name is given to them because they are in most cases *placed before* Nouns and Pronouns'. Robert Lowth is often cited as the author responsible for introducing the proscription against ending a sentence with a preposition, but in fact he tells us that the placing of a preposition at the end of a relative clause (as in 'which they are associated with' above) 'is an idiom which our language is strongly inclined to; it prevails in common conversation, and suits very well with the more familiar style in writing'. He goes on to write that 'the placing of the Preposition before the Relative is more graceful, as well as more perspicuous; and agrees much better with the solemn and elevated style'. Lowth is not telling his readers that it is incorrect or ungrammatical to end a clause or sentence with a preposition, but that it is better not to do this in formal styles. Careful reading of grammars such as Lowth's often reveals that they are not as 'prescriptive' as we have been led to believe: the more dogmatic texts tended to be the handbooks of 'polite' usage which existed alongside the more scholarly grammars in the eighteenth century, but proliferated in the nineteenth.

The grammars of English written in the eighteenth and nineteenth centuries make overt reference to matters of social class. As the economy changed to one whereby people measured their wealth in money rather than land, and the Industrial Revolution saw the rise in society of plutocrats from humble origins, language and manners came to be the only means of distinguishing between the gentry and the newly rich middle classes. As Benjamin Withers wrote in 1788, 'purity and politeness of Expression ... is the only external Distinction which remains between a Gentleman and a Valet, a Lady and a Mantua-maker'. Although Robert Lowth wrote his grammar for 'all classes' and William Cobbett aimed his at 'Soldiers, Sailors, Apprentices and Plough-boys' (1823), most grammars in the eighteenth and nineteenth centuries were written for the middle classes, the very people who would be insecure about 'correct' usage and able to afford what they saw as the means to remedy this. Withers notes that 'the importance of a correct mode of expression in *Business* is sufficiently obvious' and James Buchanan aimed his *Complete English Scholar* (1753) at boys 'who are to be put to Trades'. There are frequent references in grammars of this period to the depraved language of common people, compared to the noble and refined expressions of the gentry: the middle classes would naturally aspire to the latter. These grammars also advocated the usage of educated speakers in London: provincialisms were condemned, and the language of the Scots and Irish in particular was subject to fierce attack. This often came from writers who were themselves Scottish or Irish. In the aftermath of the Act of Union (1707), the eradication of 'scotticisms' was seen as a patriotic act, intended to unify Britain by propagating a unified standard language. Conversely, Noah Webster, writing in the period following the American War of Independence, proclaimed the virtues of American English, claiming that it was the purest and least corrupt form of the language.

Sometimes, grammarians appealed to logic, as when they condemned multiple negation: this, as we have seen, was normal in the language until the seventeenth century, leading to such sentences as Shakespeare's

> I haue one heart, one bosome, and one truth,
> And that no woman has, nor neuer none
> Shall mistris be of it, saue I alone. (*Twelfth Night*)

The correctors objected to such constructions on the logical ground that two negatives make an affirmative, and for similar reasons they condemned double comparatives and double superlatives, like Shakespeare's 'more nearer' and 'the most vnkindest cut of all'. However, although the explanation given by these grammarians is spurious, detailed study of seventeenth-century texts has revealed that, by the time the rule that 'two negatives make a positive' was first expressed, the use of multiple negation in writing by educated people had already declined significantly, so the grammarians' prescriptions were simply codifying what was already becoming standard usage. Another idea behind some prescriptions was that there is an ideal universal grammar, to which the language should be made to conform: originally, language had been divinely instituted, and mirrored actuality perfectly. Since the Tower of Babel, however, it had become much corrupted. In practice, the Universal Grammar to which English was to conform often turned out to be the grammar of Latin: this is seen, for example, in the arguments about the cases of personal pronouns (for example, 'It is me' or 'It is I'?). Some writers, more reasonably, argued from analogies within the language: disputed points of usage could be settled by examining parallels within English. This procedure would tend to regularize the language, but was often undermined by a common belief that large numbers of linguistic distinctions are necessary in order to represent distinctions in the real universe. This belief is behind the insistence that adverbs should be clearly distinguished from adjectives, so that for example the use of *quick* and *exceeding* as adverbs is condemned. Similarly, it was argued that the past tenses and past participles of strong verbs should be distinguished. As we have seen, this differentiation had disappeared in many verbs, and in the early eighteenth century some writers said such things as 'I have wrote' and 'he had chose'. The correctors argued for distinct past participles like *written* and *chosen*. Here, the influence of Latin probably also played a part. Sometimes, an appeal was made to etymology, especially in the matter of word-meanings: the 'correct' meaning of a word was the meaning of some earlier form (English or Latin) from which it was descended. So it was argued that *mutual* must mean 'reciprocal', not 'common', and that *demean* must signify 'behave', not 'debase'. Etymology was also invoked in some disputes about constructions, as when it was argued that 'averse from' is preferable to 'averse to'.

The various eighteenth-century grammarians and correctors did not, however, always agree with one another. Because of the widely differing criteria appealed to, there were often hot disputes about points of usage. But even if the correctors often disagreed with one another, they passed on a substantial body of dogma to the nineteenth century, which added to it and passed it on to the twentieth. In the past couple of hundred years, language has become the subject of serious scientific study, and there are now grammars and dictionaries which aim to record and analyse usage, not to prescribe it. But even in our own age there are still handbooks which lay down the traditional rules on such matters as prepositions ('different to/from/than'?), the position in the sentence of *only*, the difference between *may* and *can* and between *shall* and *will*, the cases of pronouns ('Who did you give it to?' or 'To whom did you give it?'?), the splitting of infinitives, the 'correct' meanings of words and so on.

The verb system

One of the constructions attacked by some eighteenth-century 'correctors' was the type 'The house is building' and 'The grammar is now printing.' Dr Johnson described this construction as 'a vitious expression, probably corrupted from a phrase more pure but now somewhat obsolete: a printing, a forging'. One reason for the persistence of the construction was that sentences like 'The house is being built' were not yet possible. This latter construction in fact arose in the late eighteenth century, and was then itself attacked by some purists, who advocated instead the very construction condemned by Dr Johnson.

The reason for the unacceptability in earlier times of 'The house is being built' is that it combines the progressive with the passive. As we have seen, by late ME times there were four main markings of the verb, namely the past, the perfect, the passive and the progressive. It gradually became possible to combine these markings in various ways in most constructions, and by the early modern period most combinations were possible. The sole exception was the combination of the progressive and the passive. So in Shakespeare we find such things as 'my Ladie Hero hath bin falselie accusde' (Perfect + Passive), 'The Iuy which had hid my princely Trunck' (Past + Perfect), 'I haue bin drincking all night' (Perfect + Progressive), 'As if the garment had bin made for me' (Past + Perfect + Passive), and 'both the Princes had bene breathing heere' (Past + Perfect + Progressive). But we never find constructions like 'She is being falsely accused' and 'The garment was being made.' These do not occur until the late eighteenth century.

Since the late eighteenth century, it has been possible to combine any two or three of the four markings. In theory, indeed, it is possible to combine all four, as in 'It had been being eaten': it may not be easy to think of a context where this is required, but it can hardly be argued that the construction is ungrammatical.

The progressive marking signals continuing action over a period ('John was working in the garden') or repeated action over a period ('Smith is scoring a lot of goals this season'), but also implies that the period in question is of limited duration. The fact that the duration is limited explains why we can say 'John was standing on the bank', but not *'London is standing on the Thames': the latter sentence implies that London may at any moment move to some other place, so we have instead to say 'London stands on the Thames.'

The perfect marking signals what W. F. Twaddell calls 'current relevance': it implies that what is said bears on the immediate situation, or the situation at the time referred to. Some handbooks of English for foreign learners say that the perfect signals completed action. That this is not so can be seen from such sentences as 'Our family have lived in this house for three hundred years, and intend to go on doing so.' Alternatively, it is sometimes said that the perfect refers to a nearer past, and the past tense to a remoter past. But this is also wrong: it's perfectly possible to say 'I've only been there once, about twenty years ago', and to receive the reply 'Oh, I went there this morning.'

If none of the four markings is used, and there is no modal auxiliary, we are left with what is traditionally called the present tense of the verb ('I go', 'he goes'). This is not a good name, however, for the so-called present tense can refer to the future ('I go to New York next week'), to habitual action ('I go to work every morning'), and even, in colloquial style, to the past ('This chap storms into the pub, bangs on the counter, and says ...'). It is preferable to call it the *unmarked* form of the verb: since it has none of the four markings, and is not accompanied by a modal auxiliary, it signals nothing but the lexical meaning of the verb in question.

During the whole of the Modern English period, the perfect and progressive markings have become increasingly common. In Early Modern English, the unmarked form of the verb is often used in situations where we feel the need for the perfect or the progressive.

In Shakespeare's *Richard III*, a character says 'Soft, he wakes', where we would say 'Sh! He's waking up', and in *King Lear* a character says 'You spoke not with her since?', where, at least in Standard British English, we would say 'You haven't spoken with her since?'

Changes in pronunciation

Figure 12 gives a vowel diagram for the pure vowels of Standard English in about the year 1700. This assumes the style of speech in which ME *ę̄* coalesced with ME *ā*, so that *meat* and *mate* were homophones. As we have seen, in the speech of educated people in London, this style was supplanted in the eighteenth century by a style of speech in which ME *ę̄* had instead coalesced with ME *ē*, so that *meat* and *meet* were homophones.

Although the late modern period saw no systematic changes in pronunciation to rival the Great Vowel Shift, there were a number of important changes which began in the speech of London and were incorporated into RP when this developed towards the end of the period. None of these changes have spread throughout Britain, or even England, and the presence or absence of the 'new'

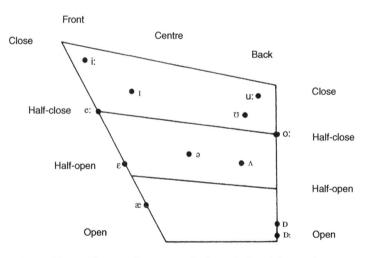

Figure 12 Vowel diagram: the pure vowels of Standard English, c. 1700

pronunciations mark some of the most important and noticeable differences between regional and/or social accents of English
today. Perhaps the most important change has been the disappearance of /r/ before consonants and before a pause. Formerly, the /r/
was always pronounced in words like *barn* and *person* and *father*.
But today, in RP and indeed in most speech in England, /r/ is never
pronounced in words like *barn* and *person*, and is pronounced in
words like *father* only if it occurs immediately before a vowel (as
in 'father and mother'). The weakening of /r/ before consonants
and before a pause had begun by the sixteenth century, but the
first evidence for the disappearance of this /r/ appears towards the
end of the eighteenth century, when the elocutionist John Walker
describes it as a feature of London speech. Even then, the loss of /r/
is not accepted as 'correct': throughout much of the nineteenth
century prescriptive handbooks on elocution condemn 'dropping'
the /r/ just as roundly as the omission of initial /h/. By the time
Daniel Jones published the first edition of his *English Pronouncing
Dictionary* in 1917, the pronunciations represented had no /r/
before consonants or word-finally.

Jones was describing the pronunciation of words in RP, but this
loss of final and preconsonantal /r/ did not take place in all varieties of English. Those varieties in which it was retained are usually
called **rhotic**, while varieties in which it was lost are **non-rhotic**.
Most North American speech is rhotic, except for varieties spoken in
some coastal areas in the south-eastern United States and in New
England and African American Vernacular English (**AAVE**). Both
Scots English and Irish English are rhotic, as is the traditional speech
of the West Country and some parts of Lancashire in England, but
Australian, New Zealand and South African English are all non-
rhotic, like RP and most other varieties within England and Wales.

Although preconsonantal and final /r/ has been lost in RP
and many other forms of English, it has left its mark on the words
where it was formerly pronounced: before disappearing, it caused
changes in the vowel which preceded it. In Middle English, *arm* was
pronounced [arm], *birch* was [bɪrtʃ] and *here* was [heːr], whereas
today they are [ɑːm], [bɜːtʃ] and [hɪə]. The /r/ has caused three
kinds of change: lengthening, change of quality and diphthongization. The changes mostly began in Early Modern English, but one

of them goes back to ME times, and many of them were not completed until the eighteenth century.

Examples of the lengthening process are *arm, bark, card* and *cord, horse, storm*. These originally had short [a] and [ɔ], which were lengthened in the seventeenth century. The lengthened [aː] was at first just an allophone of /æ/, but after the loss of /r/ it became an independent phoneme, and has developed into present-day /ɑː/: there was no /ɑː/ phoneme in Early Modern English. The lengthened [ɔː] coalesced with the vowel of words like *cause* and *law*, which in Middle English was the diphthong [aʊ], but which became a pure vowel in the course of Early Modern English, and which has developed into the present-day /ɔː/ phoneme.

In the sixteenth century, words like *herb, birth* and *curse* not only had /r/ pronounced, but also had short vowels identical with those of *bed, bid* and *puss*, their pronunciations being [ɛrb], [bɪrθ] and [kʊrs]. Under the influence of the /r/, all three vowels became [ə], the first evidence for the change taking place appearing around 1600 for [ɛr] and [ɪr], and forty or fifty years later for [ʊr]. In the later seventeenth century, therefore, the three words were pronounced [ərb], [bərθ] and [kərs]. By the end of the eighteenth century, the [ə] had been lengthened to [əː] and the /r/ lost, at least in the advanced variety spoken in London, giving the pronunciations [əːb], [bəːθ] and [kəːs]. At this stage, clearly, /əː/ had become an independent phoneme, and it has developed into the /ɜː/ phoneme of present-day English. There was no /ɜː/-type phoneme in Standard English before the eighteenth century. Neither the change of vowel-quality nor the lengthening took place if the /r/ was intervocalic, as can be seen in such words as *merry, stirrup* and *turret*. In some non-standard forms of English, the loss of /r/ took place a good deal earlier, especially before /s/, at a time when the preceding vowel had not yet been modified under the influence of the /r/. This accounts for the words *cuss* and *bust*, which are simply variants of *curse* and *burst*.

Throughout the Modern English period, there have been numerous words with alternative forms, one from ME *er* and the other from ME *ar*. In Late Middle English, *er* became *ar* in preconsonantal and final position, but this change did not take place in all varieties of speech, even in Standard English, and today we have some forms from one style of speech, some from the other. The outcome in present-day English is /ɜ:/ in one case, as in *certain, err, herd, pert,* and *servant,* but /ɑ:/ in the other, as in *clerk, farm, harvest, marvel, sergeant, star.* Formerly, two forms often existed side-by-side, as with *servant* and *sarvent,* but in most cases a single form has now been standardized. There are however a few doublets, such as *person* and *parson, university* and *varsity, perilous* and *parlous.*

When /r/ occurred after a long vowel or a diphthong, an [ə] glide developed between the vowel and the /r/. So *fire* developed from [faɪr] to ['faɪər], and *bower* from [baʊr] to ['baʊər]. When the /r/ was lost, the [ə] remained, giving ['faɪə] and ['baʊə]. In some cases the process produced new phonemes, namely the centring diphthongs /ɪə/, /ɛə/, /ʊə/ and /ɔə/, as in *here, pear, poor* and *more,* though in most people's speech the /ɔə/ has since become /ɔ:/, giving the pronunciation /mɔ:/. After long vowels, /r/ also had a lowering effect. In the Great Vowel Shift, ME *ā* and ME *ǣ* both moved to closer positions, but if /r/ followed, this movement was arrested at [ɛ:]. So *pare* and *pear,* which in the sixteenth century were [pæ:r] and [pɛ:r], both became [pɛ:r], later [pɛə]. In the case of [u:], a following /r/ caused lowering, and in many words sixteenth-century [u:r] became [ɔ:r] by the end of the seventeenth century. This has developed into present-day [ɔə] or [ɔ:]. Examples are *coarse, course, court, door, fourth, pour, sword* and *whore.* In some styles of speech, however, the lowering did not occur, and in such cases the [u:r] has developed into present-day [ʊə], which often exists as a variant pronunciation alongside [ɔ:], as in *gourd, moor* and *poor.*

Two other combinative changes of the Modern English period are worthy of mention: the rounding of vowels after /w/, and the lengthening of vowels before voiceless fricatives. Originally, as the spelling suggests, *swan* and *watch* had the same vowel as *ran* and *match,* namely ME *a.* In the eighteenth century, the /w/ caused rounding of the following vowel, which became [ɒ]. The change did not take place, however, if the vowel was followed by a velar consonant, as in *quack, quagmire, twang, wag* and *wax,* which regularly have present-day /æ/ (though in the case of *quagmire,* a word not often heard in everyday speech, an analogical pronunciation with /ɒ/ is now sometimes heard). If the group [wa] was followed by preconsonantal or final /r/, both rounding and lengthening took place, leading to present-day [ɔː], as in *war* and *quart*. If the /r/ was intervocalic, the rounding took place but the lengthening did not, as in *quarrel*, *warrant*.

Before the voiceless fricatives /f/, /s/, and /θ/, short [æ], from ME *a*, became lengthened to [æː], which later became [aː], and then [ɑː]. The lengthened vowel was originally just an allophone of /æ/, and there is evidence of this lengthening from the seventeenth century onwards, but once the /ɑː/ phoneme had arisen in words like *barn*, the lengthened [æː] was backed to [ɑː] and fell in with this new phoneme. At this point it became the object of condemnation from elocutionists such as John Walker, who wrote in 1791 that the use of the same vowel in *basket* as that of *father* was 'vulgar'. Throughout much of the nineteenth century, the pronunciation of words such as *bath*, *laugh*, *pass*, etc. with [ɑː] was condemned as 'drawling', but, like the loss of /r/, this innovation eventually found its way into RP. In regional speech, the lengthening took place only in the south of England and the South Midlands, and in words like *pass* and *path* the short vowel [a] is still common everywhere north of the Wash. Even in RP and southern English varieties, the lengthening did not take place if the voiceless fricative was immediately followed by a vowel: compare *pass* with *passage*, *path* with *mathematics*.

A similar lengthening before voiceless fricatives affected [ɔ], from ME *ǭ*, as in *often*, *cross*, *cloth*. The pronunciation of such words with /ɔː/ was condemned as 'vulgar' in the late eighteenth century, but, like /ɑː/, was used by RP speakers by the beginning of the twentieth century. However, in this case, the short vowel is now normal, and the other pronunciation sounds old-fashioned and very upper-class if used by an RP speaker.

Another pronunciation which has seen shifts in the sociolinguistic status of variants is that of final unstressed -*ing*. In Early Modern English, the normal development was from [-ɪŋg] to [-ɪŋ]. There was, however, a variant style in which it became [-ɪn]. This was not standard usage in Early Modern English, but became fashionable in the eighteenth century, and persisted until the twentieth in RP. In the nineteenth century, probably under the influence of spelling, the [-ɪn] pronunciation came to be condemned and avoided by middle-class speakers, so that it became simultaneously a feature of lower- and upper-class speech. In RP, [-ɪn] is now old-fashioned, and [-ɪŋ] normal, but [-ɪn] and [-ən] are common in regional speech.

The influence of scientific writing

The seventeenth century saw the triumph of the scientific outlook in England, and the sciences have had a pervasive influence on the language and the way it has been used in the past three hundred years. As we have seen, Latin gave way to English as the language of science and scholarship. The rise of scientific writing in English helped to establish a simple referential kind of prose as the central kind in Modern English. Other kinds of prose continued to exist, as readers of Carlyle, Ruskin or Virginia Woolf will be well aware, but a rhetorical or poetical style ceased to be the norm, and what we may call *the plain style* became central, the background against which other kinds of prose were read. The plain style is not of course confined to science, but is found in all kinds of expository writing – history, philosophy, literary criticism and so on. Nor, unfortunately, do all scientists write in a plain style. But scientific writing, and the scientific attitude in general, played a part in the establishment of this style.

In the later seventeenth century, the influence of science on the way language was used was quite conscious. In 1667 Thomas Sprat wrote a history of the Royal Society, the first scientific society in England and still the most famous. In this book he attacked rhetorical and figurative language, which he said the members of the Royal Society had rejected:

> They have therefore been most rigorous in putting in execution, the only Remedy, that can be found for this *extravagance*: and that has been, a constant Resolution, to reject all the amplifications, digressions, and swellings of style: to return back to the primitive purity, and shortness, when men delivered so many *things*, almost in an equal number of *words*. They have exacted from all their members, a close, naked, natural way of speaking; positive expressions; clear senses; a native easiness; bringing all things as near the Mathematical plainness, as they can: and preferring the language of Artizans, Countrymen and Merchants, before that of Wits, or Scholars.

Sprat's primitive purity and shortness is a myth: the kind of style he is describing is a highly sophisticated achievement, and not at all primitive. But the passage shows clearly that the scientists had their own ideas about the way language should be used. There is also an interesting contrast with the 'refiners' and 'correctors' of the language, who quite decidedly preferred the language of wits and scholars to that of artisans, countrymen and merchants.

The scientific vocabulary

The more obvious influence of science on the language, how-ever, was in the expansion of the scientific vocabulary. In the eight-eenth century came an enormous expansion in the vocabulary of the life-sciences, for this was the great age of biological descrip-tion and classification, as seen in the work of Linnaeus. From this period, therefore, stem many of the descriptive terms of botany and zoology, like *albino, anther, coleoptera, dicotyledon, fauna, habi-tat, ovate* and *pinnate*. The great changes in chemical theory in the late eighteenth century also produced many new words, includ-ing *hydrogen, molecule, nitrogen* and *oxygen*. A major part in the foundation of modern chemistry was played by French scientists, especially Lavoisier, and this is reflected in the fact that these four words all came into English from French. In the nineteenth cen-tury, the expansion of the vocabulary became explosive. Many spe-cialized fields were developing rapidly, and most of the new words have never had any circulation outside their own narrow sphere. A few, however, have come into common use, since for one reason or another they impinge on everyday life, so that we all know such words as *accumulator, aspidistra, cereal, conifer, hibernate, isobar, metabolism, ozone* and *pasteurize*.

In forming this enormous vocabulary, scientists were able to draw on various sources. One device is to take a word already in everyday use and give it a special scientific meaning, which is what the chemists have done with *salt*, the botanists with *fruit* and *pol-len* (originally 'fine flour'), the zoologists with *parasite*, the metal-lurgists with *fatigue*, and the physicists with *current, force, gravity, power, resistance* and *work*. Another way is to take over words bod-ily from another language. From Latin have come such words as *azalea, bacillus, corolla, hydrangea, sphagnum* and *tibia.* Some words have been lifted from Greek, like *acne, eczema* and *ion*, but many of these may have come into the language via Latin. A few words have been taken from German, especially in the fields of chemistry and mineralogy, such as *cobalt, paraffin* and *quartz.* And a few words are derived from the names of modern European scientists, including *amp(ère)* and *coulomb* (French), *gauss* and *ohm* (German), *ångström* (Swedish) and *volt* (Italian). These are all the names of scientific units, and the *farad*, the *kelvin* and the *watt* are similarly named in honour of Michael Faraday (an Englishman), of William Thomson, Lord Kelvin (born Belfast, educated Glasgow), and of James Watt (a Scot).

But an extremely common way of providing new scientific words is to invent them, using Greek and Latin material. From Greek, for example, are *anode, cathode, electrolysis* and *electron.* From Latin elements are formed such words as *accumulator, habitat, hibernate, invertebrate* and *transliterate.* Some Greek elements have come via Modern Latin, and many scientific words contain both Greek and Latin morphemes, for example *biosphere, haemoglobin* and *micro-species.* Latin elements are often influenced by the corresponding ones derived from French, as when, in the nineteenth century, the chemical term *valency* was formed from Latin *valentia.* Moreover, such words tend to be international, and are often coined in one language and then spread to others: *chlorophyll* came into English from French in the early nineteenth century. This word is the name of the substance in plants which gives them their green colour, and is made up from the Greek words *chlōrós* 'light green' and *phyllon* 'leaf'.

The number of such scientific words formed from classical elements is now enormous. It is sometimes argued that they have the disadvantage of being opaque, that is, that their meaning is not self-evident to a native English speaker. On the other hand, they have the advantage of being intelligible internationally. Moreover, in any specialist field, the research-workers presumably get to know the meanings of the classical elements commonly used there, so that the words are not opaque to them. Indeed, there are Greek elements that are now so commonly used in forming words that their English meaning is understood by most educated people, even if they know no Greek. Such for example are *bio* 'life', *crypto* 'hidden, secret', *graph* 'writing, drawing', *hydro* 'water', *hyper* 'over, above measure', *hypo* 'under', *macro* 'large', *mega* 'large, a million', *micro* 'small, microscopic, one millionth', *mono* 'single', *morph* 'shape, form', *phono* 'voice, sound', *photo* 'light', *pyro* 'fire', *tele* 'distant' and *thermo* 'heat, hot'. Indeed, many of these are used as affixes for forming non-scientific English words, and can be considered an active part of our processes of everyday word-formation.

The expansion of the general vocabulary

The expansion of the English vocabulary in the late modern period was not confined to scientific words. As a community changes, there is a constant demand for new words to express new concepts or new attitudes, to denote new objects or new institutions. In the late modern period, society became increasingly complex and the growth of vocabulary correspondingly great, with many new words in the fields of finance, politics, the arts, fashion and much else.

Because of the growth of world trade, and Britain's large part in it, we borrowed words from many distant countries, such as *budgerigar* from an Australian Aboriginal language, *(tea-)caddy* from Malay, *ketchup* from Chinese, *raffia* from Malagasy, a language of Madagascar, and *taboo* from Tongan. In view of the long British occupation of the Indian subcontinent, it is not surprising that a substantial number of words were borrowed from Indian languages, especially from Hindi, though also from Dravidian languages (*curry*, for example, being a sixteenth-century loan from Tamil). Examples of loans from Indian languages in the late modern period include *bangle, cashmere, chutney, dinghy, jungle, pyjamas* and *shampoo*.

Nearer home, we continued to borrow words from French, especially ones connected with the arts (*connoisseur, critique, pointillism*), with clothes and fashion (*beige, rouge, suede*), with social life (*élite, etiquette, parvenu*) and, towards the end of the period, with motoring and aviation (*chauffeur, hangar, nacelle*). From the Dutch we took a few more trading and nautical terms (*gin, taffrail*), from the Italians more words from the arts (*castrato, diva, fiasco, replica, scenario, studio* and from German words connected with mountaineering (*alpenstock, rucksack*).

The main ways of expanding the general vocabulary in the late modern period were, however, affixation, compounding and conversion. As in earlier periods, the prefix *un-* was widely used, as in *unforgiving, unfunny, unfranked* and *ungag*. The prefix *de-* was used especially for forming new verbs, like *decarbonize, deconsecrate* and *denationalize*, and could also replace another prefix, as when *demote* was coined as the opposite of *promote*. Other active prefixes include *anti-, dis-, inter-, mis-, non-, pre-, pro-* and *self-*. A common suffix is *-ize*, which is used to form verbs from adjectives (*nationalize, miniaturize, westernize*) and from nouns (*carbonize, macadamize*). From these in turn can be formed new abstract nouns in *-ization* (*miniaturization*, etc.). Other active suffixes in Late Modern English include *-able, -ee, -er, -ie* or *-y, -ist, -ly* and *-wise* (often used in American English for forming new adverbs). Most of these affixes are not of native origin: they have not come down to us from Old English, but have been taken over from Greek, Latin, or French. This is of no importance: they are now a part of the English language, and their origins are irrelevant.

Compounding, the formation of new words from free morphemes, has also played a considerable part in the late modern period, giving us numerous words like *airship, bandmaster, graveyard, offside, pigskin* and *railway*. We tend to treat such combinations as single words (a) if their meaning cannot be deduced from the sum of their parts, as in words like *blackleg* or *offside*, or (b) if they have the stress-pattern of a single word, as with *paperback* and *railway*. The importance of stress, and of the accompanying intonation-pattern, can be seen if you compare *the green house* with *the greenhouse*: the former has full stress on both the adjective and the noun, whereas in the latter the compound noun has stress only on the first syllable. And similarly with *a black bird* and *a blackbird*.

There is, however, a grey area between affixation and compounding. When a compound word has become established, it may in time undergo phonetic changes, and what was originally a free morpheme may become an affix. In some cases, the pronunciation of such an element can change so much that it is no longer recognized as identical with the original word. An example is the ending

-*ly*, used to form such adjectives as *bodily*, *kingly* and *lovely*. This goes back to an OE ending -*līc*, which was originally identical with the independent OE word *līc* 'form, shape, body', and with the same element in OE *gelīc* 'similar, equal, having the same form as'. In the unstressed form of *līc* the final consonant was lost, while in the stressed form it became [k] in the north of England and [ʧ] in the south. The southern form survives in the word *lychgate*, so called because it was the roofed gate leading into the churchyard under which the body was placed while the funeral procession awaited the arrival of the clergyman. The northern form survives in the word *like*, preposition, adjective and noun. Phonetic change and dialect variation have obscured for us the relationship between -*ly*, *lych* and *like*, which were originally the same word. And in Modern English -*ly* is a suffix, not the second half of a compound word: it is an example of the way in which a suffix can develop out of a full word. Now that we no longer feel any relationship between -*ly* and *like*, we can use the latter for forming a new series of compound words. Beside the word *lively*, which goes back to OE *līflīc*, we have the eighteenth-century formation *lifelike*, which consists of what are, historically speaking, exactly the same two elements.

Over a long period, the stressed element of a compound may also change in pronunciation, so that the origin of the word becomes obscured (though our conservative spellings often remind us of it). Examples are *breakfast* (break + fast), *garlic* (gore 'spear' + leek), *holiday* (holy + day), *sheriff* (shire + reeve), *tadpole* (toad + poll 'head') and *woman* (wife + man). The first element of *garlic* is from OE *gār* 'spear', which in Middle English came to be used for anything shaped like a spear-head, such as a triangular piece of land or the front section of a woman's skirt. The word survives as the dress-making term *gore* 'a gusset'. To the modern reader, the OE compound *wīfmann* 'woman' may seem surprising. But in Old English the word *mann* was not confined to male persons, but simply meant 'a human being', irrespective of sex or age. Most of the phonetic changes which have taken place in these words consist in the shortening of a vowel, either because it was unstressed (as in the -*līc* of *garlic*), or because it occurred before a group of consonants (*tadpole*), or because it occurred in the first syllable of a three-syllable word (*holiday*). Final consonants may also be lost, and in *woman* there has been vowel-rounding under the influence of /w/, though in the plural form *women* this was obviously inhibited by the front vowel of the following syllable.

A process which has been extremely productive in the Modern English period is that of conversion, the derivation of one word from another without any change of form. The word *market*, borrowed from Norman French in the twelfth century, was originally only a noun, as when we say 'A market is held there every Saturday.' Since the seventeenth century, however, it has also been possible to use *market* as a verb, as when we say 'ICI will market this product.' This kind of change is very rare in Old English, but is easy in Modern English, because of the loss of so many of our inflections. There is nothing in the word *market*, taken in isolation, to show what grammatical class it belongs to, whereas the Latin word *mercātus* (from which it is ultimately derived) shows immediately by its ending that it is not a verb (the related Latin verb being *mercārī* 'to trade'). In Old English, similarly, the ending of a word often proclaims its grammatical status, and related words are formed by affixation rather than by conversion. Thus there is an OE noun *dōm* 'law, judgement' and a related verb *dēman* (from earlier **dōmjan*), which have become Modern English *doom* and *deem*. But since the fifteenth century there has also been a verb *to doom*, formed from the noun. Conversely, in the seventeenth century a noun *deem* was formed from the verb (as when Shakespeare's Cressida says 'what wicked deeme is this?'), though this is now obsolete. The word *black*, on the other hand, was originally only an adjective (OE *blæc*), but in Middle English came to be used also as a noun and a verb, so that today we can 'wear black', and 'black our shoes'.

The process of conversion has been highly productive in Late Modern English, and especially in the past century. Examples of verbs formed from nouns are *to headline, to referee* and *to service*. New compound nouns are often formed by conversion from a verb phrase: from the verb *to hand out* has been formed the noun *a handout*, and similarly with *knowhow, set-up* and *walkout*. In these cases the verb phrase usually has double stress (*to hánd oút*) while the noun has single stress (*a hándout*).

Affixation, compounding and conversion are the major sources of the great expansion of the vocabulary in the late modern period, but there are also a number of minor ways in which words have been acquired. One is the process of *shortening*. This process was already productive at the beginning of the late modern period, mainly in colloquial language. Jonathan Swift objected to such slang terms as *mob* (from the Latin phrase *mobile vulgus*), *rep* (reputation) and *phyzz* (from *physiognomy*). Shortened words usually start off as colloquial, but many eventually supplant the full form, as *mob* has. Most often, the end of a word is cut off, as when *cabriolet* was shortened to *cab*, and *photograph* to *photo*. There may be successive phases of shortening: *public house* was shortened to *public* and then to *pub*, while *taximeter cab* became *taxi-cab* and then *taxi*. Occasionally it is the beginning of the word that is cut off, as when *acute* and *omnibus* became *cute* and *bus*. Other examples of shortening in the late modern period include *ad*, (advertisement), *exam* (examination), *gym* (gymnasium), *pram* (perambulator) and *van* (caravan).

Towards the end of the late modern period, a few new words were made by *blending*, that is, by combining part of one word with part of another. An example of this is *brunch* (*breakfast* and *lunch*), which was coined at the end of the nineteenth century. Such blends are sometimes called 'portmanteau words', a term taken from Lewis Carroll, who coined blends such as *slithy* (*lithe* and *slimy*) and *mimsy* (*miserable* and *flimsy*). This method of forming new words became more productive in the twentieth century.

Another minor source of word-formation in the late modern period is to create common nouns from the names of people or places. Sometimes the proper noun is combined with a suffix, as in the verb *to pasteurize* (from the name of the French scientist Louis Pasteur), and the many names of minerals formed from the name of the place where they were first discovered plus *-ite*, such as *lanarkite*, *strontianite* and *uralite*. Sometimes a pet-name is taken, as with *bobby* 'policeman', from the name of Sir Robert Peel (whence also came the slang word *peeler*). But often the proper name is taken over unchanged and used as a common noun, as with *cardigan*, *doily*, *jacquard*, *mackintosh* and *sandwich* (from the fourth Earl of Sandwich, who was reluctant to leave the gaming-table even to eat). An example from an earlier age is *derrick*, from the name of an early seventeenth-century hangman.

Yet another source of words is *back-formation*. An example of this is the verb *to sidle*, which was formed in the seventeenth century from the adverb *sideling*, which meant 'sideways, obliquely'. In a sentence like 'He came sideling down the road', *sideling* could obviously be apprehended as the present participle of a (non-existent) verb *to sidle*, and as a consequence this verb was then invented. Similarly, the verb *to beg* was a ME back-formation from the noun *beggar*, which was probably derived from the Old French *begard*. In this case, the *-ar* of *beggar* has been identified with the *-er* suffix by which agent-nouns are formed from verbs (*drinker* from *to drink*, etc.), and the verb *to beg* then invented by analogy with such forms. More recent examples of back-formation are the nineteenth-century verbs *to enthuse* and *to reminisce* (from *enthusiasm* and *reminiscence*). Probably we should also count as back-formations such verbs as *to bushwhack*, *to housekeep* and *to stage-manage*, since they appear to be derived from the compound nouns *bushwhacker*, *housekeeper* and *stage manager*.

Another means by which words come into the standard language is by borrowing from regional dialects or from the language of specialized groups within the speech community. Such borrowings are called *internal loans*. An internal loan is not a new word, of course, but it is a new acquisition as far as the *general* vocabulary of the language is concerned. The Industrial Revolution, centered on northern England and the West Midlands, brought some regional words into wider circulation. On a British railway, for example, a gradient is never a *hill*, but is often a *bank* (from northern dialect), and the extra engines used to help push a heavy train up the gradient are *banking-engines*. The word *bogie* (on railway rolling-stock) is also northern, *flange* is of obscure origin, but has probably come into the standard language from regional dialect, and *trolley* was originally a Suffolk word.

The flow of northerners, and especially Scots, to London in the past few centuries no doubt helps to explain the presence in the standard language of such northern English or Scots words as *bard, bonny, bracken, cairn, canny, eerie, glen, kipper, rowan, scone* and *tarn*. Some of these are not native English words, but are loans from Scandinavian (like *rowan* and *tarn*) or from Gaelic (like *bard* and *glen*), but they have entered the standard language via regional dialect, and so are internal loans as far as their immediate provenance is concerned. The adoption of Scots words has been facilitated by our knowledge of Scots literature, especially no doubt by the former popularity of Sir Walter Scott.

Words also creep into the standard language from lower-class speech and from the argot of occupational groups: *gadget* is first heard of as sailors' slang in the late nineteenth century, and *wangle* is first recorded as printers' slang. Such words may at first be eschewed by standard speakers, but can in time attain respectability. Many words which were once considered 'low' or 'vulgar' are now fully accepted. They include such perfectly normal words as *banter, coax, flimsy, flippant, fun, sham* and *snob*, all of which were frowned on in the eighteenth century.

Public school English

Inside England, as we have seen, one form of the language became accepted as a literary standard in the late Middle Ages, and, from at least the sixteenth century, there was a sense of a prestigious accent based on that of the court in Westminster. This does not mean that dialect differences disappeared in England: Standard English was the language of a small minority. Most speakers used a non-standard form of the language, and in each area there was a speech-hierarchy corresponding to the class-hierarchy, differing from Standard English not only in accent but also in grammar and vocabulary. The higher the socio-economic level of the speakers, the nearer their speech was likely to be to Standard English, though the degree of formality of the situation also influenced the level of speech used. Even among the upper classes, Standard English was not universal: in the plays and novels of the seventeenth and eighteenth centuries we often meet country gentlemen who are represented as using a regional variety of the language. But in the late modern period there was an increasing tendency for the English upper and upper-middle classes to adopt a uniform style of speech. One of the causes of this has been the influence of the great public schools, which dominated the education of the English gentry at least since the time of Arnold of Rugby in the early Victorian age. This 'public school' English was a variant of the prestigious educated accent of London and the south-east of England, which was advocated by the elocutionists of the late eighteenth and nineteenth centuries, such as John Walker. It ceased to be a regional dialect when upper-class boys from all over the country began to acquire it in the public schools, and subsequently became a class dialect, spoken by members of the English gentry whatever part of the country they came from. This variety was first given the name 'received pronunciation' by Alexander Ellis in 1869, when he defined this as 'the educated pronunciation of the metropolis, of the court, of the pulpit and the bar'. Explicit recognition of the link between Received Pronunciation and a public school education came at the beginning of the twentieth century, a period which was to see this variety reach the height of its prestige and influence, only to decline towards the end of the century.

10 English as a world language

Today, when English is one of the major world languages, it requires an effort of the imagination to realize that this is a relatively recent thing – that Shakespeare, for example, wrote for a speech community of only a few millions, whose language was not much valued elsewhere in Europe and was unknown to the rest of the world. Shakespeare's language was pretty-well confined to England and southern Scotland, not yet having penetrated very much into Ireland or even Wales, let alone into the world beyond. In the first place, the great expansion in the number of English speakers was due to the growth of population in England itself. At the Norman Conquest, the population of England was perhaps a million and a half. During the Middle Ages it grew to perhaps 4 or 5 million, but then was held down by recurrent plagues, and was still under 5 million in 1600. It was approaching 6 million in 1700, and 9 million in 1800. Then, with the Industrial Revolution in full flow, the population expanded rapidly to 17 million in 1850, and over 30 million by 1900.

At the same time, English penetrated more and more into the rest of the British Isles at the expense of Celtic languages, though it is only during the last two centuries that it has become the first language of most speakers in Wales, Ireland and the Scottish Highlands. In 1805, William Wordsworth wrote a poem in which he listens to the singing of a 'solitary Highland Lass', and is moved to ask 'Will no one tell me what she sings?' He cannot understand her, of course, because she is singing in Gaelic, and there is nobody at hand who is able to interpret. The spread of English was encouraged by deliberate government policy. For example, after the 1745

239

Jacobite rebellion, many schools were established in the Scottish Highlands, but the medium of instruction was English, Gaelic being forbidden. In Ireland, Brian Friel's play *Translations* (1980) provides a brilliant imaginative recreation of the workings of British colonial linguistic policy in a nineteenth-century Irish-speaking community in County Donegal. In more recent times, there has been a change of policy in all these places, with official support for the Celtic languages. Irish is a compulsory school subject in Ireland, and, within the United Kingdom, there are opportunities to learn all the Celtic languages, and to be educated in them, in their respective countries and regions.

However, English has become a world language because of its wide diffusion *outside* the British Isles, to all continents of the world, by trade, colonization and conquest. The process began with English settlements in North America in the seventeenth and eighteenth centuries. English settlements in the West Indies also began in the seventeenth century, in competition with Spanish, French and Dutch colonizers. For a couple of centuries there was intermittent warfare between these four powers for domination of the Caribbean, and by the early nineteenth century Britain had firm control of a number of the islands, including Antigua, Barbados, Jamaica, St Kitts, and Trinidad and Tobago. British domination of the Indian subcontinent dates from the second half of the eighteenth century: the East India Company was founded in 1600, and British trading-posts established from the seventeenth century onwards, but it was only from the 1770s that British rule was firmly established. British settlement in Australia began slightly later, after the American War of Independence. The expansion of British influence and power continued at an even greater rate during the nineteenth century. Early in the century, the British displaced the Dutch as the dominant power in South Africa, and during the first half of the century British rule was also established in Singapore, British Guiana, New Zealand and Hong Kong. The second half of the nineteenth century was marked by 'the scramble for Africa', in which colonial powers (Belgium, Britain, France, Germany, Portugal) competed for possessions in the African continent. As a result, British rule was established in regions of West Africa (including what is now Nigeria), East Africa (including what are now Kenya and Tanzania) and southern Africa (including what are now Zimbabwe and Botswana).

In all these areas, British English has been influential, while in the Philippines and Puerto Rico, both taken by the United States from Spain at the end of the nineteenth century, the American form of English has dominated. The great growth of population in the United States, assisted by massive immigration in the nineteenth and twentieth centuries, is one factor that has given English its present standing in the world. In 1788, when the first American census was held, there were about 4 million people in the United States, most of them of British origin. By 1830, the population was nearly 13 million; by 1850 it was 23 million, and had overtaken that of England; and then it shot ahead – to 50 million by 1880, 76 million by 1900 and 150 million by 1950. For many years, the United States authorities had an explicit linguistic policy, which insisted on the primacy of the English language: immigrants who wished to obtain United States citizenship had to pass an examination in competence in the English language. A by-product of this system was Leo Rosten's comic masterpiece *The Education of Hyman Kaplan* (1937).

This worldwide expansion of English means that it is now one of the most widely spoken languages in the world. Estimates of the numbers of speakers of English vary widely, but even the most modest of these agree that there are well over 400 million speakers for whom English is a native language and many more for whom English is a second or foreign language. The method of its spread, however, also means that there are now many varieties of English, and that it is used for many different purposes in varying social contexts. In North America, Australia, and New Zealand, there was dense settlement by English-language speakers, who outnumbered the original inhabitants (Native Americans, Australian Aboriginals, Maoris), and also dominated them politically and economically. The native languages, consequently, had hardly any influence on the language of the settlers. In South Africa, on the other hand, the community of those who speak English as a first language is comparatively small: in the 2001 census, English was recorded as the language most often spoken at home for 8.2% of the population, putting it in fifth place after IsiZulu (23.8%),

IsiXhosa (17.6%), Afrikaans (13.3%) and Sepedi (9.4%). However, this does not account for the many South Africans of various ethnic backgrounds and ancestries who will speak English as a second language.

In Australia, New Zealand and South Africa there is little regional variation in the language. There are, however, social and ethnic variations: in Australia, some speakers use a 'broader' accent, that is, one that is remoter from RP, and use more local Australian words in their vocabulary, but similar variations are found all over the country. In all three countries, there are different varieties of English associated with different ethnic groups, such as Australian Aboriginal English and Maori English. In the United States, on the other hand, there is greater regional dialect differentiation. The original English-speaking settlers on the east coast developed dialectal differences, and as the frontier was pushed westwards these dialects expanded too, so that there are fairly well-marked dialect bands. At the same time, however, they influenced one another, and became more mixed, so that in the west the differences are less sharp than on the Atlantic coast. It is usual to recognize three main dialect areas, the Northern, the Midland and the Southern. What is often called General American includes parts of all three dialect areas, but excludes the non-rhotic areas, that is, those where final and preconsonantal /r/ is not pronounced (the coastal south-east, and coastal areas of New England). Canadian English is different again, though much closer to General American than to British English.

Places in which English is spoken primarily as a native, second or foreign language have been labelled as 'inner circle, outer circle and expanding circle' areas respectively. The 'inner circle' is made up of those communities in which English has been passed down the generations as a first language, such as the United Kingdom, the USA, Canada, Australia and New Zealand. The 'outer circle' consists of areas in which English is widely used as a second language, alongside one or more local languages for public purposes, and often for communication between different language groups in the community. India, for example, has a population of over one billion, and over four hundred different languages. English is one of the official languages, alongside Hindi and twenty-two 'scheduled' regional languages, and is widely used as a language of administration and commerce. In former British colonies in sub-Saharan Africa, English usually plays a similar role, whether it is recognized as an official language or not. In Nigeria there are three main languages (Yoruba, Igbo, Hausa), and over five hundred local ones, but English is also an official language, and plays a major role in government and administration. It is also used as a language of wider communication, at any rate among the higher socio-economic groups.

The 'expanding circle' consists of those areas in which there is neither any native tradition of English speaking, nor institutional use of English, but it is learned as a foreign language, for trade, travel, etc. As English has increasingly become a global language, the number of speakers learning English as a foreign language is growing rapidly, hence the term 'expanding circle'. An example of an 'expanding circle' country is mainland China (as opposed to Hong Kong, which, as a former British colony, belongs in the 'outer circle'). In the expanding circle, the model of English taught will be either RP or General American English. In 'outer circle' countries like India, in contrast, where speakers mostly learn English as a second language, they will expect to use it mostly for communication with other Indians, and will hear it used in the speech community as a matter of course. Moreover, an Indian will most often learn a local variety of the language, taught by an Indian who speaks that variety, and not British or American English.

The distinction between second language and foreign language is not, however, a sharp one: educated people from a wide range of countries, including many European countries, may have learnt English as a foreign language, but will use it as a lingua franca in contexts such as academic conferences. Moreover, there is a considerable amount of variation in the roles played by second languages, for example in education, in the fields of discourse used, and in the giving of prestige or power. In India, although official policy was to change the medium of education in schools from English to regional languages after independence, in practice many schools and nearly all universities still use English as a medium of instruction. In Nigeria, primary schools are being built which teach in the local languages, but the secondary schools and the universities are still predominantly English-medium. In Singapore there are four official languages, Chinese (Mandarin), English, Malay and Tamil. In the 1940s and 1950s, Chinese was the most common medium of education, but, since independence (1965), English-medium education has spread until it is now universal, while Chinese, Malay and Tamil are taught as subjects.

The kind of discourse for which English is used varies a good deal. In some communities where it is mostly a second language, it is used primarily in the public domain – in administration, business, science-education, and the media. But in some places, including Nigeria, India and Singapore, it is also often used in the personal domain – within the family, and among friends. When Hong Kong was still a British colony, Chinese (Cantonese) and English had equal status as official languages, but their fields were sharply divided: English was used in the legal system, in English-medium education, in the upper reaches of commerce and industry, and in the media, but everyday discourse within the Chinese community was carried on in Cantonese, and English was seen as the language of power, while Cantonese was the language of solidarity and an expression of ethnicity. In general, English was formal, while Cantonese was intimate. Now that the British have departed, and Hong Kong has been united with the Chinese mainland, English is no longer the language of power, but will probably remain an important second language, especially in view of Hong Kong's worldwide trading activities.

Formal written English is much the same all over the world, whether in an inner-, outer- or expanding-circle country, though certain words or expressions may be associated with particular places. Speakers of English as a second or foreign language may also use structures in their speech that are unlikely to be used by native speakers. There are, however, English-based languages which depart even more radically from the standard types, namely pidgins and creoles. A pidgin is an auxiliary language used in the first place for the purposes of trade between groups that have no common language. It thus arises when two or more languages are in contact, and is a simplified form of the dominant one, with influence from the other(s). This restricted type of pidgin may, however, be extended to cover other fields of discourse, and eventually be capable of fulfilling all language-functions. This is especially likely to happen in a multilingual area, where the pidgin can perform a useful function as a lingua franca. It may even become an official language: Papua New Guinea's pidgin, called Tok Pisin, is formally acknowledged in the country's constitution. Some pidgins die out because the need for them passes, but others spread and gain wide currency, and there are numerous pidgins in the world today, many of them (though not all) based on European languages, including English. There are many English-based pidgins, especially in the coastal regions of West Africa and on the islands of the Caribbean and the Pacific.

It sometimes happens that a pidgin becomes the first language of a group. The language is then called a *creole*. There are English-based creoles in the Caribbean, for example in Barbados and Jamaica, on the north coast of South America (Guyana, Surinam), and even in the United States: the creole called Gullah is spoken by about a quarter of a million people living along the south-eastern coastal areas of the USA. It is possible, too, that African American Vernacular English is descended from a creole. Creoles have also been brought to Britain since the Second World War by immigrants from the West Indies, and local varieties have developed, such as London Jamaican. Creoles probably developed in the Caribbean because of the mixing of populations caused by the slave-trade. The slavers herded together speakers of many different West African languages. At the ports of embarkation, and on the slave-ships, the captives probably communicated with one another in some kind of West African pidgin, which in the Caribbean plantations developed into creoles.

Pidgins and creoles co-exist with standard varieties of the donor language, and the different forms are then likely to influence one another. In Jamaica, for example, an English-based creole exists alongside Standard English, and their mutual influence during the past three centuries has led to a whole spectrum of usage, a 'post-creole continuum'. Speakers often vary their speech according to the social context and the effect they wish to have, moving towards the standard ('acrolectal') end or towards the creole ('basilectal') end of the continuum. There is a tendency for more educated speakers and those of higher socio-economic groups to use the standard end of the spectrum, but this is not invariably the case, since there are countervailing forces: creole expressions can be used to proclaim ethnic identity or membership of an in-group, or to suggest informality and sincerity, and are also often used for humour and in songs.

In West Africa, similarly, pidgins exist alongside Standard English, and switching from standard to pidgin, or inserting pidgin expressions into standard speech, can have social motivation. This code-mixing or code-switching is depicted in the novels of Chinua Achebe. In *A Man of the People* (1966), the charismatic demagogue Nanga speaks both English and Nigerian Pidgin English (NPE). He uses English for formal occasions, and adjusts his speech in accordance with his hearer. He uses NPE to address lower-class characters (a chauffeur, a cook), and when he is being jocular with his friends and colleagues, or when he wants to project his image as a 'man of the people'. Mrs Nanga, however, never speaks English, but only her local language (represented in the text by Standard English), with a sprinkling of English words interspersed. Odili, the schoolteacher-narrator, uses all three languages: he uses pidgin to talk to a girlfriend who speaks a different local language, to address lower-class characters, and in informal conversation with friends, often jocular.

The development of so many varieties of English has produced problems and controversies about the language, especially in former British colonies which became independent in the second half of the twentieth century. During British colonial rule, Standard British English was the language of administration, and local departures from it were stigmatized as errors. With independence, there have been disputes in many such countries as to whether English should be retained as an official language at all, and, if it is retained, whether attempts should be made to teach Standard British English or whether the local variety of English should be adopted as a standard. Various factors have played a part in these arguments – including nationalist feeling, attachment to traditional culture, desire for advances in science and technology, and the conflicting needs for local and for international communication – but there are many cross-currents. In India, after independence, there was a movement in the Hindi-speaking north in favour of making Hindi the main official language of the country, but this was opposed by many people in the south who spoke Dravidian languages: having Hindi as the main language would give obvious economic and political advantages to northerners, and many southerners therefore favoured the retention of English.

In some former colonies, a mastery of English was the privilege of a dominant elite, who therefore supported its retention, while more radical and democratic forces argued for its replacement by one or more local languages. Many of the controversies, inevitably, have been fought out in the field of educational policy. They still go on, but there seems, at the moment, to be a trend in many countries towards continuing to accept English as an official or semi-official language. Interestingly, some of the most compelling literature in the English language in the second half of the twentieth century has come from ex-colonial areas where these arguments have gone on – for example, in East Africa the poetry of Okot p'Bitek and the novels of Ngugi wa Thiong'o, in West Africa the plays and poetry of Wole Soyinka and the novels of Chinua Achebe.

Given the numerous varieties of English in the world today, it is obviously impossible to do more than give a few examples of the differences between them. These can be considered under the headings of Phonology, Grammar and Vocabulary. Pidgins and creoles, however, will be considered separately, since they are so different from the standard varieties of English.

Phonology

Different varieties of English can differ phonologically in three main ways. First, their phonological systems can differ: for example, the inventory of phonemes may be different. Secondly, the realizations of the same phoneme can be different, that is, be pronounced differently. Thirdly, the distribution of phonemes can differ, that is, different phonemes may be selected for the pronunciation of a given word. To this can be added differences of stress and intonation.

Phonology: North America

The English of North America was separated from British English rather early, and has a somewhat different system. To some extent this results from the fact that most North American speech is rhotic, that is, /r/ is pronounced before a consonant or a pause, whereas in RP it is not pronounced in these positions. Not all North American English is rhotic: in the USA, the speech of the coastal south, of eastern New England, and the traditional dialect of New York City is to a considerable extent non-rhotic, as is African American Vernacular English (AAVE). The speech of the vast majority of Americans and Canadians, however, is rhotic, and one consequence of this is that the centring diphthongs /ɪə/, /ɛə/ and /ʊə/ do not exist in their system. For conservative RP speakers, and speakers of some other dialects of British English, the words *here, scarce* and *poor* are /hɪə/, /skɛəs/ and /pʊə/, but in General American they are /hɪr/, /skɛrs/ and /pʊr/. American speakers may indeed pronounce a diphthong such as [ʊə] as an allophone before /r/, giving a pronunciation [pʊər], but their inventory of phonemes contains no /ʊə/. In addition, RP has two phonemes, /ɒ/ and /ɑː/, where General American has only one, namely /ɑ/: so *dog* and *father* are RP /dɒg/, /ˈfɑːðə/, but General American /dɑg/, /ˈfɑðər/. There are, however, regional variations in America, with slightly different inventories of vowel-phonemes in different areas. For example, for some speakers there is no distinction between /ɑ/ and /ɔ/, so that the same vowel (usually [ɑ] or [ɒ]) is used in *cot* and in *caught*. This is characteristic of much speech in the north-west of the USA, and also in Canada. In much of the southern USA, there is no contrast between /ɛ/ and /ɪ/ before nasal consonants, so that *pin* and *pen* sound the same. The consonant systems of RP and North American English are identical in that they share the same repertoire of phonemes, though a minority of US and Canadian speakers distinguish /ʍ/ from /w/ in *which* and *witch*.

North American English also differs from RP in the realization of many phonemes, especially vowels. In General American, as we have seen, differences of vowel-length play a smaller part than in RP, and length-marks are not normally used in phonemic transcriptions. A difference in consonant realization concerns /t/ and /d/. When /t/ is intervocalic, in words like *pretty* and *letter*, Americans usually make the /t/ with a single rapid tap of the tongue, and frequently also voice it, so that to British ears it sounds like /d/. Many Americans also produce intervocalic /d/ with a single rapid tap, and if they voice their /t/ it does indeed become identical with their /d/, so that *latter* and *ladder* are homophones. The tap realization can also be used when a sonorant consonant rather than a vowel precedes the /t/ or /d/, as in *dirty* (where most Americans pronounce the *r*) and *kinder*. It is also used when the following vowel is at the beginning of the next word, in phrases like *get it*. On the other hand, the glottal and glottalized realizations of /t/ that are increasingly found in many varieties of British English, and even in the speech of younger RP speakers, are not found in General American and are rare in North American varieties.

Canadian English closely resembles General American English in pronunciation, but there is one distinctive difference of vowel realization. The phonemes /aɪ/ and /aʊ/ have the allophones [əi] and [əʊ] when they occur before a voiceless consonant. So while a Canadian pronounces *ride* and *loud* as [raɪd] and [lɑʊd], *write* and *lout* by contrast are [rəit] and [ləʊt]. Another feature of Canadian English concerns the lateral consonant /l/. In RP, there are two main allophones of /l/. 'Clear [1]' has a front kind of vowel resonance, and is used before vowels and before /j/, as in *look* and *million*. Elsewhere, as in *old* and *mill*, RP uses 'dark [l]', which has a back kind of vowel resonance, the tongue being raised towards the position used for [ʊ]. Canadian English, on the other hand, uses 'dark [l]' in all positions. American English has both clear and dark allophones, but their distribution differs from that of RP, since in General American 'dark [l]' is used in intervocalic position, in words like *Billy* and *yellow*.

The third kind of phonological difference, that of distribution in individual lexical items, often results from regular sound laws: a sound law may operate in one variety of English, but not in another, because the two varieties had already branched off from one another before the sound law operated. An example is the distribution of the phonemes /æ/ and /ɑ:/. In England, the phoneme /ɑ:/ arose in the seventeenth century, from three main sources: (1) the lengthening of ME *a* before voiceless fricatives (*staff, ask, bath*). (2) The lengthening of ME *a* before preconsonantal and, later, final /r/, and the subsequent loss of this /r/ (*barn, far*). (3) An originally non-standard development of the ME diphthong *au* (*aunt, dance, example*). This third group consists mainly of ME loans from French, in which ME *a* before nasals became ME *au* in some varieties of English, but remained *a* in others. In the eighteenth century, some forms in which the *au* had developed into [a:] entered the standard language.

American English branched off from British English too early to be affected by the lengthening before voiceless fricatives, so that General American has the same vowel in *ask* as in *hat* (/ask/, /hat/), whereas in RP the vowels are different (/ɑːsk/, /hæt/ or /hat/). The same difference between RP and General American is found in the words with variant developments of ME *a* before nasals: so *dance* is RP /dɑːns/ but American /dans/. The variety of English taken to North America was clearly one in which ME *a* had remained before nasals, and had not changed to *au*. On the other hand, ME *a* was affected by a following /r/ in American English, so that it agrees with RP in having different vowels in *hat* and *far*: RP /hæt/ or /hat/, /fɑː/, General American /hat/, /fɑr/.

Phonology: southern hemisphere

The phonological systems of Australian, New Zealand and South African English are virtually the same as that of RP, though in New Zealand there is one phoneme fewer, since /ɪ/ and /ə/ have merged, so that words like *pin* have the same vowel as the first syllable of *about*; the realization of this New Zealand phoneme is a rather close central vowel. In South African English, both /ɪ/ and /ə/ occur, but their distribution is different from that in RP: some words, especially those like *kit* in which a velar consonant precedes or follows the vowel, have /ɪ/, whilst others, like *bit*, *split*, have /ə/.

Australian English has the same inventory of phonemes as RP, but nearly all the vowels are realized differently. For example, /æ/ and /e/ are closer than in RP, so that to English ears Australian *pan* sounds like *pen*, and the /ɑː/ phoneme, in words like *park* and *path*, is realized as a front [aː] (as against the more backed [ɑː] of RP). New Zealand pronunciation is very similar to Australian, but with minor differences: for example, as we have noted above, the /ɪ/ phoneme, as in *pin*, is realized in a very retracted position, while the /e/ phoneme, as in *pen*, is very close, almost [ɪ], so that to English ears New Zealand *pen* can sound like *pin*. Some speakers diphthongize the vowel to [ɪə], or even [iə], especially after /j/: the pronunciation of the word *yes* as [jiəs], with a very close vowel and with diphthongization, is a good shibboleth for distinguishing a New Zealander from an Australian. In both Australian and New

Zealand pronunciation, the /ɜː/ phoneme, as in *turn*, is realized in a closer and more forward position than in RP, in other words nearer to [eː], and in New Zealand, moreover, it is given lip-rounding, so that it is quite similar to the [ø:] heard in such French words as *feu* 'fire'. South African English, like Australian and New Zealand English, has a closer realization than RP for the /æ/ and /e/ vowels, and a fronted and rounded realization of /ɜː/. On the other hand, its realization of the /ɑː/ phoneme, as in *park* and *path*, is a backward [ɑː], as in RP, which in broader South African speech may be rounded to [ɒː]. In broad South African, the /ɪə/ and /ɛə/ phonemes are often realized as the pure vowel [eː], so that *fear* and *fair* are both [feː]. Among the consonants, South Africans tend to realize /r/ as a single tap, rather than as an approximant as in RP, and to produce the voiceless plosives (/p/, /t/, /k/) without aspiration.

Southern hemisphere English and RP also have some differences in the distribution of phonemes in lexical items, but the differences are less great than those between RP and North American English. In Australia and New Zealand, British settlement did not begin until the end of the eighteenth century and beginning of the nineteenth century respectively. It is not surprising therefore that Antipodean English agrees with RP in using the /ɑː/ phoneme in words both of the *ask* type and of the *far* type, since, by the end of the eighteenth century, when English speakers began to settle in Australia, the /ɑː/ phoneme was being used in the south of England, where many of the first settlers came from. Most New Zealanders also use /ɑː/ in words like *aunt* and *dance*, but most Australians on the contrary use /æ/.

In unstressed syllables in which the vowel is non-final, RP has a contrast between /ɪ/ and /ə/: *offices* /ˈɒfɪsɪz/ differs from *officers* /ˈɒfɪsəz/. In most Australian speech, however, only /ə/ is used in such positions, so that *offices* and *officers* are homophones, and /ə/ is the vowel of the unstressed syllable in such words as *naked*, *rabbit*, *village* and *waited*, where RP has /ɪ/. This Australian feature is shared by most New Zealand and South African English. One result of Australian usage is that sometimes Australians make a distinction while RP does not: in RP, the words *taxes* and *taxis* are both /ˈtæksɪz/, whereas in Australian English the first is /ˈtæksəz/ while the second is /ˈtæksiːz/.

Phonology: West Indies

In the West Indies, the phonological systems of local Standard English vary somewhat from island to island. To some extent this is because some have rhotic speech (for example, Barbados) and some non-rhotic speech (for example, Trinidad), while yet others fluctuate (for example, Jamaica). Even the non-rhotic systems, however, may differ somewhat from RP: in Trinidad, for example, the standard language has only one phoneme corresponding to RP /ɪə/ and /ɛə/, so that *beer* and *bare* are homophones, being pronounced [beə]. Like many other Caribbean varieties, Trinidadian English also lacks a phoneme /ə/: in positions where RP has this unstressed vowel, it uses either [i] or [a]. West Indian English also differs from RP and General American in its intonation patterns, and by a tendency to accent syllables by means of pitch rather than stress.

Phonology: outer-circle varieties of English

Outer-circle varieties of English often differ considerably in phonological system from RP and General American. The number of phonemes is often much reduced. In many varieties of English in the outer circle, there is no difference between long and short vowels. In one common form of Nigerian English, for example, there is only one phoneme corresponding to RP /ɪ/ and /iː/, so that *bid* and *bead* are both /bid/; only one corresponding to /æ/ and /ɑː/, so that *hat* and *heart* are both /hat/; only one corresponding to /ɒ/, /ʌ/ and /ɔː/, so that *stock, stuck* and *stork* are all /stɔk/; and only one corresponding to RP /ʊ/ and /uː/, so that *look* and *Luke* are both /luk/. Moreover, there is no /ə/ phoneme, /a/ most often being used instead, so that *singer* is pronounced ['sɪŋ'ga], whereas in RP it is /'sɪŋə/. Nor is there a phoneme corresponding to RP /ɜː/, the vowel used often depending on the spelling: *work*, for example, is /wɔk/, a homophone of *walk*. There are perhaps no diphthongs, speakers tending to replace them by a sequence of two vowels: the word *ear*, for example, is [i-a], pronounced as two syllables. Even more striking, perhaps, is that Nigerian English can be described as 'syllable-timed', not (like RP and General American) 'stress-timed': in other words, all the syllables in a phrase seemingly occur at equal intervals, not just the stressed syllables.

Reduction in the number of vowel-phonemes is characteristic of most varieties of African English. Elsewhere, English as a second language tends to be nearer to RP in its phoneme system, though with local variations: in some parts of India, for example, 'broad' speakers of Indian English make no distinction between /v/ and /w/. But, as in Nigeria, a widespread characteristic of outer-circle varieties of English is the use of syllable-timing instead of stress-timing, usually accompanied by a tendency to mark syllable-accent by pitch rather than stress. Commonly, too, there is no use of intonation for contrastive stress, that is, to pick out a particular word in the sentence for emphasis. This tendency to syllable-timing is commonly found in the English spoken in South Asia, Singapore and Malaysia, and sub-Saharan Africa.

In outer-circle varieties of English, the phonemes have a wide range of different realizations. As for the distribution of phonemes, there is a tendency to use spelling-pronunciations, and especially to use other vowels suggested by the spelling where RP would have unstressed /ɪ/ and /ə/. In both Indian English and Nigerian English, suffixes like *-able* and *-ence* are often given full vowels, as are unstressed words like *to* and *of*. There are many differences of stress: often, the stress is moved away from the first syllable, as in the Nigerian pronunciation of *petrol*, stressed on the second syllable, but the opposite process is seen in some Indian pronunciations, such as *defence* and *mistake* with first-syllable stress. Analogy may also operate to cause pronunciation-variants: in Nigeria, the word *maintenance* has become *maintainance*, under the influence of the verb, and is stressed on the second syllable. (Of course, this happens in the speech of many 'inner-circle' speakers too: many British English speakers both pronounce and spell *pronunciation* as *pronounciation*, for example.) There is also a tendency in such forms of English for consonant-clusters to be simplified: in Nigeria, final clusters are often reduced, /-st/ for example becoming /-s/ (for example, in *west, passed*), whereas on the contrary the influence of the spelling causes final /-mb/ to be pronounced in words such as *bomb* and *climb*. Many speakers in northern India do not use word-initial /sp/, /st/or /sk/, instead inserting /ɪ/ or /e/ before the cluster, so that *student* becomes /ɪˈstuːdent/ or /eˈstuːdent/, and similarly with *speak* and *school*.

Phonology: stress and intonation

Different varieties of English also differ in patterns of stress and intonation. We have already seen that English as a second language is very often syllable-timed instead of stress-timed, lacks the use of contrastive stress, and tends to use pitch rather than stress to mark syllable-accent, features that are to some extent shared by West Indian English. But there are also differences between the standard stress-timed varieties of the language. RP uses fewer stressed syllables: where an RP speaker gives a word one heavy stress and several weak ones, an American or an Australian often gives it a secondary stress on one of the weak syllables. For example, words ending in *-ary*, like *customary* and *military*, have only one stress in RP, but in North America and Australia are normally given a secondary stress on the *a* of *-ary*, which therefore has a full vowel (whereas in RP it is either /ə/ or is lost completely). In addition, more words in a sentence may be stressed than in RP. An example (given by A. G. Mitchell) is the sentence *Thank you very much*, in which an RP speaker usually stresses only *Thank* and *much*, while an Australian also stresses *very*. The use of more stresses means that an utterance moves more slowly, and Australian speech in particular sounds very slow-moving to RP speakers. Some regional English speech shares in this propensity to stress more syllables, and so also moves more slowly than RP. For example, in northern England the word *industry*, which in RP is stressed only on the first syllable, is often also given a stress on the second, while words like *distributive*, which in RP have a single stress on the second syllable, may instead be stressed on the first and the third.

Grammar

There are only minor grammatical differences between the main standard forms of English. American English differs from British English, but the differences are minor. Among past tenses of verbs, some American English has the forms *dove, fit* and *snuck* (British *dived, fitted, sneaked*), and in a number of forms uses /-d/ where British English has /-t/ (for example, *burned, learned, spelled, spilled*), though the forms with /-d/ are increasingly found in British English.

In some verbs of this latter type, British English changes the stem-vowel from /iː/ to /e/ in the past tense, whereas in American English it remains /i/ (such as *dreamed, kneeled, leaped*). An American often uses *do have* where a Briton is more likely to use *have got* ('Do you have the time?', 'Have you got the time?'). Traditionally, *do have* has also been used in Britain, but has been restricted to certain contexts, especially to refer to habitual action ('Do you have dances in your village-hall?'). In recent years, the more extended American usage has been spreading to the UK. American English has two different past participles for the verb *to get*, namely *got* and *gotten*, where Standard British English has only the first. Formerly, American *I have got* meant 'I have', while *I have gotten* was restricted to 'I have obtained', but in recent years *gotten* has come to be used in a wider range of contexts. Prepositions, too, are sometimes used differently: in Britain people tend to live *in* Sunset Avenue, whereas an American usually lives *on* it, and British people tend to cater *for* people, while Americans cater *to* them. There are often also different preferences in the choice of auxiliaries. But, while examples of this kind could be multiplied, they are minor things: in all essentials, British and American grammar are the same. Even where differences exist, British speakers and writers are increasingly using the American variants instead of or alongside the British ones.

In the West Indies, where there is a creole–English continuum, there is a tendency for creole grammatical features to occur sporadically even in educated speech, especially when it is informal. Such features include the omission of many inflections (especially the plural and possessive markings of nouns and the third-person singular and past-tense markings of verbs) and the omission of *is* and other parts of the verb *to be*.

In countries where English is a second language, similar differences from British and American grammar are even commoner. A feature frequently found is the sporadic omission of the verb *to be* (for example, in East Africa, Ghana, India and the Philippines), giving sentences such as *We waiting for the flight*. In some varieties there is sporadic omission of the definite and indefinite article (as in West Africa, Singapore), and of the noun- and verb-inflections (as in Singapore). A number of features are found in both India and Nigeria. These include the use of the progressive verb-tenses where

British speakers use unmarked forms ('He is going to his office every morning', 'I am having a cold'), plural forms of nouns which in British English are uncountables (*furnitures, litters* 'rubbish'), and the use of *isn't it?* as a universal tag-question ('She is living here, isn't it?', 'We should wait for him, isn't it?'). This last usage, which resembles French *n'est-ce pas?*, is also common among Welsh speakers, and, in the form *innit*, is becoming increasingly common amongst younger speakers in the UK, possibly as a result of Indian English influence in multicultural communities.

Vocabulary

It is perhaps in vocabulary that we see the greatest divergences between the different varieties of English as a first language. Expanding across the vast North American continent, with new flora and fauna and different natural features from those of Europe, building up a new society, with its own political institutions, its own social customs, its own recreations, its various ways of earning a living, the Americans were impelled to adapt old words or invent new ones to meet their many needs. The very names for topographical features evoke a specifically American atmosphere, and words like *bluff, creek* (in the sense of 'stream' rather than 'inlet'), and *gulch*, seem as much out of place east of the Atlantic as *coomb, fen, heath* and *moor* do west of it. In the southern hemisphere, similarly, the English-speaking communities developed their lexicon to meet the needs of a new society and new environment. Subsequently, many of the new words have been exported to the UK and to other English-speaking countries.

One common way of forming this new vocabulary has been by loans from other languages. In North America, the first contacts of the settlers were with the Native Americans, and a few words were borrowed from them, especially in the seventeenth century. Many of these words were shortened and simplified by the borrowers: *pawcohiccora* was borrowed as *hickory*, and *segankw* became *skunk*. Occasionally, the word was altered to give it English elements with a meaning of their own, as when *wuchak* was borrowed as *woodchuck* (a process known as 'popular etymology'). Like these three words, many of the loans are the names of

American flora and fauna, such as *sequoia* and *terrapin* (though the former was originally a Cherokee personal name). Others were for words connected with Native American culture, like *totem, wampum* and *wigwam*. The word *powwow* originally meant 'medicine-man, sorcerer', and passed through a series of meaning-changes before reaching its present one of '(informal) conference, consultation'. Among other words borrowed are some in the sphere of politics, like *caucus* and *Tammany*. Some American place-names and river-names are also Native American: *Mississippi* means 'big river', and *Chicago* perhaps means 'place of wild onions'.

Similar loans from local languages are found in the southern hemisphere: for example, Australian *billabong, dingo* and *woomera* (from Aboriginal languages), New Zealand *pakeha* 'white person' and *puckeroo* 'broken, useless' (from Maori) and South African *impi* 'a body of Bantu warriors' (from Zulu).

Since the British were not the only nation engaged in colonization, there were also loans made locally from other European languages, especially in North America. The Americans borrowed several hundred words from the Spaniards, who had very early established permanent settlements in the New World, borrowings being especially common in the south-west of the United States. Many of the loans go back to the seventeenth century, though there are also a large number from the nineteenth. Some of them are topographical, like *canyon* and *sierra*, or words for flora and fauna, like *alfalfa, armadillo* and *cockroach* (adapted by popular etymology from *cucaracha*). A considerable number come from ranch life, like *bronco, corral, lasso, mustang, ranch* and *stampede*, with which we can perhaps group words for clothing like *poncho* and *sombrero* (though the latter had already been borrowed into metropolitan English in the sixteenth century with a different meaning, 'oriental umbrella or parasol'). Another interest of the Spanish settlers, mining, is reflected in such loans as *bonanza* and *placer* 'deposit in a stream-bed'. Miscellaneous loans include *filibuster, hombre, pronto, stevedore, vamoose* and *vigilante*.

In the northern part of North America, there was contact right from the beginning with the French, and a number of words were borrowed from them, especially in the eighteenth century. They again include topographical words, like *prairie* and *rapids*, and flora and fauna, like *pumpkin* and perhaps *gopher*. This last word may be from French *gaufre* 'honeycomb', borrowed as the name of a small rodent because of its honeycomb of burrows. There were also some borrowings from the Dutch settlers in North America, who were centred on New Amsterdam (which in 1644 was taken by the British and became New York). The loans include food names (*cookie*, *waffle*), miscellaneous words (*boodle*, *boss*, *dope*, *snoop*) and possibly *Yankee*, which may be a diminutive of Dutch *Jan* 'John', and so a patronizing name given by the Dutch to the British settlers in New England. Later, in the nineteenth and twentieth centuries, large numbers of immigrants of many nationalities entered the United States, but their contribution to the American vocabulary is remarkably small, because the languages of the immigrants had low prestige, and they were usually anxious to Americanize them-selves as quickly as possible. The largest number of loans are from German, for the German influx in the nineteenth century was mas-sive, and there is still a German-speaking population in the United States. The borrowings include food names like *delicatessen*, educa-tional terms like *semester* and *seminar*, and a number of miscellan-eous words like *loafer* and *nix*.

The Australians and New Zealanders lacked any such regular con-tact with other European languages, but in South Africa there have been borrowings from Afrikaans, the South African form of Dutch. These include *apartheid* 'racial segregation', *dorp* 'small town', *kraal* 'village', and *veld* (earlier *veldt*) 'open country'. This last word is cog-nate with English *field*, while *kraal* is cognate with *corral*, which we have already encountered as a Spanish loan into American English. The Afrikaans word was a borrowing from Portuguese *corral* and *curral*, and the Spanish and Portuguese words had themselves been borrowed from a Khoisan language of south-west Africa.

Many of the new words, however, are not loans, but have been created by the normal processes of word-formation – affixation, compounding, shortening, back-formation – often with different results in different countries. So there are Australian compounds like *outback*, *stockman* and *tuckerbox*, and American ones like *bull-frog* and *groundhog*. Some such coinages are for objects peculiar to the new country, but sometimes, inevitably, different words have been coined for the same thing. So while a Briton puts rubbish in the dustbin for collection by the dustman, an American is likely to put trash or garbage in the trash- or garbage-can for collection by the trashman or garbage-collector. And whereas a Briton puts petrol in the car and drives on the motorway, an American will put in gas and drive on the freeway. Alternatively, the Briton may travel by tram or by railway, while the American travels by streetcar or by railroad. Moreover, existing English words were sometimes given new meanings in the new environment, like Australian *bush* 'woodland, rural areas', *wattle* 'acacia' and *paddock* (used for any piece of fenced land, whatever its size). In America, similarly, the word *robin* was applied to a bird of the thrush family, which happens to have a red breast. Occasionally, a word which was lost in England was retained elsewhere, like Australian *fossick* 'rummage, seek around', *larrikin* (at one time 'hooligan', now rather 'a bit of a lad') and perhaps *wowser* 'fanatical puritan'. In some cases earlier forms of English had alternative words, one of which has been retained in Britain and the other elsewhere. The words *autumn* (a fourteenth-century loan from French) and *fall* (*of the leaf*) (recorded from the mid-sixteenth century) both existed in Shakespeare's time with the same meaning, but one is now the normal form in Britain and the other in America.

In countries where English is spoken as a second language, new words are often introduced from the local languages, and existing English words and phrases given new meanings. Many such words are found in the countries of the Indian subcontinent. From the closely related Hindi and Urdu, the main languages of the northern part of the Indian subcontinent, have come such words as *dhobi* 'washerman', *dhoti* 'loin-cloth' and *lathi* 'long heavy stick', *almirah* 'cupboard, cabinet' (this word came to India from Portuguese), *jawan* 'soldier', *ryot* 'peasant', *sahib* 'sir, master' and *tank* 'pool, reservoir'. New words may be coined from existing English elements, like *co-brother* 'wife's sister's husband' and *tiffin* 'lunch' (perhaps from the slang word *tiff* 'to sip'), or formed by conversion, like *extern* 'to banish' (from the noun or adjective). Existing English words may be given new meanings, like *backside* 'at the back of' and *demit* 'to resign', and words or meanings which have gone out of use in the UK may still survive, like *stepney* 'spare wheel' and *stir* 'public disturbance, demonstration'.

In sub-Saharan Africa, what is striking is not the borrowing or coining of new words, but rather the development of new meanings, the survival of usages which are now old-fashioned in the UK, and the formation of whole new phrases. So, in Nigeria, your Yoruba friend Titi may stop and offer you a lift in her *motor* by saying *Enter!* 'Get in!', whereupon you may find it necessary to say to the other passengers *Dress!* 'Move over!' Titi tells you that she is *very much eager* to introduce you to another Nigerian – *He's bearing Tunji* 'His name is Tunji'. Tunji, she tells you, is *a worker*. You ask whether that simply means that Tunji has a job, and Titi replies *In fact!* 'That's right.' Tunji, she says, is one of those people who *try their possible best* 'do their utmost' in everything. When you get out of the car, you slip and fall on the road, and Titi says *Sorry!* – which is not an apology, but an expression of condolence or sympathy. To help you to recover, she suggests that you might like *a hot drink*, which doesn't mean tea or coffee, but whisky or something similarly spirituous, also known as a [ʃɔt] (a 'short' or a 'shot'). Some months later, when you are back home, Titi sends you a letter, beginning *I am very worried to read from you* 'I'm extremely anxious to hear from you.'

Pidgins and creoles

There are numerous pidgins and creoles in the world today, probably well over two hundred. They are based on many different languages, including Swahili, Arabic, Malay and Japanese, as well as on many European languages. Pidgins and creoles, however, are hybrid language systems, and the 'donor language' is not the only source, though it is the dominant one.

A particularly large number are based on English: there are about forty areas where so-called 'English-based' pidgins and creoles are spoken, and in some of these areas several different varieties exist. They fall into two main groups, the Atlantic and the Pacific. The Atlantic varieties include those of the Caribbean, of Guyana and of West Africa (the Gambia, Sierra Leone, Liberia, Ghana, Nigeria, Cameroon), and the Pacific varieties those of the South Sea islands, of Australia, and of the coasts of South-East Asia.

The distinction between pidgins and creoles is not a sharp one, for sometimes a variety is used by some groups as an auxiliary language and by others as a first language. This is particularly true in West Africa, where the co-existence of more than four hundred different languages means that pidgins are especially useful. Even when used as an auxiliary language, a pidgin can fulfil a wide range of functions: in West Africa, English-based pidgins are used for all normal language functions, alongside Standard English and the local languages, and some speakers use a pidgin more frequently than their native language. In this situation, the pidgin remains under the influence of the standard language, and will tend to evolve towards it. If, however, the pidgin loses contact with the donor-language, as happened with the English-based creoles of Surinam, it may evolve away from it, though perhaps retaining archaic features which have been lost by the donor language.

In English-based pidgins, the main features taken over into the pidgin are lexical: the new language system draws on English for vocabulary, but only minimally for phonology, and hardly at all for grammar. Indeed, what is striking is that the various pidgins in the world often resemble one another in structure much more than they resemble the dominant languages from which they are derived. A pidgin tends to preserve the absolutely minimal grammatical structures needed for effective communication, and reduces redundancy to almost nil. One result of this typically pidgin structure is that an English-based pidgin is generally not considered to be a dialect of English, but to be a different language in its own right, though there is an area of overlap: in Jamaica, with its continuum of usage from creole to Standard English, the intermediate varieties ('mesolects') probably *are* to be thought of as dialects of English.

The great simplification of pidgin–creole structures as compared with the donor language is seen in both phonology and grammar. The number of phonemes is usually reduced: for example, in Jamaican Creole many speakers use the same vowel in *block* as in *black* (both [blak]), the same vowel in *beer* as in *bare* (both [biɛr]), the same vowel in *pour* as in *poor* (both [po:r]), the same vowel [a:] in *caught*, *cross*, *farm* and *form*, and the same vowel in both syllables of *matter* (which is ['mata]). Among the consonants, /θ/ and /ð/ are phonemes of a type rare outside English, and in pidgins and creoles they are commonly replaced by /t/ and /d/. Thus in Jamaican Creole *thin* is [tɪn] and *father* is ['fa:da]. There is also a tendency to simplify consonant-clusters: in Jamaican Creole, the final consonant is dropped from such words as *act*, *bend* and *left*. It is also common for /h/ to be lost, even in stressed syllables, so that *health* is [ɛlt].

The morphological system, similarly, is much simplified in pidgins and creoles. Both nouns and verbs commonly have only one form. There is thus no distinction in nouns between singular and plural: in West African pidgin, for example, 'one person' is *wan man*, 'ten persons' *ten man*, and 'many persons' *plenti man*. In verbs, the third-person inflection *-es* is missing, so that the same verb-form is used throughout the present tense: *a kari* or *mi kari* 'I carry', *yu kari* 'you carry', *i kari* 'he/she/it carries', etc. Since the verb has only one form, tenses and aspects are shown either by adverbs or by special particles placed before or after the verb: for example, in West African pidgin, *bin* can be placed before the verb to mark the past tense (*i bin kam* 'he came'), *don* to mark the perfect (*i don kam* 'he has come') and *go* to mark the future (*i go kam* 'he will come'). There is usually a simplification of the pronoun system: a single form like *i* is often found for *he*, *she* and *it*. Often there is a single form for the nominative and accusative of the pronoun and also for the pronoun-determiner: so *wi* may mean 'we', 'us' and 'our', and *dem* may mean 'they', 'them' and 'their'. On the other hand, many pidgins make a pronoun-distinction not found in Standard English, by having separate forms for the second-person singular and second-person plural (just as many speakers of Irish English and several British English dialects distinguish between *you* and *yous*): in West African pidgin, *yu* is 'you (singular)' and *una* or *wuna* 'you (plural)'. Negation is achieved without the use of auxiliary *do*, some such particle as *no* being used instead, as in *wi no sabi* 'we don't know'. Interrogation is also achieved without auxiliary *do* and without change of word-order, simply by intonation: *yu get plet?* 'have you got a plate?' It will be seen that pidgins are extreme forms of analytic languages: they mostly lack inflections, and rely on free morphemes to indicate grammatical relations. For this reason, word-order is of great importance, and is strictly adhered to.

English-based pidgins and creoles may draw most of their vocabulary from English, but they make changes to it. Words are often used with new meanings, like West African *chop* 'to eat' and *bif* 'animal, meat'. Conversion is common, the same word often being used as noun, verb and adjective. New compounds are formed: for example, *die* and *man* are combined as *daiman* 'corpse', a form found in both Atlantic and Pacific pidgins. A common device is reduplication or repetition: in Jamaican Creole, *smal* means 'small', and *smalsmal* means 'very small'. As could be expected from their origins, all English-based pidgins have a nautical element in their vocabulary, but again with new meanings: for example, from *heave* come forms meaning 'push, lift', from *capsize* forms meaning 'overturn, spill', and in Cameroon is found a word from *man-of-war* meaning 'wasp'. Inevitably, a few words also come into pidgins from the local languages, like West African *akara* 'kind of pancake', from Yoruba. In addition, all English-based pidgins seem to have words derived from Portuguese, especially *saber* 'to know' and *pequeno* 'small, little', the latter often producing a word meaning 'child'. The Portuguese were among the earliest European explorers and colonizers, and it has been suggested that many English-based pidgins were originally Portuguese-based, and were 'relexified' when English presence and influence replaced Portuguese.

As an example of pidgin, let us look at a short piece of Nigerian pidgin, recorded in Port Harcourt by Dr Loreto Todd in 1985. It is an Igbo speaker's translation of the end of the parable of the Prodigal Son (Luke XV.31–2), and you may find it interesting to compare it with other versions of the same passage which we have looked at earlier (pp. 32–6 above).

> Di papa bin tɔk sei: 'Ma pikin, yu sabi sei yu dei wit mi eni dei eni dei, an ɔl ting wei a gɛtam na yu on. Bɔt i gud mek wi hapi, bikɔs dis yu brɔda bin dɔn dai an i dɔn wikɔp fɔ dai agɛn; i bin dɔn lɔs an wi bin luk i agɛn.'

This is given in a 'semi-phonetic' transcription, often used for this purpose, in which the vowel-symbols are phonetic but the consonant symbols correspond to English spelling. In the passage, *bin tɔk sei* means 'said', *bin* being the past-tense marker and *sei* a particle which follows verbs of saying and thinking. Then come the two common words derived from Portuguese, *pikin* 'child' and *sabi* 'know', followed by *sei yu dei wit mi* 'that you are with me' (in which *sei* is rather like the conjunction 'that', while *dei* is one of the words corresponding to the verb 'to be'). The phrase *eni dei* means 'every day', and when reduplicated, as here, means 'always'. The word *wei* is a relative, meaning 'who, which, that', but in addition *-am* 'it, him, her, them' is added to the verb *gɛt* 'have', the whole phrase meaning 'everything that I have'. Another word for the verb 'to be' is *na*, and *na yu on* means 'is your own'. No distinction is made between 'you' and 'your', as is also seen in *dis you brɔda* 'this your brother'. In *bin dɔn dai*, both the past-tense and the perfect-tense markers are used, so that it means 'had died', but the perfect marker alone is used in *i dɔn wikɔp* 'he has returned (woken up)'. The same word is used for *die* and *death*, so that *fɔ dai* means 'from death'. Pidgin tends to use only a small number of prepositions, and the two commonest ones in Nigerian pidgin both occur in the passage, *wit* and *fɔ*.

Standard English

There have always been different varieties of English, and, as the language has spread across the world over the last four hundred years, many more have arisen. The pidgins and creoles that have developed from English are so different that they can be thought of as separate languages rather than varieties of English. But we are still left with a wide range of varieties of English used as a first or second language.

Fortunately there is a solid core of common usage which makes it possible to talk of 'standard world English'. Regional variations are especially marked in the spoken language, many of them being a matter of accent, and are greatest in informal speech. There is also a tendency for regional differences to be smaller in the usage of speakers belonging to higher social classes. But if we examine the more formal uses of language, and especially if we confine ourselves to a formal style of *written* language, the differences become small. In formal writing, the essential structure of the language is practically the same throughout the English-speaking world; the differences in vocabulary are perceptible but not enormous; and the differences in spelling negligible. There is, therefore, a standard written variety which is very much the same throughout the English-speaking community, and it is this, if anything, which deserves to be called Standard English.

11 English today and tomorrow

In the English language today we can see both centrifugal and centripetal tendencies. On the one hand, as we saw in the previous chapter, a range of 'national' varieties of English has emerged. In 'inner-circle' countries like Australia and New Zealand, RP was the prestigious accent in the first half of the twentieth century, but by the end of that century endogenous standards of pronunciation had taken over. On the other hand, processes of levelling and diffusion are respectively reducing the local diversity of dialects within the UK and spreading certain linguistic features over a wide area, in some cases throughout much of the UK and in others throughout the 'inner circle'. This has been partly due to the great development of communications (aircraft, telegraph, telephone, the internet) and the rise of mass media (the popular press, the cinema, radio, television). The mutual influence between different national varieties of English shows itself especially in vocabulary. Many people are surprised to learn that some commonly used words are of American origin (chapter 10): words like *cockroach*, *loafer*, *stevedore* and *tornado* are so familiar that we do not think of them as Americanisms, and the same is true, or rapidly becoming true, of more recent importations like *blurb*, *cagey*, *gimmick* and *rugged* (in the sense of 'robust' as in 'rugged individual'). American slang and colloquial words are particularly appealing, like *hassle* 'quarrel, difficulty, fuss', *heist* 'hold-up, robbery', *hype* 'confidence-trick, swindle', *scam* 'ruse, swindle' and *to zap* 'attack suddenly, move quickly'. This kind of American lexical influence goes on constantly, but other varieties of English are increasingly influencing British English: from Australia, for example, we have imported *bush telegraph*, *uni* (for 'university') and many slang terms such as *chunder* ('vomit'), whilst New Zealand has given us terms for adventurous leisure pursuits, such as *zorbing*. In recent times, along with the 'globalization' apparent in the worldwide spread of companies, fast-food outlets, etc., a phenomenon of linguistic globalization has been noticed. Features which originate in one 'inner-circle' variety rapidly spread to others, where, because they are associated with the speech of young people, they have become a source of irritation to older, more conservative speakers. One example of this is the spread of the 'new quotatives': whereas older speakers, when telling a story, would introduce a quote by saying 'and I said …' or, more colloquially, 'and I went', younger people sometimes say 'and I'm like …', 'and I'm …' or, more recently 'and I'm all …'. This phenomenon was first noticed in the USA in the 1980s, where it was perceived as typical of the 'Valley Girl' speech attributed to affluent young women in California's 'Silicone Valley'. Through the 1990s it spread to Canada, the UK, Australia, New Zealand and South Africa, in all of which places it tended to be first used by young, middle-class women. Another feature which is heard in the speech of young people from a wide range of 'inner-circle' countries is what has been variously termed 'High Rising Tone', 'Australian Question Intonation' and 'Uptalk'. All these labels refer to a pattern of speech in which the final syllable(s) of a declarative utterance have the rising tone usually associated with questions. Although the first serious studies of this intonation pattern were conducted in Australia and New Zealand, and folk-linguistic statements attribute its spread in the UK to the popularity of Australian soap-operas such as *Neighbours*, it was also, like the 'new quotatives' noticed as a feature of 'Valley Girl' speech on the Pacific coast of the USA, from the 1980s. Both these features, rising intonation and the 'new quotatives', have become markers of 'youth' speech throughout the 'inner circle'. Their spread may be due to a combination of factors associated with global youth culture, including the media and electronic communication using social network sites.

Dialect levelling

A similar kind of process of convergence is going on inside Britain: the different dialects are being mixed and levelled. In addition to the influence of the mass media, there has been that of universal and compulsory education, dating from the last quarter of the nineteenth century, which has worked against the broader dialect elements, both regional and social. Moreover, the population has been more mobile: the small self-contained community has practically disappeared, there has been continuing migration to the larger towns and cities, and in two world wars there was mixing of men in enormous conscript armies. In 1948, very soon after the end of the Second World War, Harold Orton inaugurated the *Survey of English Dialects* as a last-gasp attempt to record the 'genuine, traditional' dialects of England before they were wiped out by the joint forces of compulsory education and communication. More recently, a great deal of attention has been paid, by both linguists and the media, to the phenomenon of 'dialect levelling'. This is a process whereby, over a large area, distinctive features of local dialect give way to more wide-ranging 'regional' ones. Social and demographic factors such as the creation of 'new towns' like Milton Keynes, relocation and commuting, have brought together speakers of different dialects. Mutual accommodation between these speakers has led to the loss of features associated with a particular location, and used by a minority of speakers in the 'new' community, in favour of those that are more widespread. Alongside this 'levelling' process, some linguistic features, mainly associated with the London area, have become widespread throughout the UK, especially in the speech of younger people. Like the 'global' features discussed in the previous section, these have been the source of much negative comment from older people. This process, whereby features spread from a specific point of origin over a wide area, is known as 'diffusion'. Examples of 'diffusing' features are glottalization, especially of medial and final /t/ and the use of /f/ and /v/ where RP would have /θ/ and /ð/ as in *yoof* for 'youth' and *bovvered* for 'bothered'. This does not mean, of course, that regional and social differences have disappeared: Manchester speech is still different from London speech, even if younger people in both places use glottal stops and say *bovvered*. In particular, speakers from the north of England sound different from those in the south and Midlands, and, of course, most educated speakers in Scotland, Wales and Ireland sound different from those in England. In each region, there is a speech-hierarchy, corresponding fairly closely to socio-economic class. The variations are not just a matter of accent, but also of grammar and vocabulary. The speech of the top of the hierarchy is closest to Standard English in grammar and vocabulary, and to RP in pronunciation. As you go down the hierarchy, the differences from standard usage become increasingly great. The degree of difference, however, is also influenced by sex, by age and by style: women diverge less from the standard than men of the same socio-economic group, and in all groups the difference is greatest in colloquial and informal style, and smallest in formal situations.

Two very common grammatical features in non-standard speech are the use of past participles as past-tense forms (*I seen him* 'I saw him', *they never done it* 'they didn't do it'), and the use of the same form for adjectives and adverbs (*the lads played real good* 'the boys played really well'). Standard speakers sometimes describe such usages as 'ungrammatical'. This, however, is not a good description. Non-standard speakers have as strict and complete a grammar as standard speakers, but it just happens to be a different one: in their grammar, for example, *seen* and *done* may be the regular past-tense forms of *see* and *do*. Indeed, these usages are very much what could be expected from the general development of the language. One intriguing possibility is that such non-standard usages could become standard: as young people's role-models increasingly become pop-stars and professional footballers, whose speech often comes from the lower socio-economic regions, the stigmatized usage of today may become the accepted usage of tomorrow. But here much depends on general social history, which we can't predict.

In the meantime, we still have in Britain variations of regional and social usage, but the general mixing and levelling effect means that the range of variations has been reduced, and the more idiosyncratic usages are disappearing. And all the varieties are undergoing constant change. In what follows, we shall try to point to some of the changes going on in our own lifetimes, and shall, of necessity, confine ourselves to the changes taking place in Britain (though many of them no doubt have parallels in the rest of the English-speaking world).

Received Pronunciation and regional accents

As we have seen, Received Pronunciation (RP), a non-regional accent based on the speech of the great public schools, has been accepted as a standard inside England for well over a century. Increasingly, however, RP has lost some of its prestige, as people educated at public schools have lost their monopoly of power and education. A considerable part has been played by the great post-war expansion of higher education. Today, the majority of university students are not speakers of RP, and it is from them that a large part of the English professional classes are recruited. Most schoolteachers, too, do not use RP, but an educated regional accent, so that the influence of the schools is towards this rather than towards RP.

This is not to say that RP has lost all its magic. Since it has been so fully described, it is the accent usually taught to foreigners learning British English. But the public schools are no longer felt to have a monopoly of 'correct speech', and the prestige of educated regional speech has risen enormously during the past half-century. Much has been written in the media about 'Estuary English', a variety used by educated speakers in the south-east of England and beyond, which incorporates the diffusing 'youth' features discussed above. It is the accent used, for example, by many radio and television announcers and presenters. On the other hand, there has been a rise in the prestige of *all* national and regional accents in Britain: some of the most respected broadcasters on the BBC, formerly a bastion of RP, now have educated Welsh and Scottish accents. There is still considerable prejudice against 'broad' regional accents, but what are popularly known as 'soft' accents are now in many contexts more acceptable than RP. There is consequently a tendency in present-day Britain to draw the boundaries of 'acceptable pronunciation', and indeed of 'Standard English' generally, rather wider than formerly, and to take into account the usages of a larger part of the population. Some of the changes that seem to be taking place in the language are therefore more apparent than real: they may be changes in acceptance, rather than actual substantive changes. What formerly existed as a usage in some group, but was considered non-standard, may now come to be accepted as standard, because of the changing definition of 'standard'. Christian Mair has noticed a phenomenon which he calls 'colloquialization', whereby features which had been associated with informal and/or spoken usage, such as contractions, are becoming acceptable in more 'formal' registers, and, conversely, 'formal' structures such as the passive, are being disfavoured. It does seem, however, that there are substantive changes going on, in pronunciation, in grammar and in vocabulary.

Changes in vocabulary

The expansion of the vocabulary seems to be going on at a great rate in our time. Many new words continue to be coined from Greek and Latin morphemes for use in science and technology, and some of these get into the general vocabulary, like *cosmonaut* and *stereophonic* (now shortened to *stereo*). Especially in fields such as medicine, there is an ongoing tendency to use Latin and/or Greek elements when naming new discoveries. Thus, in 1995, a new anti-obesity drug was named *leptin* from the Greek *leptos*, meaning 'thin'. Not all new scientific and technical words are coined from Latin and Greek elements: there is an increasing tendency, especially in 'newer' technologies such as computing, to prefer words coined from existing English elements, often in a playful way. This often involves extending the meaning of existing words, such as *mouse*, *spam*, *web*, *to surf*, etc., but new words can also be created by compounding, as *chatroom*, *homepage*, *spell-check* and *weblog*. The last of these is more usually shortened to *blog*, and various shortening processes are used to create new words in this and other fields. Thus *telnet* and *digicam* are formed by compounding the first elements of *tele* and *network* and *digital* and *camera* respectively. Acronyms, words created from the initial letters of the words in a phrase, are also very common in computing vocabulary. The *stereo* referred to above has now been superseded in many households by the *MP3*, the name for which was itself formed from the acronym MPEG, taken from the Moving Picture Experts Group who defined this standard for encoding video and audio. Other acronyms used in computing are *FAQ* (Frequently Asked Questions) and *SQL* (Structured Query Language). Some computing terms seem to have been coined arbitrarily or punningly: *phish* is a respelling of *fish* to describe the illegal act of 'angling' for personal information online, *cookie* to describe a small data file that tracks the user's movements, so called because these were randomly assigned from a 'cookie jar', and *Trojan*, as in 'Trojan Horse', to describe a virus which infects a system by being disguised as something harmless. Once a new word is coined, it can quickly be transferred from one word class to another: modern English is particularly conducive to this process because there are very few inflections that identify a word as a particular part of speech. Thus, according to the *OED Online*, the noun *blog* and the verb *to blog* were both first cited in 1999, along with the agentive noun *blogger* and the verbal noun *blogging*. The proprietary name *Google* was given to a search engine so popular that the word soon became used as a transitive verb: to *google* somebody or something meaning to search for him, her or it on Google. Affixation is still one of the favourite methods of word-formation. Fashionable prefixes in recent years include *cyber-* (*cyber-café*, *cybernaut*, *cyberpet*), *mini* (*minibar*, *mini-break*, *minidisk*) and *nano-* (*nanodevice*, *nanosecond*, *nanotechnology*), but more traditional prefixes also continue to be productive, as in *anti-poll-tax*, *debug*, *non-event* and *undelete*. Active suffixes are illustrated by the words *ageism*, *brinkmanship*, *techie* 'technician' or 'technology enthusiast', *circuitry*, *privatize*, *sexist* and *skateboarder*.

Loans are not a major source of new words, but a few continue to drift in. For example, in the last decade of the twentieth century, according to the *OED Online*, English imported *pressé* from French; *limoncello* from Italian; *jilbab* from Persian; *sudoku* from Japanese; and *wiki* from Hawaiian.

Change of meaning

One common cause of semantic change in our time appears to be formal influence: the form of a word causes it to be confused with another word, which influences its meaning. An example is the word *format*. This is a technical term of bibliography, referring to the way the sheets of paper are folded in making a book (quarto format, folio format, etc.) – the only meaning recorded in the original edition of the *OED*. Now, however, people use it to mean 'layout, design' (for example, of a page, a poster), and even more generally to mean 'arrangement, mode of procedure, form': we hear about the format of a lecture-course, a meeting, a conference, a cricket tournament, a symphony. Such a development is common when a word moves out of a specialized field of discourse into the general vocabulary, but it is also probable that *format* has been influenced by another word, namely *form*: for many people, indeed, *format* is now merely a variant of *form*.

Other pairs of words where semantic influence appears to be taking place include *adopt/adapt, amoral/immoral, cautionary/cautious, differential/difference, diffuse/defuse, fallacious/false, flaunt/flout, humanitarian/humane, incredulous/incredible, legalistic/legal, masterful/masterly, mitigate/militate, nationalistic/national, perpetrate/perpetuate, prescribe/proscribe, psychiatric/psychological, realistic/real, secretive/secret* and *sociological/social*. Usually, it is the first word of each pair which takes on the meaning of the second, so that, for example, people say *a masterful ('masterly') sculptor, realistic ('real') progress, psychiatric ('mental') illness* and *sociological ('social') problems*. Some of these changes are still seen as malapropisms, but others are now commonly accepted.

Among the other changes of meaning in recent times, let us pick out just a few examples. The word *ethnic* frequently occurs in the phrase *ethnic minority*, and is now often used to mean 'having to do with an ethnic minority', as when people speak of *ethnic music*. The noun *exercise* 'practice-operation, task performed as training' is commonly generalized to mean 'operation, task', as in the expression *the object of the exercise* 'the aim or purpose of the task in question'. The usage perhaps arose in military circles, as a deliberate understatement. The adjective *forensic* 'judicial, having to do with the law courts' often occurs in the expressions *forensic science* and *forensic scientist*, and many people now use it to mean 'scientific' (though always in a judicial context): so *forensic tests* are 'scientific tests carried out to help solve a crime', and *a forensic expert* is 'a scientist who helps police-investigations'. Words also change their meaning through pejoration and amelioration as their connotations become more negative or positive. A recent example is perhaps the word *obscene*: formerly this was rather a strong word, meaning 'abominable, loathsome', but is now sometimes used as a vague epithet of disapproval, especially in political journalism, so that footballers are accused of earning 'obscene' amounts of money. Conversely, words that were once pejorative can take on more positive meanings, such as *wicked* used by young people as a term of approval. One noticeable tendency is for words with more neutral or pleasant connotations to be used as euphemisms, especially when referring to war or death. Thus genocide becomes *ethnic cleansing* and the accidental killing of a comrade or ally is attributed to *friendly fire*.

Changes in pronunciation

In the educated speech of south-eastern England, the long vowels /iː/ (as in *see*) and /uː/ (as in *too*) are often diphthongized to [ɪi] and [ʊu]. To check your own pronunciation, look into a mirror and say 'ee-ee-ee-ee': if you use a pure vowel your lips and tongue will remain stationary, but if you use a diphthong they will move with each 'ee'. Repeat with 'oo-oo-oo-oo'. Try, too, to *hear* whether or not your vowel is a diphthong. In non-standard speech, these diphthongs often begin at an even opener and more central position, becoming [əi] and [əu].

This change can be seen as a continuation of the Great Vowel Shift: the long close vowels of Middle English, ME ī and ME ū, became diphthongized, and now the vowels that moved up and took their place are being diphthongized in turn. A similar continuation can be seen in the development of the /ɔː/ phoneme (as in *law*), which is becoming closer in quality. In the vowel diagram in figure 4 (p. 12 above), this phoneme is shown as half-open. Some older speakers use a slightly more open vowel than that, but many younger ones give it a much closer realization, nearer to [oː] (as in French *chose*).

In the earlier part of the twentieth century, words like *off*, *cloth* and *cross* were pronounced with a long vowel /ɔː/ by RP speakers, but this pronunciation is now considered very old-fashioned and most RP speakers would use a short /ɒ/ in these words.

More recent changes include the fronting of /ʊ/ and /uː/, the lowering of /e/ and /æ/ to /ɛ/ and /a/, and the monophthongization of 'centring' diphthongs /ʊə/ and /ɔə / so that, for instance *poor*, *pore* and *paw* become homophones.

Two vocalic changes which are a matter of a change of acceptance are the spread of /ə/ at the expense of /ɪ/ in unstressed syllables, and the use of word-final /-iː/ instead of the more conservative /-ɪ/. Many speakers, for example, use /ə/ instead of /ɪ/ in the unstressed syllables of *kitchen*, *remain*, *system*, *waitress* and *women*. Sometimes it replaces other vowels too, for example in words like *boycott* and *sawdust*. The former Prime Minister, Tony Blair, was known to use /ə/ in every unstressed syllable of the word *conservatives*. The use of /-iː/ in words like *happy* and *city* is common in the south and Midlands, and in other areas such as the north-east of England, Humberside and Merseyside. In the south and Midlands, the vowel is often diphthongized, as it is in other positions. It is probable, however, that these two changes do not represent recent innovations: the variant pronunciations are quite old ones, and the change is one of acceptability. It is notable that the same pronunciations are common in Australia, and were presumably taken there from southern England in the eighteenth and nineteenth centuries.

A change which does appear to have been in progress in the twentieth century is the redistribution of /juː/ and /uː/ Words like *new* and *use* had ME *iu*, which was the falling diphthong [iʊ]. Round about 1600, this changed into /juː/, giving the pronunciations /njuː/, /juːz/. But in some positions the [iʊ] instead became /uː/, namely after /tʃ/, /dʒ/, /r/ and Consonant + /l/, as in *chew*, *June*, *rude*, *blew*. Later, however, the /juː/ became /uː/ in other positions, especially after /s/, /l/ and /θ/. This did not happen in all speech groups, however, and today there are double forms of such words as *suit*, *lute*, and *enthusiasm*, though the /juː/ forms seem increasingly old-fashioned. The present trend seems to be for the /uː/-forms to spread at the expense of the /juː/-forms, so that increasingly *suit* and *lute* are /suːt/, /luːt/, rather than /sjuːt/, /ljuːt/. In much regional English speech, and in American English, /uː/ replaced /juː/ in even more phonetic contexts, and some of these /uː/-forms show signs of entering standard British pronunciation: for example, *resume* is occasionally heard as /rɪˈzuːm/.

Among the consonants, there are two trends affecting /r/, namely the extension of intrusive /r/, and the loss of /r/, in unstressed syllables. Intrusive /r/, heard in expressions like *the idear of it* and *the lawr of the sea*, arises by analogy with words like *father*, which quite regularly have a final /r/ before a vowel, but not before a consonant or a pause. For a long time, intrusive /r/ has been normal in educated speech after /ə/, so that *the idear of it* and *Ghanar and India* are perfectly acceptable. Until relatively recently, however, intrusive /r/ was stigmatized when it occurred after other vowels, so that *the Shahr of Persia* and *the lawr of the sea* were considered vulgar. This now seems to have changed, however, and intrusive /r/ is widespread in educated speech after any vowel. Sometimes the intrusive /r/ goes on to attach itself permanently to the stem of the word, leading to such forms as *drawring board* and *withdrawral*. These are quite common, but probably not yet accepted as standard.

There is a tendency for /r/ to be lost in unstressed syllables. This has long been the case where there are two successive occurrences of /r/, as in *February*, *library*, *temporary* and *secretary* (the first /r/ being the one that goes). Now, however, in colloquial speech /r/ is often lost in unstressed syllables where there is no other /r/. A TV weather-forecaster has been heard to say /dʒʊənə 'nait 'tempətʃəz 'dʒenəli: … / ('during the night, temperatures generally …'). Such pronunciations, indeed, are not universally accepted, but they are perhaps straws in the wind.

Two further consonantal changes have been attributed to the influence of 'Estuary English' on RP. Glottalization of /t/, especially in word-final position, is now common in the speech of younger RP speakers, even members of the Royal Family. Another consonantal feature said to be spreading from 'below' is the velarization of /l/ in words like *cool*, *hill* and *Paul*, so that it sounds like a vowel /ʊ/.

Changes are taking place in the way words are stressed. There is a long-term trend in two-syllable words for the stress to be moved from the second syllable to the first: this has happened in living memory in such words as *adult*, *alloy*, *ally* and *garage*. It is still going on, especially where there are related noun–verb pairs. There are many pairs where the noun has first-syllable stress, and the verb second-syllable stress, and in such cases many speakers now stress the verb also on the first syllable: examples are *annex*, *contest*, *contract*, *escort*, *export*, *import*, *increase*, *progress*, *protest* and *transfer*. In cases where both the noun and the verb have second-syllable stress, there is a tendency for the noun to be given first-syllable stress, as with *discharge, dispute, redress* and *research*; occasionally the verb may also be given first-syllable stress. When the stress is moved on to the first syllable of a verb, it is usually also moved in words derived from it, like *protester*.

In words of more than two syllables, there is an apparent tendency to move the stress from the first to the second syllable, as with *aristocrat, communal, controversy, doctrinal, formidable, hospitable* and *pejorative*. The forms with second-syllable stress, however, are not new ones, and here we are dealing with a potential change of acceptance rather than a substantive change. The pronunciations with first-syllable stress are traditional standard ones, and the other forms are permeating from below, as part of the dialect-mixing of our times. The words *cigarette, ice-cream* and *magazine*, on the other hand, are normally pronounced in Britain with the main stress on the final syllable, but nowadays some speakers instead put it on the first, probably as a result of American influence.

A trend which has been encouraged by the spread of higher education and of foreign travel is the adoption of what can be called 'continental pronunciations'. Words borrowed from other languages soon get assimilated to an English style of pronunciation, either by passing through normal English sound changes or because of the influence of the spelling. Nowadays, however, such words are often given a 'foreign' kind of pronunciation again. In the traditional pronunciation, the words *armada, Copenhagen, gala* and *Gaza* had their stressed *a* pronounced /eɪ/, but it is now common for /ɑː/ to be used instead, and in *armada* this pronunciation is universal. Similarly, *beret, richochet* and *valet* are now commonly pronounced without their final /t/, *proviso* sometimes has /iː/ instead of /aɪ/, Marlowe's *Dr Faustus* is given the /aʊ/ of the German *Faust* instead of the traditional English /ɔː/, and *chivalry* is almost universally pronounced with /ʃ/ instead of the traditional /tʃ/. The new pronunciations are not always based on a genuine knowledge of the other language: the word *Raj* was traditionally /rɑːdʒ/, but is now often /rɑːʒ/, a pronunciation which probably owes more to a knowledge of French than to a knowledge of Hindi, while the new pronunciation of *Copenhagen* bears very little resemblance to the Danish.

This 'continental' influence is perhaps reinforced by the 'new' pronunciation of Classical Latin, which has continental-style vowels, whereas the 'old' pronunciation had anglicized vowels. Almost any English person today who has learnt Latin will have learnt the 'new' style of pronunciation. This perhaps explains why many people are reluctant to use the traditional pronunciation of those Latin tags which commonly occur in English, like *a priori*, *quasi* and *sine die* (traditionally /'eɪ praɪɔːraɪ/, /'kweɪzaɪ/, /'saɪnɪ'daɪiː/). These sound wrong, and people often instead use an approximation to the 'new' Latin pronunciation. This even affects proper names: there is no likelihood that a well-known name like *Julius Caesar* will lose its traditional pronunciation, but Shakespeare's *Coriolanus* is now often pronounced with /ɑː/ instead of /eɪ/.

The same change of vowel is sometimes heard in *apparatus*, *status* and *stratum*, and even occasionally in *data*. Besides affecting words which are obviously direct from Latin, the 'new Latin' influence also affects a few words more remotely derived from Latin. Thus the words *deity*, *spontaneity* and *vehicle* traditionally had their *e* pronounced as /iː/, but nowadays it is often pronounced /eɪ/. The 'new Latin' and 'continental' tendencies must obviously reinforce one another.

Changes in grammar

On the whole, noun- and verb-forms have remained very stable during the Later Modern English period, because of the influence of the standard literary language and of the educational system. One exception is the group of learned nouns borrowed from Greek and Latin complete with their original plural forms (*dogma/dogmata*, *formula/formulae*, *genus/genera*, *syllabus/syllabi*, etc.). Such words are more and more often given analogical plurals in *-(e)s* (*formulas*, *genuses*, etc.), though sometimes a distinction is made between technical and popular usage: technical *formulae*, popular *formulas*. A slightly different development is seen in nouns which have a learned plural in *-a*, like *bacterium*, *criterion*, *datum*, *medium*, *phenomenon* and *stratum*. These words are often used in the plural (we seldom need to talk about one bacterium, for example), and the plural form, lacking the standard English *-es* marking, has been apprehended by many people as a singular. This happened long ago to *data*, which for years has been regularly used by scientists as a singular, but it is now happening to other similar words as well. So now it is quite common to hear or read such expressions as 'the mass media is responsible', 'this criteria', and 'a bacteria'. The decline of the classics in English education has obviously played a part here, but at the same time the change is absolutely in line with the general development of the language: for nearly a thousand years, the whole trend in English noun-plurals has been for the -(*e*)*s* morpheme to be standardized, an obviously economical development. A parallel case is that of the Italian loanword *graffiti*. The singular *graffito* is recorded by the *OED* from 1851, but now that the word has moved out of the specialist archaeological sphere, and is frequently used for modern wall-scribblings (especially in lavatories), the plural *graffiti* has taken over, and is commonly used as a singular. The word is thus going the same way as earlier Italian loans like *macaroni*. A more recent example is *panini*, which, in Italian, is the plural of *panino* 'a bread roll', but in English is used to refer to a single sandwich, so that a new plural *paninis* has been created.

There have been several recent developments in the use of modal verbs, such as the tendency for people to use auxiliary *may* instead of *might*. In 1968, an account of a football-match in a 'quality' English newspaper contained the sentence 'Just before half-time, Leeds United may have scored a goal.' This was baffling, since the obvious meaning is 'Leeds United perhaps scored a goal.' Had the reporter perhaps gone away to the bar, and didn't know what had happened? What the writer in fact meant was that they *might* have scored a goal (but had failed to do so). Since then, examples have proliferated, especially (though not exclusively) when the auxiliary is followed by *have* plus past participle. For many of the younger generation, indeed, auxiliary *might* now hardly exists, either *may* or *could* being used instead.

The modals *shall* and *must* are likewise increasingly rare. *Shall* tends to be replaced by *will*, '*ll*, or *be going to*, whilst, possibly for pragmatic reasons such as the wish to sound more polite and less dictatorial, *must* is giving ground to *need to*.

Another change going on among the auxiliaries is that *dare* and *need* are ceasing to be auxiliaries, and are coming more and more to be used as ordinary lexical verbs. Thus it is increasingly normal to say 'Do you need to go?' and 'I don't dare (to) go', rather than 'Need you go?' and 'I dare not go.' In some non-standard speech, the same thing has happened to the auxiliaries *ought to* and *used to*, so that you hear expressions like 'She didn't ought to' and 'He didn't used to'.

We saw in chapter 9 that, in the course of the late modern period, the use of the progressive became increasingly frequent and spread to constructions such as the progressive passive ('the house is being built') where it had previously been considered ungrammatical. This process has continued in recent times: the progressive is no longer restricted to verbs which can refer to continuous action, and is now even heard with verbs of emotion, as in 'I'm loving this music.'

We referred above to the process which Christian Mair has identified as 'colloquialization', whereby structures formerly restricted to spoken and/or informal usage are increasingly used in more formal registers. Thus contractions such as *I'll, he'd* and *didn't* were once proscribed in formal written English but are now becoming more common. Conversely, formal structures such as the passive and long, complex sentences are now actually proscribed in many written genres. Style-guides such as online grammar checks advise against these, and have perhaps contributed to the decline in their use. The formal passive, as in 'the manager was fired' is giving way to the construction with *get*, as in 'the manager got fired', or is avoided altogether, as in 'the board fired the manager'.

One grammatical change that can be attributed to external influence is the increasing use of *they* with a singular verb, as in 'Anyone who goes there knows that they will have a good time.' Until relatively recently, it was acceptable to use masculine pronouns when the gender of the person being referred to was unknown, but the rise of feminism and equal opportunities legislation in the late twentieth century has led to the preference for 'gender-neutral' language. Since phrases such as 'he or she,' or constructions like 's/he' seem awkward, the existing but proscribed expedient of using 'they' as a gender-neutral singular pronoun has become acceptable.

English tomorrow

It's dangerous to extrapolate or to prophesy, and none of us can guess what the English language will be like in a hundred years' time. The changes of recent decades suggest what forces are at work in the language today and the likely shape of things in the next few decades, but the history of the language in the coming century will depend on the history of the community itself.

One of the striking things at the moment is the expansion going on in the vocabulary. If this continues, the change over a century will be comparable to that of such earlier periods as 1300 to 1400 or 1550 to 1650. Another trend is dialect-mixing: unless some global disaster disrupts world communications, this is likely to continue, and the divergent tendencies in the language to be held in check. Inside England, public-school English seems already to have been supplanted by educated south-eastern usage or even 'Estuary English' and other educated regional varieties of the language have achieved parity of esteem: it has for some time been normal for local radio and TV services in the English regions to have announcers and presenters who use the local form of the language, and it is no longer the case that all broadcasters on national radio and TV stations are RP speakers. In the British Isles outside England, such regional standards are well established. In pronunciation, such trends as the diphthongization of the long close vowels may well continue, and could lead to further changes in the vowel system. In grammar, the trends of the past thousand years continue in small ways. More substantial changes could be caused by the permeation of the standard language by usages which at present are informal and/or non-standard. In grammar, for example, past-tense forms like 'I done' might become acceptable, as might the conflation of adjective and adverb forms. Perhaps more controversially, the reduced forms used in electronic communications such as text messaging and e-mail, such as l8 for 'late' and LOL for 'laugh out loud', might find their way into other kinds of written usage. What we can be sure of is that the process of change, which we have traced from the early Indo-European records up to modern times, is still going on, and will continue. It requires an effort of detachment to recognize current change for what it is. We are so thoroughly trained in one form of the language that we are likely to dismiss innovations as mistakes or vulgarisms. On the other hand, if our own elders make similar deprecating noises about *our* use of the language, we probably dismiss them as stuffy old fuddyduddies. Such conservatism is inevitable, and indeed necessary for the stability of the language, but we need to step outside such attitudes and view the whole speech community with scientific detachment. We shall then recognize that our behaviour is simply that of one group at one point in time, and that in the next generation the innovations that we deplore may well have become completely respectable, and indeed uniquely right for the users.

Moreover, why not *enjoy* the language that you speak? As speakers of English, we're fortunate in being inside a language of enormous richness and variety: it can be great fun simply to listen to English of many different kinds – from different parts of the world, different social groups, different occupations – and also to enjoy the ways in which the language is changing. In a universe of change, it's natural to long for stability, to want to pin things down and fix them. But it can't be done. The whole of nature is in flux, and so is the whole of human life, and we might as well make the best of the fact. It's not really much good clinging to the bank: we have to push out into the flux and swim.

Notes and suggestions for further reading

1 What is language?
Good general introductions to linguistics are Aitchison 1987a and Atkinson, Kilby and Roca 1988; Lyons 1968 is still useful. Works of the twentieth century which have been landmarks in the subject include de Saussure 1916, Sapir 1921, Bloomfield 1933 and Chomsky 1957, 1965. The standard work on the phonetics of present-day British English is Gimson 1989, the most recent edition of which is Cruttenden 2001; a good introductory work is Roach 1991. Accents of English worldwide: Wells 1982. English intonation: Wells 2006. Introductions to the structure of English: Hill 1958 and (shorter) Strang 1968. In word-order typology and linguistic universals, the pioneer work was Greenberg 1966; a good introduction is Comrie 1989; Hawkins 1983, 1988 and Croft 1990 are more advanced. On stress-timing in English poetry see Barber 1983.

2 The flux of language
Historical and comparative linguistics generally: Bynon 1983, Hock 1986, Anttila 1989, Trask 1994. Linguistic change and its causes: Lehmann 1973, Aitchison 1991, McMahon 1994, Labov 1994, 2001. History of English: Strang 1970, Smith 1996, Fennell 2001, Baugh and Cable 2002, Hogg and Denison 2006.

3 The Indo-European languages
Indo-European languages: Lockwood 1969, Baldi 1983. For a survey of recent problems in Indo-European linguistics see Szemerényi 1985. A good introductory guide to various aspects of Indo-European language and culture is Fortson 2004. The Indo-European homeland: Schrader 1890, Childe 1926, Gimbutas 1970, Renfrew 1987, Gamkrelidze and Ivanov 1990, 1995. On lexicostatistics and glottochronology see McMahon and McMahon

2005; Dyen's lexicostatistical dataset is no longer readily available, but was last available at www.ntu.edu.au/education/langs/ielex/.

4 The Germanic languages

For Proto-Germanic phonology and morphology see Streitberg 1943, Prokosch 1939 and Voyles 1992. An introduction to the Scandinavian languages: Walshe 1965. Lockwood 1976 is a history of the German language, but also contains chapters on Dutch, Afrikaans and Frisian. On the Germanic languages more generally see Robinson 1992. An excellent guide to the cultural evidence provided by Germanic lexis is Green 1998.

5 Old English

Standard works are Stenton 1971 on Anglo-Saxon history, Campbell 1962 on OE morphology and phonology, Hogg 1992 on OE phonology, and Mitchell 1987 on OE syntax. Of the many OE readers, see especially Mitchell and Robinson 2007, which, in addition to annotated texts, contains an excellent introductory section on the language. A good general introduction to OE literature is provided by Godden and Lapidge 1991, while Campbell 1982 is a lavishly illustrated introduction to Anglo-Saxon cultural history more generally. On English place-names see Reaney 1960, Ekwall 1960, Cameron 1977, Smith 1970, Gelling 1988, Mills 2003, and the various county-volumes of the English Place-Name Society, as well as the volumes of the Vocabulary of English Place-Names project. On the impact of Christianity on Old English lexis see Green 1998. On runes see Elliott 1989, Page 1973 and Parsons 1999; a shorter work is Page 1987, in the admirable British Museum series 'Reading the Past'.

6 Norsemen and Normans

For further information on the Vikings see Jones 1984, 1986 and Sawyer 1971, 1982, and on Scandinavian loanwords Björkman 1900–2. On loanwords in English more generally see Serjeantson 1935. The Edinburgh work on late medieval dialects has been published as Mcintosh, Samuels and Benskin 1986. On the establishment of Standard English see Leith 1983. For an introduction to the Old Norse language see Barnes 2007.

7 Middle English

An introduction to Middle English is provided by Mossé 1952; more elementary is Wardale 1937. For ME phonology see Jordan 1968, 1974. For ME morphology and phonology, Wright and Wright 1928 is still useful; shorter works include Brunner 1963 and Fisiak 1968; Jones 1972 uses a transformational-generative approach. On ME syntax see Mustanoja 1960. A good ME reader is Burrow and Turville-Petre 1992, which has a useful introduction on the language. For valuable discussions of the development of 'she' and Middle English open syllable lengthening see Smith 1996. On Scots see Murison 1977, Aitken and McArthur 1979. On the supplanting of Standard Scots by the standard southern language see Devitt 1989.

8 Early Modern English

Works devoted specifically to Early Modern English are Barber 1976, Görlach 1991 and Nevalainen 2006. Attitudes to English, and the relationship between English and Latin, are handled by Jones 1953, but a more recent discussion of this can be found in Blank 1996. On the auxiliary *do* see Ellegård 1953 and the discussion in Denison 1993. The standard work on Early Modern English phonology is Dobson 1968, but this is a work for the specialist; more accessible is Cercignani 1981, but the general reader will do better to rely on the phonology sections of more general works, especially volume 3 of the Cambridge History of the English Language (ed. Lass 1999). A good introduction to the historical phonology and morphology of the whole Modern English period is provided by Ekwall 1975. An interesting account of attitudes to regional and national dialects in the early modern period can be found in Blank 1996, whilst Nevalainen and Raumolin-Brunberg 2003 provide a socio-historical account of variation and change in the Tudor period. There are several works dealing with the language of Shakespeare, the most recent of which are Adamson et al. 2001 and Hope 2003.

9 Late Modern English

Works specifically devoted to parts of this period are Görlach 2001, which deals with the eighteenth century, and Bailey 1996 and Görlach 1999, both of which are concerned with nineteenth-century English. Volume 4 of the Cambridge History of the English Language (ed. Romaine 1998) covers the period from 1776 to 1997. The only volume that concentrates on the whole of this period is Beal 2004. A monumental historical grammar and phonology of Modern English is Jespersen 1909–49; shorter works include Wyld 1936, Robertson 1954 and Ekwall 1975. More recent works devoted to the phonology of this period are Beal 1999 and Jones 2006. On English spelling see Vallins 1965 and Scragg 1974. For standardization, codification and prescriptivism see Leonard 1929, Leith 1983, Milroy and Milroy 1985 and Crowley 2003. On the history of English grammars see

Michael 1970, and of English dictionaries, Starnes and Noyes 1991 and Stein 1985. On the vocabulary of science see Savory 1967 and on vocabulary in general, Sheard 1954.

10 English as a world language

For further reading on the history of American English, see Dillard 1992 and Algeo 2001. Wolfram and Schilling-Estes 1998 provide an account of dialect variation in American English. The history of African American English is dealt with in Poplack 1999 and Wolfram and Thomas 2002. On Antipodean English see Ramson 1970, Turner 1972, Blair and Collins 2000 and Gordon et al. 2004. On Jamaican English see Cassidy 1961 and Bailey 1966, and on the Caribbean, Görlach and Holm 1986. Works covering many varieties of English worldwide include Bailey and Görlach 1982 and Cheshire 1991; useful elementary introductions are Trudgill and Hannah 2002 and Jenkins 2003. Wells 1982 is a monumental account of English phonology worldwide, but the most comprehensive account of varieties of English within and beyond the British Isles is Kortmann and Schneider 2004. Holm 1988–9 is a substantial survey of pidgins and creoles, while Todd 1990 and Singh 2000 are admirable introductory works. Sebba 1997 deals with the linguistic, historical and social aspects of the development of pidgin and creole languages. Romaine 1988 is especially concerned with the theoretical questions raised by pidgins and creoles, and their bearing on the problem of language acquisition and linguistic universals.

11 English today and tomorrow

On changes in English in the twentieth century see Barber 1964, 1985, Foster 1968 and Potter 1969. Bauer 1994 and Mair 2006 provide more up-to-date accounts, including developments in the late twentieth century. A comprehensive account of present-day English worldwide is given in Kortmann and Schneider (eds.) 2004. A substantial grammar of present-day English is Quirk, Greenbaum, Leech and Svartvik 1972; a useful shorter version is Greenbaum and Quirk 1990. On recent developments in variation and change in British English, see Foulkes and Docherty 1999 and Britain 2007.

Bibliography

1. Primary sources

Andrew, M. and Waldron, R. (eds.), *The Poems of the Pearl Manuscript: Pearl, Cleanness, Patience, Sir Gawain and the Green Knight*, Exeter: University of Exeter Press, 1987

Bede, the Venerable, *Ecclesiastical History of the English People*, ed. B. Colgrave and R. A. B. Mynors, Oxford: Clarendon Press, 1969

Bible, *The Holy Bible, conteyning the Old Testament, and the New* ('The King James Bible'), London, 1611

Bible, *The New English Bible*, Oxford: Oxford University Press and Cambridge University Press, 1970

Bond, D. F. (ed.), *The Spectator*, 5 vols., Oxford: Clarendon Press, 1965

Bright, J. W. (ed.), *The Gospel of Saint Luke in West-Saxon*, Boston: D.C. Heath, 1906

Chaucer, G., *The Canterbury Tales. A Facsimile and Transcription of the Hengwrt Manuscript*, ed. Paul G. Ruggiers, Norman: University of Oklahoma Press, Folkestone: Wm Dawson and Sons, 1978

Chaucer, G., *The Riverside Chaucer*, ed. Larry D. Benson, third edition, Oxford: Oxford University Press, 1988

Clark, C. (ed.), *The Peterborough Chronicle: 1070–1154*, second edition, London: Oxford University Press, 1970

Dickens, B. and Wilson, R. M. (eds), *Early Middle English Texts*, London: Bowes and Bowes, 1951

Franzen, C. (ed.), *Worcester Manuscripts*, Anglo-Saxon Manuscripts in Microfiche Facsimile 6, Tempe: Arizona Center for Medieval and Renaissance Studies, 1998

Henryson, R., *The Poems*, ed. Denton Fox, Oxford: Clarendon Press, 1981

Higden, Ranulf, *Polychronicon*, ed. C. Babington and J. R. Lumby, 9 vols., London: Longmans, 1865–86

Klaeber, F. (ed.), *Beowulf and the Fight at Finnsburg*, third edition, with supplements, London: D.C. Heath, 1950

Krapp, G. P. and Dobbie, E. V. K. (eds.), *The Anglo-Saxon Poetic Records*, 6 vols., New York: Columbia University Press, 1931–42

Plummer, C., *Two of the Saxon Chronicles Parallel*, 2 vols., Oxford: Clarendon Press, 1892–9

Scragg, D. G. (ed.), *The Battle of Maldon*, Manchester: Manchester University Press, 1981

Schmidt, A. V. C. (ed.), *The Vision of Piers Plowman*, London: Dent, 1978

Shakespeare W., *The History of Henrie the Fourth*, London, 1598

Shakespeare W., *Henry the Fifth*, London, 1600

Shakespeare W., *Mr. William Shakespeares Comedies, Histories and Tragedies*, London, 1623

Sisam, K. (ed.), *Fourteenth Century Verse and Prose*, Oxford: Clarendon Press, 1921

Sprat, Thomas, *The History of the Royal-Society of London*, London, 1667

Sweet, H. (ed.), *King Alfred's Orosius*, London: Early English Text Society, 1883

Sweet, H. (ed.), *Sweet's Anglo-Saxon Reader*, rev. Dorothy Whitelock, Oxford: Clarendon Press, 1967

Tacitus, *On Britain and Germany*, trans. H. Mattingly, West Drayton: Penguin Books, 1948

Timmer, B. J. (ed.), *Judith*, Exeter: University of Exeter Press, 1978

Wright, W. A. (ed.), *The Metrical Chronicle of Robert of Gloucester*, 2 vols., London: H.M. Stationery Office, 1887

Wycliffe, John, *The Holy Bible translated by Wycliffe and his followers*, ed. J. Forshall and F. Madden, 4 vols., Oxford: Oxford University Press, 1850

2. Secondary sources

Adams, V. (1973). *An Introduction to Modern English Word-Formation*, London: Longman

Adamson, S., Hunter, L., Magnusson, L., Thompson, A. and Wales, K. (2001). *Reading Shakespeare's Dramatic Language* (The Arden Shakespeare), London: Thomson Learning

Aitchison, J. (1987a). *Linguistics*, third edition, London: Hodder and Stoughton

Aitchison, J. (1987b). *Words in the Mind*, Oxford: Blackwell

Aitchison, J. (1989). *The Articulate Mammal*, third edition, London: Unwin Hyman/Routledge

Aitchison, J. (1991). *Language Change: Progress or Decay?*, second edition, Cambridge: Cambridge University Press

Aitken, A. J. and Mcarthur, T. (1979). *Languages of Scotland*, Edinburgh: Chambers

Algeo, J. (ed.) (2001). *The Cambridge History of the English Language*, vol. 6: *English in North America*, Cambridge: Cambridge University Press

Anttila, R. (1989). *Historical and Comparative Linguistics*, second edition, Amsterdam: John Benjamins

Atkinson, M., Kilby, D. and Roca, I. (1988). *Foundations of General Linguistics*, second edition, London: Allen and Unwin

Bailey, C.-J. N. and Harris, R. (eds.) (1985). *Developmental Mechanisms of Language*, Oxford: Pergamon Press

Bailey, B. L. (1966). *Jamaican Creole Syntax*, Cambridge: Cambridge University Press

Bailey, R. W. (1996). *Nineteenth-century English*, Ann Arbor: University of Michigan Press

Bailey, R. W. and Görlach, M. (1982). *English as a World Language*, Ann Arbor: Michigan University Press

Baldi, P. (1983). *An Introduction to the Indo-European Languages*, Carbondale, IL: Southern Illinois University Press

Barber, C. (1964). *Linguistic Change in Present-day English*, Edinburgh: Oliver and Boyd

Barber, C. (1976). *Early Modern English*, London: Deutsch

Barber, C. (1983). *Poetry in English: an Introduction*. London: Macmillan

Barber, C. (1985). 'Linguistic Change in Present-Day English. Some Afterthoughts', in *Papers on Language and Literature*, ed. S. Backman and G. Kjellmer, Göteborg: University of Gothenburg, 36–45

Barnes, M.P. (2007). *A New Introduction to Old Norse*, part I: *Grammar*, third edition, London: Viking Society for Northern Research

Bauer, L. (1983). *English Word Formation*, Cambridge: Cambridge University Press

Bauer, L. (1994). *Watching English Change: an Introduction to the Study of Linguistic Change in Standard Englishes in the Twentieth Century*, London: Longman

Baugh, A.C. and Cable, T. (2002). *A History of the English Language*, fifth edition, London: Routledge

Beal, J. C. (1999). *English Pronunciation in the Eighteenth Century*, Oxford: Clarendon Press

Beal, J. C. (2004). *English in Modern Times 1700–1945*, London: Arnold

Björkman, E. (1900–2). *Scandinavian Loan Words in Middle English*, Halle: Niemeyer

Blair, D. and Collins, P. (eds.) (2000). *English in Australia*, Philadelphia, PA: Benjamins

Blank, P. (1996). *Broken English: Dialects and the Politics of Language in Renaissance Writings*, London: Routledge

Bloomfield, L. (1933). *Language*, New York: Holt, Rinehart and Winston; London: Allen and Unwin

Bosworth, J. and Toller, T. N. (1898). *An Anglo-Saxon Dictionary*, London: Oxford University Press

Britain, D. (ed.) (2007). *Language in the British Isles*, Cambridge: Cambridge University Press

Brugmann, K. (1888–95). *Elements of the Comparative Grammar of the Indo-Germanic Languages*, trans. J. Wright, R. S. Conway and W. H. D. Rouse, 5 vols., London: Kegan Paul

Brunner, K. (1963). *An Outline of Middle English Grammar*, trans. G. K. W. Johnston, Oxford: Blackwell

Burchfield, R. (ed.) (1994). *The Cambridge History of the English Language*, vol. 5: *English in Britain and Overseas: Origin and Development*, Cambridge: Cambridge University Press

Burrow, J. A. and Turville-Petre, T. (eds.) (1992). *A Book of Middle English*, Oxford: Blackwell

Bynon, T. (1983). *Historical Linguistics*, new edition, Cambridge: Cambridge University Press

Cameron, K. (1977). *English Place-Names*, third edition, London: Batsford

Campanile, E. (1998). 'The Indo-Europeans: Origins and Culture', in Ramat and Ramat (eds.), 1–24

Campbell, A. (1962). *Old English Grammar*, reprinted with corrections, London: Oxford University Press

Campbell, J. (ed.) (1982). *The Anglo-Saxons*, Oxford: Phaidon

Cardona, G., Hoenigswald, H. M. and Senn, A. (eds.) (1970). *Indo-European and Indo-Europeans*, Philadelphia: University of Pennsylvania Press

Cassidy, F.G. (1961). *Jamaica Talk*, London: Macmillan

Cercignani, F. (1981). *Shakespeare's Works and Elizabethan Pronunciation*, Oxford: Clarendon Press

Cheshire, J. (ed.) (1991). *English around the World*, Cambridge: Cambridge University Press

Childe, V. G. (1926). *The Aryans*, London: Kegan Paul, Trench, Trubner

Chomsky, N. (1957). *Syntactic Structures*, The Hague: Mouton

Chomsky, N. (1965). *Aspects of the Theory of Syntax*, Cambridge, MA: MIT Press

Chomsky, N. and Halle, M. (1968). *The Sound Pattern of English*, New York: Harper and Row

Comrie, B. (1989). *Language Universals and Linguistic Typology*, second edition, Oxford: Blackwell

Croft, W. (1990). *Typology and Universals*, Cambridge: Cambridge University Press

Crowley, T. (2003). *Standard English and the Politics of Language*, second edition, Basingstoke: Palgrave Macmillan

Cruttenden, A. (2001). *Gimson's Pronunciation of English: revised by Alan Cruttenden*, sixth edition, London: Arnold

Crystal, D. (1969). *Prosodic Systems and Intonation in English*, Cambridge: Cambridge University Press

Denison, D. (1993). *English Historical Syntax: Verbal Construction*, London: Longman

Devitt, A. (1989). *Standardizing Written English*, Cambridge: Cambridge University Press

Dillard, J. L. (1992), *A History of American English*, London: Longman

Dobson. E. J. (1968). *English Pronunciation 1500–1700*, 2 vols., second edition. Oxford: Clarendon Press

Dyen, I., Kruskal, J. B. and Black, P. (1992). *An Indoeuropean Classification: a Lexicostatistical Experiment*, Transactions of the American Philosophical Society, n.s. vol. 82, part 5, Philadelphia: American Philosophical Society

Ekwall, E. (1960). *The Concise Oxford Dictionary of English Place-Names*, fourth edition, Oxford: Clarendon Press

Ekwall, E. (1975). *A History of Modern English Sounds and Morphology*, trans. Allan Ward, Oxford: Blackwell

Ellegård, A. (1953). *The Auxiliary Do*, Stockholm: Almqvist and Wiksell

Elliott, R. W. V. (1989). *Runes: an Introduction*, second edition, Manchester: Manchester University Press

Fennell, B. (2001). *A History of English: a Sociolinguistic Approach*, Oxford: Blackwell

Fisiak, J. (1968). *A Short Grammar of Middle English*, London: Oxford University Press

Fortson, B. W., IV. (2004). *Indo-European Language and Culture: an Introduction*, Oxford: Blackwell

Foster, B. (1968). *The Changing English Language*, Harmondsworth, Middlesex: Penguin Books

Foulkes, P. and Docherty, G. J. (eds.) (1999). *Urban Voices: Accent Studies in the British Isles*, London: Arnold

Francis, A. N. (1958). *The Structure of American English*, New York: Ronald Press

Gamkrelidze, T. V. and Ivanov, V. V. (1990). 'The Early History of Indo-European Languages', *Scientific American*, March, 82–9

Gamkrelidze, T. V. and Ivanov, V. V. (1995). *Indo-European and the Indo-Europeans: a Reconstruction and Historical Analysis of a Proto-Language and a Proto-Culture*, 2 vols., trans. Johanna Nichols, Berlin: de Gruyter

Gelling, M. (1988). *Signposts to the Past: Place-Names and the History of England*, second edition, Chichester: Phillimore

Gelling, M. and Cole, A. (2000). *The Landscape of Place-Names*, Stamford: Shaun Tyas

Gimbutas, M. (1970). 'Proto-Indo-European Culture: the Kurgan Culture during the Fifth, Fourth, and Third Millennia B.C.', in Cardona, Hoenigswald, and Senn (eds.), 155–97

Gimson. A. C. (1989). *An Introduction to the Pronunciation of English*, fourth edition, London: Edward Arnold

Godden, M. and Lapidge, M. (eds.) (1991). *The Cambridge Companion to Old English Literature*, Cambridge: Cambridge University Press

Gordon, E., Campbell, L., Hay, J., Maclagan, M., Sudbury, A. and Trudgill, P. (2004). *New Zealand English: its Origin and Evolution*, Cambridge: Cambridge University Press

Görlach, M. (1991). *Introduction to Early Modern English*, Cambridge: Cambridge University Press

Görlach, M. (1999). *English in Nineteenth-century England*, Cambridge: Cambridge University Press

Görlach, M. (2001). *Eighteenth-century English*, Heidelberg: Winter

Görlach, M. and Holm, J. (eds.) (1986). *Focus on the Caribbean*, Amsterdam: Benjamins

Gray, R. D. and Atkinson, Q. D. (2003). 'Language-Tree Divergence Times Support the Anatolian Theory of Indo-European Origin', *Nature*, 426: 435–9

Green, D. H. (1998). *Language and History in the Early Germanic World*, Cambridge: Cambridge University Press

Greenbaum, S. and Quirk, R. (1990). *A Student's Grammar of the English Language*, London: Longman

Greenberg, J. H. (1966). 'Some Universals of Grammar with Particular Reference to the Order of Meaningful Elements', in *Universals of Language*, ed. J. H. Greenberg, second edition, Cambridge, MA: MIT Press

Hawkins, J. (1983). *Word Order Universals*, New York: Academic Press

Hawkins, J. (ed.) (1988). *Explaining Language Universals*, Oxford: Blackwood

Hill, A. A. (1958). *Introduction to Linguistic Structures*, New York: Harcourt Brace

Hock, H. H. (1986). *Principles of Historical Linguistics*, Berlin: Mouton

Hogg, R. M. (1992). *A Grammar of Old English*, Oxford: Blackwell

Hogg, R. M. and Denison, D. (eds.) (2006). *A History of the English Language*, Cambridge: Cambridge University Press

Holm, J. (1988–9). *Pidgins and Creoles*, 2 vols., Cambridge: Cambridge University Press

Holmberg, B. (1964). *On the Concept of Standard English and the History of Modern English Pronunciation*, Lund: CWK Gleerup

Holthausen, F. (1909–49). *A Modern English Grammar on Historical Principles*, 7 vols., London: Allen and Unwin

Holthausen, F. (1934). *Altenglisches etymologisches Wörterbuch*, Heidelberg: Carl Winter

Hope, J. (2003). *Shakespeare's Grammar* (The Arden Shakespeare), London: Thomson Learning

Jenkins, J. (2003). *World Englishes: a Resource Book for Students*, London: Routledge

Jespersen, O. (1909–49). *A Modern English Grammar on Historical Principles*, Heidelberg: Winter: Copenhagen: Munksgaard

Jones, C. (1972). *An Introduction to Middle English*, New York: Holt, Rinehart and Winston

Jones, C. (2006). *English Pronunciation in the Eighteenth and Nineteenth Centuries*, Basingstoke: Palgrave Macmillan

Jones, D. (1962). *The Phoneme: its Nature and Use*, second edition, Cambridge: Heffer

Jones, G. (1984). *A History of the Vikings*, second edition, Oxford: Oxford University Press

Jones, G. (1986). *The Norse Atlantic Saga*, second edition, Oxford: Oxford University Press

Jones, R. F. (1953). *The Triumph of the English Language*, London: Oxford University Press

Jordan, R. (1968). *Handbuch der mittelenglischen Grammatik*, third edition, Heidelberg: Carl Winter

Jordan, R. (1974). *Handbook of Middle English Grammar: Phonology*, translated and revised by Eugene J. Crook, The Hague: Mouton

Kortmann, B. and Schneider, E. W. (eds.) (2004). *A Handbook of Varieties of English*, vol. 1: *Phonology*; vol. 2: *Morphology and Syntax*, Berlin: Mouton de Gruyter

Kurath, H., Kuhn, S. M. and Lewis, R. E. (1952–). *Middle English Dictionary*, 15 vols., Ann Arbor: University of Michigan Press: continuing

Labov, W. (1972). *Sociolinguistic Patterns*, Philadelphia: University of Pennsylvania Press

Labov, W. (1994). *Principles of Linguistic Change*, vol. 1: *Internal Factors*, Oxford: Blackwell

Labov, W. (2001). *Principles of Linguistic Change*, vol. 2: *Social Factors*, Oxford: Blackwell

Lass, R. (ed.) (1999). *The Cambridge History of the English Language*, vol. 3: *1476–1776*, Cambridge: Cambridge University Press

Lehmann, W. P. (1952). *Proto-Indo-European Phonology*, Austin: University of Texas Press

Lehmann, W. P. (1973). *Historical Linguistics: an Introduction*, second edition, New York: Holt, Rinehart and Winston

Lehmann, W. P. (1974). *Proto-Indo-European Syntax*, Austin: University of Texas Press

Leith, D. (1983). *A Social History of English*, London: Routledge and Kegan Paul

Leonard, S. A. (1929). *The Doctrine of Correctness in English Usage 1700–1800*, New York: Russell

Lieberman, P. (1984). *The Biology and Evolution of Language*, Cambridge, MA: Harvard University Press

Lockwood, W. B. (1969). *Indo-European Philology*, London: Hutchinson

Lockwood, W. B. (1975). *Languages of the British Isles Past and Present*, London: Deutsch

Lockwood, W. B. (1976). *An Informal History of the German Language*, London: Deutsch

Luick, K. (1914–21). *Historische Grammatik der englischen Sprache*, Leipzig: Tauchnitz

Lyons, J. (1968). *Introduction to Theoretical Linguistics*, Cambridge: Cambridge University Press

McIntosh. A., Samuels, M. L. and Benskin, M. (1986). *A Linguistic Atlas of Late Mediaeval English*, 4 vols., Aberdeen: Aberdeen University Press

McMahon, A. M. S. (1994). *Understanding Language Change*, Cambridge: Cambridge University Press

McMahon, A. M. S. and McMahon, R. (2005). *Language Classification by Numbers*, Oxford: Oxford University Press

Mair, C. (2006). *Twentieth-century English: History, Variation and Standardization*, Cambridge: Cambridge University Press

Marchand, H. (1969). *The Categories and Types of Present-day English Word-formation*, second edition, Munich: C.H. Beck

Marckwardt, A. H. (1980). *American English*, second edition, New York: Oxford University Press

Martinet, A. (1955). *Economie des changements phonétiques*, Berne: Francke Verlag

Michael, I. L. (1970). *Grammatical Categories and the Tradition to 1800*, Cambridge: Cambridge University Press

Mills, A. D. (2003). *A Dictionary of British Place-Names*, Oxford: Oxford University Press

Milroy, J. and Milroy, L. (1985). *Authority in Language*, London: Routledge and Kegan Paul

Mitchell, B. (1987). *Old English Syntax*, 2 vols: reprinted with corrections, Oxford: Clarendon Press

Mitchell. B. and Robinson, F. C. (2007). *A Guide to Old English*, seventh edition, Oxford: Blackwell

Mossé, F. (1952). *A Handbook of Middle English*, trans. J. A. Walker, Baltimore: Johns Hopkins University Press

Murison, D. (1977). *The Guid Scots Tongue*, Edinburgh: Blackwood

Mustanoja, T. F. (1960). *A Middle English Syntax*, part I, Helsinki: Mémoires de la Société Néophilologique de Helsinki

Nevalainen, T. (2006). *An Introduction to Early Modern English*, Edinburgh: Edinburgh University Press

Nevalainen, T. and Raumolin-Brunberg, H. (2003) *Historical Sociolinguistics: Language Change in Tudor and Stuart England*, London: Longman

Odumuh, A. E. (1987). *Nigerian English (NigE)*, Zaria: Ahmadu Bello University Press

Onions, C. T. (1966). *The Oxford Dictionary of English Etymology*, Oxford: Clarendon Press

Oppenheimer, S. (2006). *The Origins of the British: a Genetic Detective Story*, London: Constable

Orton, H. and Dieth, E. (1962–71). *Survey of English Dialects*, 5 vols., Leeds: Edward Arnold

The Oxford English Dictionary (1989). second edition, 20 vols., Oxford: Clarendon Press

Page, R. I. (1973). *An Introduction to English Runes*, London: Methuen

Page, R. I. (1987). *Runes*, London: British Museum

Parsons, D. N. (1999). *Recasting the Runes: the Reform of the Anglo-Saxon Furthorc*, Uppsala: Institutionen för nordiska språk

Poplack, S. (ed.) (1999). *The English History of African-American English*, Oxford: Blackwell

Potter, S. (1969). *Changing English*, London: Deutsch

Prokosch, E. (1939). *A Comparative Germanic Grammar*, Philadelphia: Linguistic Society of America, University of Pennsylvania

Quirk, R., Greenbaum, S., Leech, G. and Svartvik, J. (1972). *A Grammar of Contemporary English*, London: Longman

Quirk, R., Greenbaum, S., Leech, G. and Svartvik, J. (1985). *A Comprehensive Grammar of the English Language*, London: Longman

Quirk, R. and Wrenn, C. L. (1957). *An Old English Grammar*, second edition, London: Methuen

Ramat, A. G. and Ramat, P. (eds.) (1998). *The Indo-European Languages*, London: Routledge

Ramson, W. S. (ed.) (1970). *English Transported: Essays on Australasian English*, Canberra: Australian National University Press

Reaney, P. H. (1960). *The Origin of English Place-Names*, London: Routledge and Kegan Paul

Renfrew, C. (1987). *Archaeology and Language: the Puzzle of Indo-European Origins*, London: Jonathan Cape

Renfrew, C. (1989). 'Models of Change in Language and Archaeology', *Transactions of the Philological Society*, 87(2): 103–55

Roach, P. (1991). *English Phonetics and Phonology*, second edition, Cambridge: Cambridge University Press

Robertson, S. (1954). *The Development of Modern English*, second edition, rev. F. G. Cassidy, New York: Prentice-Hall

Robinson, O. W. (1992). *Old English and Its Closest Relatives*, London: Routledge

Romaine, S. (1988). *Pidgin and Creole Languages*, London: Longman

Romaine, S. (ed.) (1998). *The Cambridge History of the English Language*, vol. 4: *1776–1997*, Cambridge: Cambridge University Press.

Ruhlen, M. (1991). *A Guide to the World's Languages*, vol. 1: *Classification*, London: Edward Arnold

Sapir, E. (1921). *Language*, London: Oxford University Press

Saussure, F. de (1916). *Cours de linguistique générale*, Paris: Payot

Saussure, F. de (1960). *Course in General Linguistics*, London: Owen

Savory, T. H. (1967). *The Language of Science*, revised edition, London: Deutsch

Sawyer, P. H. (1971). *The Age of the Vikings*, second edition, London: Arnold

Sawyer, P. H. (1982). *Kings and Vikings: Scandinavia and Europe AD 700–1100*, London: Methuen

Schrader, O. (1890). *Prehistoric Antiquities of the Aryan Peoples*, London: Griffin

Scragg, D. G. (1974). *A History of English Spelling*, Manchester: Manchester University Press

Sebba, M. (1997). *Contact Languages: Pidgins and Creoles*, London: Macmillan

Serjeantson, M. S. (1935). *A History of Foreign Words in English*, London: Routledge and Kegan Paul

Sheard, J. A. (1954). *The Words We Use*, London: Deutsch

Singh, I. (2000). *Pidgins and Creoles: an Introduction*, London: Arnold

Smith, A. H. (1970). *The Place-Name Elements*, 2 vols., Cambridge: Cambridge University Press

Smith, J. (1996). *An Historical Study of English: Function, Form and Change*, London: Routledge

Starnes, W. T. and Noyes, G. E. (1991). *The English Dictionary from Cawdrey to Johnson*, new edition by Gabriele Stein, Amsterdam: Benjamins

Stein, G. (1985). *The English Dictionary Before Cawdrey*, Tübingen: M. Niemeyer

Stenton, F. M. (1971). *Anglo-Saxon England*, third edition, Oxford: Clarendon Press

Strang, B. M. H. (1968). *Modern English Structure*, second edition, London: Edward Arnold

Strang, B. M. H. (1970). *A History of English*, London: Methuen

Stratmann, F. H. and Bradley, H. (1891). *A Middle-English Dictionary*, Oxford: Clarendon Press

Streitberg, W. (1943). *Urgermanische Grammatik*, Heidelberg: Carl Winter

Szemerényi, O. J. L. (1985). 'Recent Developments in Indo-European Linguistics', *Transactions of the Philological Society*, 1–71

Todd. L. (1990). *Pidgins and Creoles*, second edition, London: Routledge

Toller. T. N. (1921). *An Anglo-Saxon Dictionary. Supplement*, Oxford: Clarendon Press

Trask, R. L. (1994). *Language Change*, London: Routledge

Traugott, E. C. (1972). *A History of English Syntax*, New York: Holt, Rinehart and Winston

Trudgill, P. and Hannah, J. (2002). *International English*, fourth edition, London: Edward Arnold

Turner, G. W. (1972). *The English Language in Australia and New Zealand*, second edition, London: Longman

Vallins, G. H. (1965). *Spelling*, revised by D. G. Scragg. London: Deutsch

Visser, F. T. (1963–73). *An Historical Syntax of the English Language*, 3 parts in 5 volumes, Leiden: E. J. Brill

Voyles, J. B. (1992). *Early Germanic Grammar: Pre-, Proto-, and Post-Germanic Languages*, San Diego: Academic Press

Walshe, M. O'C. (1965). *Introduction to the Scandinavian Languages*, London: Deutsch

Wardale, E. E. (1937). *An Introduction to Middle English*, London: Routledge and Kegan Paul

Wells. J. C. (1982). *Accents of English*, 3 vols., Cambridge: Cambridge University Press

Wells. J. C. (2006). *English Intonation: an Introduction*, Cambridge: Cambridge University Press

Wolfram, W. and Schilling-Estes, N. (1998). *American English: Dialects and Variation*, Oxford: Blackwell

Wolfram, W. and Thomas, E. (2002). *The Development of African-American English*, Oxford: Blackwell

Wright, J. and Wright, E. M. (1925). *Old English Grammar*, third edition, London: Oxford University Press

Wright, J. and Wright, E. M. (1928). *An Elementary Middle English Grammar*, second edition, London: Oxford University Press

Wright, L. B. (1935). *Middle-Class Culture in Elizabethan England*, Chapel Hill: University of North Carolina Press

Wyld, H. C. (1936). *A History of Modern Colloquial English*, third edition, Oxford: Blackwell

3. Electronic resources

A Key to English Place-Names www.nottingham.ac.uk/english/ins/epntest/intro.html [accessed January 2008]

Dipaolo Healey, A. (ed.). *Dictionary of Old English Web Corpus* quod.lib.umich.edu/o/oec/ [accessed January 2008]

Gordon, R. G., Jr. (ed.) (2005). *Ethnologue: Languages of the World*, fifteenth edition, Dallas: SIL International. Online version: www.ethnologue.com/ [accessed January 2008]

Kurath, H. and others (eds.). *Middle English Dictionary* quod.lib.umich.edu/m/med/ [accessed January 2008]

Simpson, John, (ed.). (2000). *Oxford English Dictionary*, third edition online, Oxford: Oxford University Press. dictionary.oed.com [accessed January 2008]

Index